THE LIMITS OF INSTITUTIONAL REFORM IN DEVELOPMENT

Billions of dollars of institutional reforms have been introduced to improve governments in developing countries. Unfortunately, many governments remain dysfunctional despite these reforms. This book asks why reforms seem to have been limited and how they can be improved to yield better results in the future.

In answering the questions, the book argues that reforms face limits when they are introduced as short-term signals to make governments look better, not as realistic solutions to make governments perform better. Reforms as signals introduce unrealistic best practices that do not fit developing country contexts and are not considered relevant by implementing agents. The result is a set of new forms that do not function.

Reforms are not always subject to such limits, however. Realistic solutions are emerging from institutional reforms in some contexts and are yielding more functional governments in the process. Lessons from these experiences suggest that reform limits can be overcome by focusing change on problem solving, through an incremental process that involves multiple agents. The book combines these lessons into a new approach to doing institutional reform in development, called problem-driven iterative adaptation (PDIA). It suggests that PDIA offers a better way of fostering reform to governments across the developing world and beyond.

Matt Andrews is an Associate Professor at the Harvard Kennedy School and a Fellow at the School's Center for International Development. His work has appeared in journals such as *Governance,* the *International Public Management Journal, Public Administration Review, Oxford Development Studies, Public Administration and Development,* and the *Journal of Development Studies.* Professor Andrews was previously a World Bank staff member and prior to that he supported various government leaders in South Africa during the transition from apartheid. He has worked in more than twenty-five developing and transitional countries. Professor Andrews received his PhD from the Maxwell School at Syracuse University.

The Limits of Institutional Reform in Development

Changing Rules for Realistic Solutions

MATT ANDREWS

Harvard Kennedy School of Government

CAMBRIDGE
UNIVERSITY PRESS

32 Avenue of the Americas, New York NY 10013-2473, USA

Cambridge University Press is part of the University of Cambridge.

It furthers the University's mission by disseminating knowledge in the pursuit of education, learning and research at the highest international levels of excellence.

www.cambridge.org
Information on this title: www.cambridge.org/9781107684881

First published 2013
First paperback edition 2013

A catalogue record for this publication is available from the British Library

Library of Congress Cataloguing in Publication data

Andrews, Matt, 1972–
The limits of institutional reform in development : changing rules for realistic solutions / Matt Andrews, Kennedy School of Government, Harvard University.
page cm
Includes bibliographical references and index.
ISBN 978-1-107-01633-0
1. Institution building – Developing countries. 2. Developing countries – Economic conditions. 3. Economic development – Developing countries. I. Title.
HC59.7.A7945 2013
338.9009172´4–dc23   2012029381

ISBN 978-1-107-01633-0 Hardback
ISBN 978-1-107-68488-1 Paperback

Contents

Acknowledgments

This book has emerged over a number of years, drawing on the support and inspiration of multiple people to whom I owe many debts of gratitude. I am particularly grateful for the opportunities I have had to work on institutional reforms in a variety of developing countries. I have encountered many excellent people in the development community as a result, from whom I have learned a great deal (especially my friends in the World Bank and the governments undergoing reform). I also have incredible colleagues and students at the Harvard Kennedy School who have helped shape and sharpen my ideas over the past few years. My greatest debt is to Jean, Samuel, Joshua, and Daniel. They have always been generous in accepting my long and frequent absences and early morning writing habits. The book is dedicated to them, with deep and enduring thanks.

Preface

This book emerged in response to mounting evidence that institutional reforms in development often do not work. Case studies and multicountry analyses show that many governments in developing nations are not becoming more functional, even after decades and hundreds of millions of dollars of externally sponsored reforms. These studies increasingly suggest that disappointing results cannot be explained by routine excuses, either. One cannot simply blame governments in these countries for not doing reforms, because many governments remain deeply dysfunctional even after many satisfactorily completed projects introducing best practices advocated by international organizations. The work on institutional reform in development has seldom explored reasons for failure beyond such excuses, however. This has created a gap in the literature, which is important from academic and practical perspectives. The academic challenge is to see if theory and evidence can help promote a better understanding of why many reforms do not lead to better governments. The practical imperative is more fundamental: Can a better understanding of past experience help improve the likelihood of more institutional reform success in more developing countries in the future? Driven by these questions, the book seeks to provide a product that is useful to academics and practitioners in the development field. It combines ideas from various streams of institutional theory to analyze a diverse set of institutional reform experiences. This analysis yields an argument that reforms are limited when governments adopt them as signals to garner short-term support. Such reforms are often unrealistic; they may produce new laws that make governments look better, but these are seldom implemented and governments are not really better after the reforms. The analysis points to examples where reforms are not simply adopted as signals, however, and have helped make governments more functional. These experiences inform an alternative approach to doing institutional reform called problem-driven iterative adaptation (PDIA), which yields realistic reforms that actually produce better governments over time.

ONE

Change Rules, Change Governments, and Develop?

SQUARE PEG REFORMS IN ROUND HOLE GOVERNMENTS

Government often dominates developing countries. Sometimes government is the only game in town. Countries suffer when rules of this game are deficient and governments are ineffective or predatory. Because this frequently seems to be the case, public sector institutional reforms have emerged as central to development. These reforms are an essential element of interventions by players like the World Bank and other multilateral and bilateral agencies. They focus on improving governmental rules of the game and establishing effective governments that facilitate economic growth. These goals are often not met, however, even when countries adopt advised reforms, at considerable expense, and with great anticipation. *This book asks why institutional reforms in development often do not lead to improved governments and how they can be better structured to achieve such goal.*

These questions emerge when looking at recent cases. Consider Afghanistan, where the international community proposed in 2003 that institutional reform would help "within seven years ... [to] build a stable centralized state ... arranged around the rule of law and a technocratic administration."[1] Seven years; billions of dollars; and many new laws, regulations, and structures later, the government is still criticized as corrupt and inefficient. Although promises suggested the country could be a new Korea, "[i]t is now hoped that good development in Afghanistan might allow it over decades to draw level with Pakistan."[2] Think also of Georgia, where government streamlined taxes, reorganized public organizations, and cut regulations in 2004 to catalyze private industry and create jobs – with talk of becoming a Caucasian Singapore. Georgia's government received the

[1] Stewart 2010, 1.
[2] Ibid.

1

World Bank's *Doing Business* Most Improved Business Reformer award in 2008 and enjoyed rapid growth between 2004 and 2007. Unfortunately, this was driven by foreigners buying up privatized assets and not by expanded local economic activity.[3] Domestic innovation, market competition, and employment stagnated between 2004 and 2008.[4] Government regulations may no longer burden entrepreneurs, but reforms have not led to a government that effectively catalyzes employment-generating production either. Why? What could be done differently in the future?

These are important questions to ask in many countries beyond Afghanistan and Georgia, where public sector institutional reforms have not delivered better government. As a matter of fact, this book is not the first piece of work to ask these questions. Others have raised them before, with different opinions on why reforms do not work. The list of critics is long and includes prominent voices like Bill Easterly, Dani Rodrik, Peter Evans, and Merilee Grindle.[5] The list of reasons offered for failure is even longer, and these are often presented as exclusive of each other, with limited explanation for why reform persists despite mixed and often disappointing results.[6] This book builds on such work. It offers a specific argument about why many reforms fail, and draws on lessons from more successful experiences to identify a potentially new, improved approach to doing reform in the future:

- The argument builds on existing views that reforms often fail because they do not fit many developing country contexts – looking like square pegs in round holes. It provides a novel explanation for why this poor fit is common and recurrent: many reforms are introduced as short-term

---

[3] See the International Finance Corporation (IFC) 2009 Sector Competitiveness Overview, http://www.ifc.org/ifcext/georgiasme.nsf/AttachmentsByTitle/1GeorgiaManufacturingSe ctorCompetitivenessAssessmentEng/$FILE/1GeorgiaSectorCompetitivenessAssessmentF inalReportEng.pdf.

[4] Georgia ranks 5 for ease of doing business but 90 on the World Economic Forum's Global Competitiveness Index, 115 of 133 on internal competition, 98 on market dominance, and 125 for "monopoly problems." See http://www.weforum.org/pdf/GCR09/GCR20092010 fullrankings.pdf. Unemployment rates in 2010 ranged from 16.5 percent officially to 29 percent in Transparency International's estimates. See http://www.transparency.ge/en/ blog/p2-2-5-georgias-official-statistics-and-unfolding-greek-tragedyp.

[5] Rodrik (2007, 2) opens *One Economics Many Recipes* with a story similar to the Afghan and Georgian vignettes and asks, "What had gone wrong?" Consider also Andrews 2010; Chang 2003; Easterly 2001; Evans 2004; Goldsmith 2010; Grindle 2004; Pritchett and Woolcock 2004; and World Bank 2008.

[6] Some claim, for example, that reforms impose inappropriate ideological models on governments. Others argue that appropriate reforms are not sufficiently owned, or that reforms fail because of capacity constraints, and so on.

signals that ensure developing countries attain and retain external support and legitimacy. The argument posits that reforms introduced as signals are commonly designed with limited attention to context, involve impressive-looking but hard-to-reproduce best practice interventions, and emerge through narrow engagements with agents that outsiders consider champions. Such reforms are prone to having limited success, however. They may produce new forms (like laws) in the short term, but these typically have poor functionality. Governments look better after reform but often are not better.

- An improved reform approach takes shape after the analysis of interventions that have yielded more functional governments. This approach, called problem-driven iterative adaptation (PDIA),[7] is akin to the way one imagines carpenters craft pegs to fit real holes – where the process is as important as the product. This process begins with problem identification, given the argument that reforms are more likely to fit their contexts when crafted as responses to locally defined problems. Relevant solutions – those that are politically acceptable and practically possible – emerge through a gradual process of step-by-step experimentation to solve such problems. This process yields solutions that resemble bricolaged hybrids blending external and internal ideas. The solutions arise through engagements between many agents playing multiple functional roles, and not solitary champions.

The book uses institutional theory to frame the argument and inform this new approach. It not only takes ideas from the new institutional economics as a starting point but also draws from broader work in new institutional theory, applying ideas about institutional logics, isomorphism, institutional entrepreneurship, and decoupling. Such ideas are common in studies crossing political science, sociology, and management fields. They have yet to be applied prominently in the development domain, however, and are presented here to show how interdisciplinary thinking can enrich the development dialogue. The theory is accompanied by empirical studies to illustrate and validate arguments.

Before outlining the book's content in more detail, this chapter introduces the topic and shows why it matters. A first section argues that institutional reforms have become pervasive in development and thus demand attention. A second section shows that reforms involve similar types of interventions across different contexts, reflecting confidence in a specific agenda of action. The third section notes that results of these reforms are varied and often

[7] Andrews, Pritchett, and Woolcock 2012.

lower than anticipated, raising questions about how effective the new agenda really is.

INSTITUTIONAL REFORMS ARE NEW AND PERVASIVE

New institutional economics has informed public sector reform in developing countries since the 1980s. This theory posits that formal and informal rules – institutions – influence all people, organizations, and economies. Governments are the hub of many such rules, bound by some and the maker and enforcer of others. Think of civil service laws, budget rules, norms of information disclosure, building permit requirements, or the tests government inspectors use to assess whether one should get a driver's license. These "rules of the game" determine the size, scope, operation, and influence of government.

Theorists claim that different institutions create incentives for different behavior, leading to different outcomes. A strict driving test may create better incentives for safe driving than a lax one, for example, which impacts the safety of public streets. In so shaping behavior, theory posits that different institutions have different effects on social and economic progress – the sine qua non of development. The key to development, this argument suggests, is "finding the right institutional framework" or rules of the game.[8] Governments have been the focus of this search, and many efforts to improve public organizations are thus called institutional reforms.

In developing countries, these reforms are frequently influenced by external entities like the International Monetary Fund (IMF), World Bank, regional development banks, and bilateral agencies. The influence manifests in many ways. It comes, for example, through external identification of what the right rules are, and through financing, facilitation, and sometimes even implementation of interventions intended to introduce these rules. Such reforms target improvements in core public administration processes, the way governments interface with business, and service delivery mechanisms in areas like health and education.

These reforms are relatively new to development, featuring in fewer than 1 percent of World Bank projects before 1980.[9] This reflected a policy of nonpolitical engagement that dominated international development at the

---

[8] World Bank 2000a; Yeager 1999, 113.

[9] This is the number of projects benefiting activities in the public administration, law, and justice (PAL&J) sector. This approach to measuring World Bank–sponsored institutional reforms builds on work by Kim Moloney (2009). Only 18 of the 2,782 World Bank projects started before 1980 were classified as such.

time.[10] Such policy kept many development organizations out of the business of government in developing countries. Interventions focused rather on building infrastructure and productive economic sectors, with little attention to rules of the game affecting the use and impact of these assets and sectors.[11] This started changing in the late 1970s, when international organizations noted that governments had become key players in developing countries. A 1988 World Bank report states, for instance, that "[t]he public sector now appears to be as important in developing countries as in industrial countries."[12]

Public sectors were in turmoil during this period, many burdened with overwhelming debt and facing economic slowdown. International organizations offered assistance in various forms. These included much-discussed structural adjustment operations, which contributed to an expansion of institutional reform activities in the 1980s. Such projects constituted about a fifth of World Bank loans in the decade.[13] This was only one part of a growing engagement, however, which was boosted by the Soviet Union's dissolution and various global, regional, and country-specific crises in the 1990s and 2000s. New governments emerged from these events, or replaced old governments that had lost legitimacy. There was a general sense that many of these new states were looking for help in discerning and adopting the kind of institutions that could ensure their effectiveness.

As a result of such events, the last twenty years have seen a number of multilateral and bilateral agencies introducing institutional reform strategies and advisory, aid, and lending mechanisms. Great Britain's Department for International Development has engaged in such reforms since the early 1990s, for instance, and first formalized a strategy on the topic in the mid-1990s.[14] The Asian Development Bank introduced a governance policy to guide such interventions in 1995,[15] and the African Development Bank did the same in 2000.[16]

Engagements like these have ensured the continued growth and influence of public sector institutional reforms in development. These reforms are

---

[10] Wright and Winters 2010.

[11] More than 750 World Bank projects before 1980 sought to strengthen rural infrastructure and agriculture sectors. A total of 550 constructed railroads, highways, and seaports; 350 established electric power and energy sources; 300 built schools and hospitals; and 220 developed water and telecommunications infrastructure.

[12] World Bank 1988, 5.

[13] A total of 469 World Bank projects had PAL&J sector content in this decade.

[14] Department for International Development 2011.

[15] Asian Development Bank 2006, i.

[16] African Development Bank 2012, 15.

now a major line of business for most development agencies. They can be identified in more than half of the operations carried out by Great Britain's Department for International Development between 2004 and 2010.[17] They are also evident in more than half of the Asian and African Development Banks' project portfolios in the late 2000s,[18] having comprised less than 10 percent of interventions prior to the 1990s.[19] The emergence of such activities is probably most obvious when considering World Bank experience, where projects likely to incorporate public sector institutional reforms comprised 65 percent of all operations between 2000 and 2010.[20] In some respects, these reforms are now the most common part of the organization's agenda.[21] They featured in more than $50 billion worth of World Bank–sponsored projects between 2006 and 2011, a quarter of spending in the period.[22]

The pervasive nature of these reforms is further evidenced in the variety of affected countries. Bilateral agencies and regional development banks typically sponsor such interventions in more than one hundred countries.[23] World Bank projects supporting these reforms can be identified in more than 140 countries.[24] A randomly selected sample of forty countries illustrates the variety of these contexts.[25] It includes Afghanistan, Algeria, Angola, Argentina, Azerbaijan, Benin, Bolivia, Bulgaria, Burundi, Cape Verde,

---

[17] Spending on governance accounted for about 20 percent of the Department for International Development's (DFID) activities, whereas more than 20 percent of the spending focused on economic reforms tended to involve interventions at the interface of the public and private sectors. Beyond this, DFID documents note that institutional reforms are common in sectoral engagements (like water supply and sanitation, health, and education). Department for International Development 2010, 2011.

[18] African Development Bank 2012; Asian Development Bank 2012, 34.

[19] Governance operations in the African Development Bank between 1967 and 2006 accounted for 15 percent of all loans. Most took place after the mid-1990s. African Development Bank 2012.

[20] More than 3,200 projects had some spending in the PAL&J sector in the decade.

[21] The World Bank had supported 13,121 projects as of April 2011; 5,981 of these had activities in the PAL&J sector. Essentially, therefore, about one in two projects has sponsored institutional reforms. This exceeds the World Bank focus in any other sector. Fewer than a third of projects have incorporated an agricultural sector focus. Fewer than one in five disbursed in the education, health, transportation, electricity, and water sectors.

[22] This is the project spending benefiting activities in the PAL&J sector, as reported in the World Bank's 2012 financial report. The amount could be much greater if capturing institutional reform content in various thematic areas. For instance, $28 billion was spent on the public sector governance, $1.7 billion on rule of law reforms, and more than $51 billion on financial and private sector reforms.

[23] African Development Bank 2012; Asian Development Bank 2012; Department for International Development 2010; Inter-American Development Bank 2012.

[24] One can see this when searching for projects in the PAL&J sector in the World Bank projects database.

[25] The forty-country sample was chosen using a random number technique.

Central African Republic, Chile, China, Georgia, Ghana, Guinea, Haiti, Honduras, Kyrgyz, Laos, Madagascar, Malawi, Mauritius, Moldova, Mongolia, Mozambique, Nicaragua, Niger, Poland, Rwanda, Samoa, Senegal, Serbia, Sri Lanka, Tanzania, Thailand, Togo, Uganda, Ukraine, and Uruguay. One can think of the incredible variation in the countries listed here – in economic size and complexity, political and social structures, geography, and history. One thing they all share, however, is the recent experience of having engaged with external donors to introduce public sector institutional reforms.

INSTITUTIONAL REFORMS ARE SIMILAR, EVEN IN DIFFERENT CONTEXTS

The country coverage of these reforms is impressive, especially considering their relative newness. One consequence of this is that multilateral and bilateral development organizations are increasingly shaping the ideas, opportunities, demand, and supply of public sector institutional reforms in developing countries. Many would expect this influence to be varied, with different reform types across the wide range of affected countries. This reflects a belief that the "right rules" are different for different contexts. Such sentiment is regularly voiced in formal pronouncements on reform by development organizations like the World Bank. These typically decry attempts to generalize government reform solutions.[26] A more skeptical set of observers argues that generic models do, however, exist and actually dominate reform designs supported by development agencies.[27] Some refer to a strong neoliberal influence on reform content.[28] Others infer that interventions commonly impose modern managerial solutions on developing countries.[29] Although many hold to these beliefs, they are seldom supported by empirical research beyond isolated case studies.[30]

A number of sources facilitate more rigorous identification of similarities, however. World Bank project documents provide information about the way

---

[26] A 1992 World Bank document notes, "The institutional characteristics for managing development [varies] widely among countries and do[es] not permit easy generalization" (World Bank 1992, 7). Ahrens (2001, 54) writes: "There are still no clear or settled ideas about how effective governance should be defined, let alone how key governance issues can be appropriately incorporated into externally-financed programmes."

[27] Andrews 2010; Chang 2003; Grindle 2004.

[28] Rodrik (2007, 182) claims that a "'neoliberal' socio-economic model" pervades development.

[29] Kenny 2008.

[30] World Bank (2008, 38) argues, for example, that reforms are "likely to be one size fits all," but does not show evidence for such or explain what the generic model looks like.

reforms are designed, for instance. Recent studies of these documents note two common practices:[31]

- First, central agents like government ministers and their policy departments are seen as the key reformers. By contrast, broader constituencies needed to implement reforms are seldom mentioned. For example, budget departments are often identified as vital to budget reform, but agencies affected by such reforms are not considered important reform partners. This suggests that centralized rule makers must lead institutional reform, but it is not important to engage those who must ultimately abide by or implement new rules.
- Second, projects use formal mechanisms to effect institutional change. These include laws, procedures, and systems. This approach underscores a bias toward formal institutions. Such bias is evident in the 1990s literature on fiscal institutions,[32] which describes budgetary institutions as "all the rules" affecting budgeting but only focuses on official processes and laws. Informal mechanisms like political traditions are ignored. This suggests that informal mechanisms do not matter or are actually problematic and need to be replaced by more neutral, technical formal devices.[33]

Beyond these process similarities, one can also identify patterns in the content of institutional reforms. These manifest when examining the reform strategies of development organizations and the themes commonly introduced through externally supported projects. The World Bank project database is particularly valuable in this regard, providing information about themes pursued in more than five thousand projects incorporating public sector institutional reforms.[34] Three reform similarities appear when examining these sources.

First, reforms aim to foster market-friendly governments through interventions like privatization, deregulation, trade liberalization, and the establishment of government entities needed to promote competitive markets. Such interventions address the way governments engage with the private

---

[31] See Andrews 2011a; 2011b; 2012c. These papers, which examined a set of World Bank project documents, see process commonalities. Design and completion reports provided narratives about reform content and results.

[32] Alesina and Perotti 1999, 14.

[33] As an example, consider the way in which the influential public finance scholar Alan Schick identifies informality as a problem in developing countries. He prescribes basic aspects of formality as a solution – external rules that are routinely enforced by strong central rule makers. See Schick 1998.

[34] As discussed, these are reforms incorporating activity in the PAL&J sector.

sector and are a focal point in 44 percent of all World Bank projects targeting institutional reform.[35] The British development agency explains that these interventions address a "state failure" to facilitate vibrant markets.[36] The African Development Bank considers them necessary to improve the "investment climate and business environment."[37] They were initiated in the first few World Bank projects addressing public sector institutional reforms in all forty sample countries,[38] suggesting that market-friendly rules are a key and consistent element of institutional reforms in development. They are not only the generically relevant "right rules" to adopt in reforms, but they are the common right rules to start reform with – in all countries, no matter when the start date is or what the context looks like. This view is borne out by the fact that such interventions dominated reform in Chile in the 1970s, Uganda in the 1980s, Azerbaijan in the 1990s, and Afghanistan in the 2000s.

Second, reforms aim to create disciplined governments. Examples include staff rationalization mechanisms and budget controls that facilitate spending accountability, touted as vital in the Inter-American Development Bank's 2003 "Modernization of the State" document.[39] Such mechanisms are evident in more than 30 percent of World Bank–projects focused on reforming governments.[40] Ninety percent of the forty sample countries took steps to discipline their public finances and civil service regimes and to streamline debt in the first four years of World Bank–sponsored institutional reform.[41] This timing suggests that reforms intended to discipline

---

[35] This reflects 2,432 projects with at least one major thematic reference to "financial and private sector development," "rule of law," and "trade and integration" of 5,610 PAL&J projects.

[36] Department for International Development 2010, 17.

[37] African Development Bank 2012, 19.

[38] This is apparent when one breaks reform experiences down into defined periods of mostly two years and identifies the period in which a country started its public sector reform and what it did in this and ensuing periods. Azerbaijan's PAL&J reforms began in 1994, for example, and 37 projects with 151 themes have been pursued in eight periods since then. Afghanistan had its first public sector reform in 2002. It initiated more than 40 projects addressing issues in more than 150 thematic areas in the four ensuing periods. In both examples the first four periods of reform were dominated by activities establishing the rules of market-friendly government.

[39] Inter-American Development Bank 2003.

[40] A key World Bank theme reflecting this is called "Economic Management" and was referenced in 640 projects. The "Public Sector Governance" theme was cited in 1,976 projects, and a large portion of these interventions emphasized creating disciplined civil service and budgetary regimes. Based on these statistics, one can assume that improved discipline was a focal point of as many as a third of 5,610 projects addressing institutional reforms.

[41] Madagascar's 1989 *Economic Management and Social Action* project is an example. It formalized budget, fiscal policy, and investment processes. Mozambique's 1994 *Second*

governments go hand in hand with efforts to establish market-friendly government structures. In fact, both types of activities are often integrated in the same early-period operations.[42] They reflect ideas that seem to be at the heart – and start – of public sector institutional reform.

Third, reforms aim to modernize and formalize government processes. In this respect, the Asian Development Bank's 2000 action plan lists various modern solutions for governments to introduce in areas like public financial management and decentralization.[43] Similar documents emerged even earlier from the Inter-American Development Bank and World Bank,[44] advocating the adoption of modern mechanisms like fiscal rules, medium-term budgeting frameworks, and internal audit regimes. Such solutions are the focus of about a third of the World Bank projects fostering public sector institutional reform.[45] These engagements feature prominently in all periods of reform in the forty sample countries. This is not to say that reforms looked the same in all periods, however. Early-period interventions typically reflect what some call first-generation interventions that bring centralized, *ex ante* control to public financial management and administrative processes.[46] Later-period reforms are often different, reflecting "second-generation" interventions that introduce cutting-edge mechanisms like performance management and devolved organizational structures, all slated to improve efficiency.[47]

Economic Recovery Credit aimed to develop a strong macro-monetary capability within the central bank and ensure disciplined fiscal policy. Georgia's 1995 *Rehabilitation Loan* supported a program to restore macroeconomic stability and liberalize prices.

[42] Madagascar's early fiscal policy reforms were aligned with efforts to liquidate or privatize public enterprises. Bulgaria's *Rehabilitation Loan* sought to improve monetary policy mechanisms and accelerate privatization.

[43] Asian Development Bank 2000.

[44] Inter-American Development Bank 2003; World Bank 2000b.

[45] A total of 1,976 World Bank projects addressing the "Public Sector Governance" theme introduced new laws, processes and systems to modernize and formalize government, as did many projects stressing reforms in the "Urban Development" thematic area (which was a key theme in 920 projects).

[46] First-generation reforms include standardized annual budgeting and treasury processes, basic procurement rules and cash-based expenditure controls, control and rationalization of the wage bill, and formalization of pay and employment systems. One sees such initiatives in Argentina's 1991 *Public Sector Technical Assistance Loan*, Tanzania's 1992 *Parastatal and Public Sector Reform Project* and the 2004 *Second Emergency Public Administration Project* in Afghanistan. They also characterize content in Lao's 1992 *Structural Adjustment Credit* and Georgia and Moldova's 1999 *Structural Adjustment* operations.

[47] Recent projects in Argentina, for instance, introduce performance management, monitoring and evaluation, e-government and other modern processes. Tanzania's 1999 *Public Sector Reform Program* is another example, focused on policy de-concentration, performance monitoring, and establishing meritocratic civil service processes. Afghanistan's

Prominent Indicators Reinforce Reform Agendas

This discussion should not be read to say that all countries' reform experiences look exactly the same or that the identified goals of reform are either right or wrong. It simply argues that a large part of every country's institutional reform agenda seems focused on producing some common version of a market-friendly, disciplined, and modernized government. These three themes dominate more than 70 percent of World Bank-supported projects incorporating institutional reform and are regularly touted in the strategies of other development agencies.[48] They seem to provide the reform content that development organizations have decided constitutes the "right rules" needed to facilitate effective government.

Such content is reinforced by prominent indicators used to assess the quality of developing country governments. The Worldwide Governance Indicators (WGIs) are an example. A team of World Bank economists produced these in the late 1990s to provide measures of different dimensions of governance, including "regulatory quality" and "government effectiveness." Described by Christopher Pollitt as "the best-known international measures of governance,"[49] these indicators synthesize data from more than thirty largely subjective sources. Their intellectual foundation is described as "[t]he norms of limited government that protect private property from predation by the state."[50] The following reflects part of what the indicators portray as an "effective government"[51]:

> It is small and limited in engagement, formalized in mission and process and drawing limited revenues primarily from domestic sources. High-quality personnel devise and implement needed programs and deliver efficient and effective services via participatory processes and through formalized, disciplined, efficient and targeted financial management. Responsiveness to the citizenry's changing needs is high, effected through transparent, decentralized and politically neutral structures; consistently, even during political instability, without impeding (indeed supporting) the private sector.

Many will find this word picture appealing – the kind of government one might comfortably call "good." One should note how clearly it reflects the

most recent reforms introduce multiyear budgeting and other modern mechanisms. Laos, Moldova, and Georgia have taken similar steps to adopt current best practice IT-based management systems, internal audit processes, and medium-term expenditure frameworks.

[48] A total of 4,091 World Bank PAL&J projects cite at least one of the themes reflected in the three areas discussed in the text.

[49] Pollitt 2008, 11.

[50] Kaufmann, Kraay, and Mastruzzi 2007, 2.

[51] Andrews 2008, 382.

three themes discussed earlier as dominant in institutional reform experiences; both reforms and indicators emphasize market-friendly, disciplined, and modernized governments. One should also note that these characteristics are considered generically relevant and good for all countries.

Other indicators are similar. The World Bank's Country Policy and Institutional Assessment (CPIA) grades countries against common characteristics in twenty areas that represent "policy and institutional dimensions of an effective poverty reduction and growth strategy."[52] The CPIA criteria reflect the belief that "[g]ood policies and institutions are expected to lead, over time, to favorable growth and poverty reduction outcomes."[53] These criteria are detailed and considered generically relevant for all countries. The criterion used to assess a country's trade regime penalizes countries with high tariff rates and complex tariff structures, for instance, and the presence of other trade taxes and rules or standards that might limit trade, perceptions of corruption in customs, and the lack of modern mechanisms like risk management and electronic systems in the customs administration.[54]

These and other indicators constitute pictures of good government and good practice. The pictures provide a view of the "right rules" of government that is both common and consistent with the dominant design of institutional reforms in development. Indicators thus reinforce reforms and embed a model of what government should look like to facilitate development. This model is dominant regardless of statements to the contrary by development organizations and promises by these organizations not to pursue such.

INSTITUTIONAL REFORMS PRODUCE MIXED, AND OFTEN DISAPPOINTING, RESULTS

The common content in reforms and indicators suggests that the development community is confident that it has identified the solutions needed to foster effective government in developing countries. The question is whether reform results support such confidence. Answering this question requires assessing whether reforms have led to (or are fostering) better governments in developing countries. Although all measures of government quality are controversial, development organizations have attempted to answer this question by examining the way reforms impact the indicators discussed earlier.

[52] http://siteresources.worldbank.org/IDA/Resources/CPIA2007Questionnaire.pdf, 1.
[53] http://siteresources.worldbank.org/IDA/Resources/CPIA2007Questionnaire.pdf, 4.
[54] World Bank 2010, 10.

A 2008 World Bank evaluation of public sector reforms used CPIA measures to assess the impact of reforms introduced through World Bank–sponsored projects between 1999 and 2006.[55] It found that two-thirds of governments improved their overall governance scores after adopting reforms through these projects. Success rates varied across specific areas related to the governance agenda, however. Although 60 percent of countries improved public financial management scores after reforms, only 50 percent saw better corruption, transparency, and accountability scores, and just 40 percent registered gains in the quality of public administration. This means that between 40 and 60 percent of countries did not see better post-reform scores in important areas targeted by these interventions.

In revisiting such results, a 2011 study found even more disappointment.[56] Fewer than 40 percent of the eighty countries receiving World Bank support for public sector reform between 2007 and 2009 registered improved CPIA governance scores in that period. A quarter of these countries actually saw such scores decline, whereas more than a third stayed the same. The quality of public administration was higher after reforms in only 13 percent of reforming countries, dropping in about the same-sized group.[57] The study found cause for concern in even the higher-performance area of public financial management. It noted that 60 percent of countries targeted by reforms in this area have not been able to improve their institutions sufficiently to impact government functionality. According to the CPIA criteria, this level accords with a score of 4 (of 6), which only 46 of 137 countries had achieved by 2009. Reforms in other governments have yielded improvements that seem limited to better forms – like laws, systems, and processes – but are unlikely to have a "noticeable positive effect on the overall performance of the public sector."[58]

Similar observations emerge with regard to results of other World Bank–sponsored institutional reforms. Only forty-seven of eighty-one countries scored 4 or above in the 2009 CPIA assessment of country trade regimes, for instance. This means that more than 40 percent of reforming countries had not yet reached a level of progress that CPIA guidelines suggest will facilitate better performance. Importantly, the set of countries scoring below this level in 2009 was almost exactly the same as that in 2005, regardless of reforms before and after 2005. Countries in this set have complied with reform requirements to a point, but progress seems to have stalled before

---

[55] World Bank 2008, 46.
[56] World Bank 2011d, 68–76.
[57] World Bank 2011d, 71.
[58] World Bank 2011d, 73.

realizing gains of improved functionality. A 2006 World Bank evaluation notes a potential result of this, finding that economic outcomes were not evident after many apparently successful trade reforms. It laments that fewer than half of the countries with "a strong compliance record" in this area experienced improved exports or growth after reform.[59] Even some governments with higher CPIA scores have registered disappointing economic results and are still waiting to see gains from reforms.[60]

The evidence suggests that many countries are improving the rules of their public sector and trading games but are not seeing tangible results from such improvements, either because reforms are stalling or because reforms prove to be ineffective solutions to the problems countries are actually facing. Similar story lines could be told about interventions in a variety of other areas, providing a more comprehensive picture of the impact reforms are having on government as a whole.[61] Recent studies from two influential regional development banks use World Governance Indicators to give this broader perspective. For example, the African Development Bank refers to government effectiveness and regulatory quality indicator scores of Sub-Saharan African countries in introducing its 2012 governance strategy.[62] It shows that average country scores in these two areas declined between 1998 and 2006, despite substantial reforms in most countries. A 2008 paper from the Asian Development Bank Institute looks at the same two measures, calling WGIs "[t]he most comprehensive and reliable source of information on government performance."[63] The study finds that "[a]lmost across the board, regulatory quality in the region has gone down" and shows that government effectiveness scores have not improved either.[64] It summarizes these results in saying that "Asia is struggling" to meet the challenge of "implementing institutional reform."[65]

Authors of the World Governance Indicators caution against using their measures in the way African and Asian development bank authors have

---

[59] World Bank 2006, 23.

[60] An example is Honduras.

[61] After decades of reform, for example, few countries score four or above on CPIA scores in key areas like the financial sector and business regulatory environment. World Bank evaluations in such areas find key results are also often not significantly better in reformers than they are in nonreformers. A 2005 study found, for instance, that countries with World Bank financial sector reforms had lower ex-post facto rates of credit provision to the private sector than others. Such reforms were judged to have improved financial systems in affected countries but were falling short of fostering the kind of results one would expect from fully functional financial sectors. (See World Bank 2007.)

[62] African Development Bank 2012, 19.

[63] Stone 2008, 10.

[64] Ibid., 11.

[65] Ibid., 13.

done – comparing country scores over time. The main concern is that sources of data used to construct indicators differ between years. The indicators are, however, often used in time series research.[66] Accepting that scores might not be strictly comparable across years, many authors note that intertemporal patterns are probably still valid. Assuming such, and building on the two development bank studies already cited, government effectiveness scores were compared between 1998 and 2008 for 145 countries. All of the countries had undertaken institutional reforms with the World Bank and other agencies, and one can expect similarities in their reform agendas given earlier discussion.[67] Results look varied, however. Seventy-two countries had declining government effectiveness scores in the period, whereas an almost equivalent number, seventy-three, registered improved scores.

The basic story line is that half of 145 countries that have had donor-sponsored reforms in place saw declines in indicators of government effectiveness over a recent ten-year period. Interestingly, a similar story holds when looking only at the forty countries identified earlier. Twenty-one of these countries went backward on government effectiveness scores between 1998 and 2008. A smaller set of nineteen countries saw improved indicators. Cape Verde dropped from 0.35 to 0.05, even though the country had pursued reforms in twenty-eight World Bank projects that started in 1992 and cost $122 million. Senegal's scores dropped by a quarter of a point, even though it had undertaken seventy-five projects with institutional reform content costing more than $1 billion.[68] Senegal's reform activities were consistently pursued as well, with sixteen projects in the 1980s, twenty-six in the 1990s, and twenty-one between 2000 and 2008. A total of $526 million was committed to projects between 1998 and 2008 alone, the period in which government effectiveness scores fell. Nicaragua engaged in World Bank–sponsored institutional reforms costing $355 million between 1998 and 2008, building on about $290 million worth of prior engagements, but saw government effectiveness scores dip by more than half a point.

REFORMS WITH VARIED RESULTS AND THE REST OF THIS BOOK

These results serve to conclude a simple introductory narrative about institutional reforms in development. The story tells of reforms that have

---

[66] There are more than two thousand references to the Governance Matters studies in Google scholar after 2008. A large number of these studies use the indicators as either dependent or independent variables in longitudinal research.

[67] All 145 countries had benefited from World Bank PAL&J sector projects at some time since the 1980s.

[68] These were the projects classified in the PAL&J sector.

emerged from nowhere to dominate development dialogue and practice. These reforms have become associated with common interventions that all countries are encouraged to adopt regardless of context. Interventions are not commonly successful, however. Many countries do not see improved scores on prominent indicators of government effectiveness even after adopting millions of dollars worth of externally influenced reforms. Between 40 and 60 percent of interventions do not seem to yield these improvements, whether one is looking at CPIA or WGIs, specific areas of reform, or governance reforms as a whole.

This kind of evidence typically yields mixed responses. Some may point to the fact that many countries have seen improved government effectiveness scores and ask what lessons their experience might offer. Others will focus on those countries with declining scores and think about deconstructing reasons why they seem to be going backward, despite reforms. A third group will question the analysis itself, suggesting that the story might be different if success were measured differently or if common explanations of reform failure were considered.

The rest of this book speaks to all three perspectives. Chapter 2 addresses those who have qualms with the approach presented. It shows that countries with reform agendas have mixed results on more than just WGIs and CPIA scores. Evidence also suggests that mixed results are not easily explained by commonly referenced factors. Countries with similar reform quantity and quality have different results, and reforms do not seem to have a deeper impact over time, as many might expect. The chapter offers an explanation for this puzzling evidence: Institutional reforms are often adopted as signals to gain short-term support, not long-term solutions to real problems. Think of a carpenter producing thousands of large square pegs that win awards for their design but never fill the small round holes that need filling.

The next four chapters build on this idea, explaining why "reforms as signals" do not lead to better governments. Chapters 3 through 5 argue that such reforms typically overlook contextual realities that determine how much change is possible, emphasize best practice interventions beyond the reach of developing countries, and focus on narrow groups of "champions" that can seldom facilitate implementation and diffusion. Chapter 6 posits that the results of such reforms are limited to areas that are visible to outsiders and under the control of champions; what you see is not what you get.

The final four chapters suggest ways in which institutional reforms could be designed to have greater impact. They draw on examples of reforms that seem to be effecting real change in governments, going beyond square pegs in round holes and reforms as signals. Chapters 7 through 9 point to three important characteristics of such reforms: they emerge from problem-led learning processes, facilitate finding and fitting of context-specific solutions, and engage broad groups to ensure that new institutions are shared and embedded. The picture one should have is of a carpenter who crafts a peg for the hole that needs to be filled, experimenting along the way, and working with others to make sure the fit is right.

The book's last chapter combines ideas from Chapters 7 through 9 into a potentially new approach for doing institutional reforms in development. As noted, this is called problem-driven iterative adaptation, or PDIA, and calls for interventions to focus on solving problems through purposive muddling that includes active, ongoing, and experiential learning, with engagement by broad sets of agents who together ensure that reforms are viable and relevant. Elements of this approach are already emerging across the world of development, raising hope that change may, in fact, be happening. The chapter acknowledges that the challenge of poorly fitted institutional reform in development cannot be solved by simply proposing a new approach, however. Organizations like the World Bank, Asian Development Bank, and other bilateral agencies have embedded ways of thinking about and doing such reforms already. These embedded rules of the game have posed constraints to change in the past and promise to do so again.

Such constraints are evident in recent admissions from these organizations about their poor record of reform and change, even in the face of internal and external criticisms. These admissions note that the organizations regularly introduce strategies to do things differently but that these do not dramatically alter the way business is done.[69] This is much like a carpenter acknowledging that his pegs do not fit gaping holes but insisting that the process he follows is correct and does not require adjustment. "I don't need to change," he might say. "It would be great if all the pegs fit into all the holes, but give me some credit for what I have done. Look at all the nice pegs I have created, and remember that some of the holes were filled by the pegs. I am sure more pegs will fit more holes in time." The book closes by tackling this argument, identifying why development organizations and developing country governments keep producing so many institutional reforms with limits. It ultimately presents some practical ideas to address these issues – *changing the rules of development itself.*

---

[69] Asian Development Bank 2006; World Bank 2008.

TWO

Deconstructing the Puzzling Evidence of Reform

REFORMS WITH LIMITED RESULTS

Niger emerged from the 1990s as a poor African country attempting to introduce democracy, a modern economy, and an effective government. Part of this effort involved reforming its financial management system, with procurement being a particular focal point. Government worked with the World Bank to introduce transparent, competitive procurement practices in a 1999 project. A 2003 report was enthusiastic about results: new legislation was in place and an oversight agency had been established (the ARMP).[1] A second project followed. It received a less-enthusiastic evaluation in 2005, which pointed out that the ARMP had never been funded, no appointments had been made, and there was no publication of procurement procedures or awards (required by the 2002 law).[2] The reform that was so promising in 2003 proved limited by 2005. It was replaced in 2008, when a new World Bank project introduced a new law and a new agency. There is no evidence that this new institutional solution will work better than its predecessor.

Chapter 1 noted that institutional reforms often suffer the same fate as Niger's World Bank–sponsored efforts at improving procurement. Many governments that adopt these reforms, at great cost and with great anticipation, do not see better government as a result. Some readers may dispute this, rejecting the idea that governments remained ineffective in many countries where far-reaching reform agendas were in place. Surely, at least, there are simple explanations. Countries with declining governments were probably those that did not reform, or did very little, or are yet to see results.

This approach reflects a belief that governments should get better after reform and that there are valid excuses when this does not happen. This

[1] World Bank 2003a.
[2] World Bank 2005a.

chapter addresses such belief. The first section draws on varied evidence to reinforce the message that many reforms are not yielding better governments. A second section shows that conventional explanations do not account for this mixed reform record. The emerging evidence is puzzling. It suggests that countries do not necessarily see better reform results if they have more interventions, or higher levels of satisfactory interventions, or contexts that appear more reform friendly, or a longer legacy of reform.

A third section explores the narratives of selected reform experiences to better understand this puzzling evidence. These narratives reveal a tendency of many governments to treat reforms as signals, which external agencies readily reward – often through improved governance indicator scores at the time reforms are devised. The problem is that reforms as signals promise impressive changes that often prove un-implementable in many contexts. This leads to failing reforms four to six years into a project – as seen in Niger's procurement intervention. Instead of rethinking reforms at this stage, governments often reengage in the same ideas and start signaling again, just as Niger's recent reforms introduced a new new law and a new new agency. This is like a carpenter repeatedly producing square pegs that win immediate design awards but ultimately fail to fit into round holes that need filling.

INSTITUTIONAL REFORMS DO HAVE VARIED IMPACTS

Chapter 1 referenced recent studies that show mixed results for institutional reforms in development; many of these results are disappointing. The studies reveal that between 40 and 60 percent of reforming countries do not register improved scores on prominent indicators of government effectiveness. These include various dimensions of the World Bank's Country Policy and Institutional Assessment (CPIA) and the Worldwide Governance Indicators (WGI) government effectiveness measures. The discussion noted that even countries with better scores often fail to achieve improved government functionality or economic gains. Many governments have progressed with trade reforms but exports are still not growing, for instance. Some readers might question whether a broader set of experiences or measures will temper this story line. This is a valid question, especially given the many problems involved in examining reforms and their impact.

Broader experience is referenced in a recent portfolio review by Great Britain's Department for International Development. It uses internal measures to assess performance of different programs and finds variable results.[3] Public financial management (PFM) and taxation engagements achieve a score of 68 of 100, and national government reforms register only 60. Both scores suggest that reform objectives were likely to be partially to largely achieved, with particularly questionable performance in the area of core administrative reform. This finding is similar to that in the World Bank 2008 review cited in Chapter 1. The portfolio assessment does not assess reform impacts beyond these measures, but it does note that many reforms – especially those based on technical solutions alone – "have a limited sustained value."[4] This also reinforces a crucial message in Chapter 1: reforms are often not implemented deeply enough to make a functional impact.

The message is also supported by multiple references to reform limits in a 2011 Asian Development Bank review. This notes that efforts to deregulate and facilitate formal business start-ups slowed after initial success, because "further achievements are harder to achieve and require more difficult actions."[5] The review document further describes only "marginal improvements" in governance and public sector management indicators.[6] Referring to indicators like the World Bank CPIAs, it states that reforms have yielded better results addressing budget and financial management issues than transparency, accountability, and corruption challenges.[7] This, again, confirms evidence discussed in Chapter 1.

The story of varied reform results can also be told using aggregate indicators of government effectiveness similar to the WGIs referenced in Chapter 1. The Quality of Government (QoG) measure is an example. It is available from the Quality of Government Institute at the University of Gothenburg (www.qog.pol.gu.se) and is one of many sources used to calculate WGI effectiveness measures. The QoG measure is a subjective index created by summing three sets of data on corruption in government, bureaucratic quality, and the rule of law. When summed, the indicator ranges from zero to one and is widely used in academic research to reflect the quality of government.[8] Taken as such, one might expect these scores to improve over time in most of the countries with active institutional reforms in place. When looking at the experience of 106 countries that pursued such reforms, however, one

---

[3] Department for International Development 2011.
[4] Department for International Development 2010, 4.
[5] Asian Development Bank 2011, 16.
[6] Ibid., 16.
[7] Ibid., 16.
[8] There are more than five hundred references to this measure on Google Scholar between 2009 and 2011 alone.

sees that the picture is very different. Seventy percent of the countries experienced declines in quality of government scores between 1998 and 2008.

This evidence again reinforces the message in Chapter 1 that many countries have adopted reforms without seeing improved measures of government effectiveness or quality. The proportion of declining countries – 70 percent – is in fact higher with the QoG measure than it was for the WGI. A similar proportion of the forty sample countries identified in Chapter 1 saw declining quality of government scores. Data are available only for twenty-nine of these countries, and scores dropped in nineteen, held steady in one, and improved in nine. The biggest gain was in Serbia, which increased its score from 0.34 to 0.47. At the other extreme, Argentina fell from 0.69 to 0.52. Serbia had adopted twenty-two World Bank projects with institutional reform content in the 1998 to 2008 period, costing $217 million. Argentina engaged in forty-six such projects in the period, costing more than $4 billion.

Mixed results like this are evident with regard to other measures of government effectiveness as well. Economic growth could be considered such a measure, not because governments drive all growth but because this is a bottom-line indicator that many believe citizens value. Ronald Reagan's 1980 election campaign famously noted that an administration's success was reflected in whether people felt better off because of the government's presence. Bill Clinton's 1992 election slogan reinforced the idea, proclaiming, "It's the economy, stupid" when describing what citizens expect of their governments. Given such, it is important to note that most countries' economies grew over the 1998 to 2008 period, and most of the world's citizens could access more value in 2008 than they could in 1998. However, many countries grew at rates slower than those of their comparators, suggesting variation in factors like the quality of government and market institutions. Gross domestic product (GDP) per capita, measured in constant terms, increased by about 20 percent in Bolivia between 1998 and 2008, for instance, less than the mean growth rate for lower-middle-income countries. Similarly, Malawi's citizens saw personal incomes grow at about 10 percent over the entire period, far below the average of low-income countries. Incomes increased by about 50 percent in comparable-income Mozambique, which shares Malawi's southern border. Countries like Bolivia and Malawi were performing less effectively than comparators. Using a sports metaphor, they were boxing below their income weight – looking like middleweights but punching like flyweights.

More than 60 percent of 132 developing and transitional economies underperformed in this way, growing at rates lower than their comparators showed was possible in the period. Twenty-five of the forty randomly selected countries fell into this category as well. One obviously cannot attribute these results simply to low-quality government, but the poor performance does reflect partly on such – at least subjectively. As with many other countries, Malawi's government did not ensure the same growth as neighboring Mozambique between 1998 and 2008, a lackluster performance that many would surely call ineffective. This weak record was achieved even though the country adopted twenty-three World Bank projects with institutional reform content amounting to about $550 million in the period, not to mention a swathe of additional reforms supported by other agencies.

COMMON ARGUMENTS DO NOT EXPLAIN VARIED AND POOR RESULTS

The evidence presented thus far shows simply that institutional reforms have produced varying results in developing countries, which often are quite poor. The evidence does not explain why reforms have limited impacts in many countries. There are, however, common arguments to consider in this respect. Countries with disappointing results may just have had fewer or less satisfactory reforms than others, for instance. These countries might also constitute more difficult and demanding contexts where institutional change is harder to achieve. The countries might also have started reforms late, such that results can only be expected in the future. This section explores evidence related to all of these arguments.

Mixed Results and the Quantity and Quality of Reform

Two groups of countries can be identified in the sample of forty identified in Chapter 1, given their performance over time on QoG and government effectiveness measures. The decliners include eighteen countries that regressed on these indicators between 1998 and 2008.[9] They contrast with nineteen improver group countries that have done better on the indicators in this time.[10] Some might posit that the difference between these two groups relates to the number of reforms they introduced. Perhaps the latter

---

[9] These are Argentina, Benin, Bolivia, Cape Verde, Guinea, Haiti, Honduras, Madagascar, Malawi, Moldova, Mongolia, Nicaragua, Samoa, Senegal, Sri Lanka, Thailand, Togo, and Uruguay.

[10] These are Afghanistan, Algeria, Angola, Azerbaijan, Bulgaria, Burundi, Chile, China, Georgia, Ghana, Mauritius, Mozambique, Niger, Poland, Rwanda, Serbia, Tanzania, Uganda, and Ukraine.

group simply had more interventions over past decades? This is difficult to test, partly because it is tricky to identify what constitutes a reform and how many reforms countries have pursued. There is an imperfect approach to this problem, however, which involves testing whether countries in the improver group had a greater number of World Bank projects incorporating some kind of institutional reform content than others. World Bank project numbers obviously do not account for internal engagements or those sponsored by other external agencies. They do, nonetheless, reflect reform activities sponsored by the biggest actor in the field, as well as the influence this actor has had on a country's reforms.

Given this approach, the average number of World Bank projects with institutional reform content was 58 for countries in the improver group.[11] A *t*-test shows that this was not statistically different from the average of fifty-two projects in declining group countries.[12] Beyond the raw data, one can contrast individual country experiences to get a qualitative perspective on the issue. A declining score country, Uruguay, started World Bank–sponsored institutional reform projects in 1988 and had thirty-eight such operations that cost more than $900 million, but saw drops in QoG and government effectiveness scores between 1998 and 2008 and slow economic growth in that time.[13] Azerbaijan, by contrast, adopted a similar thirty-seven projects with institutional reform content starting in 1995 and costing $342 million. It saw improved QoG and government effectiveness scores and strong economic growth in recent years.[14]

Comparing countries like Azerbaijan and Uruguay in this way obviously has its limits. The data capture nothing of the quality and commitment in either country's reform experience, for instance. Perhaps projects in Azerbaijan were adopted and implemented with more commitment than those in Uruguay? Maybe this is the key difference between improving and declining countries? It is difficult to test this argument as well, but World Bank project completion reports do provide some insight, given that they evaluate project quality. One can look at these evaluations and determine

---

[11] These were projects sponsoring activities in the public administration, law, and justice sector.

[12] *t*-tests suggest that there was no significant difference in the number of projects between these groups ($t = -0.63$, Satterthwaite's df = 27.74) or the cost of these projects ($t = 0.20$, Satterthwaite's df = 21.52).

[13] WGI government effectiveness scores fell from 0.62 to 0.48 in this period; QoG evaluations also declined; and economic growth was at 27 percent for the decade, less than the average for upper-middle-income countries.

[14] WGI government effectiveness scores increased by more than 0.25, and per capita income quadrupled in this period.

whether improving countries had a lower level of unsatisfactory projects than countries in the declining group.[15]

One is led to expect that project quality and commitment matter when considering evaluations from Azerbaijan. One hundred percent of the World Bank projects supporting institutional reforms in this country were deemed marginally satisfactory or better on completion. However, this is not true for all countries in the improver group. Only 70 percent of Burundi's evaluated projects were considered marginally satisfactory or better.[16] The Central African Republic experienced improved government effectiveness scores between 1998 and 2008, regardless of having eight unsatisfactory institutional reform projects of twenty-five. By contrast, a number of declining group countries had stellar records of project success. Mongolia and Cape Verde saw declining government effectiveness and QoG scores even with no unsatisfactory institutional reform projects, for instance. When considering all countries, the declining group does have a slightly higher rate of unsatisfactory projects (about 23 percent on average), but this is not significantly different from the average of the improving group (about 19 percent). The bottom line is that most projects were considered satisfactorily completed in most countries, and there is no real evidence to show that decliners had systematically weaker-quality projects or reform agendas.[17]

This suggests that governments across the developing world have adopted most of the laws, decrees, systems, organizational units, and such prescribed by external agents like the World Bank. They have been rewarded for doing so with records of generally satisfactory project completion and subsequent access to new projects, money, and support. The rewards of reform have also arguably included more functional governments in some places. However, the data analyzed here suggest that such rewards have been absent from the story line of about half (or more) of the countries involved. One of these is Honduras. This country engaged in fifty-nine World Bank projects

---

[15] Project completion reports were accessed from the World Bank project database. About half of more than two thousand projects with PAL&J content in the forty countries had reports. Two-thirds were rated satisfactory or highly satisfactory; 15 percent were marginally satisfactory.

[16] Based on the author's analysis of Burundi's PAL&J project documents in the World Bank's project database.

[17] This finding is partly due to the incomplete nature of the evidence. Nearly half of the projects did not have completion reports. Existing assessments lack variation; two-thirds of projects with completion reports were rated satisfactory or better. This is consistent with numbers in World Bank (2008), in which 79 percent of projects completed between 1999 and 2006 were satisfactory or better. Public sector reform projects succeeded at a lower rate of 43 percent. The 65 percent number reflects public sector projects and other projects in the sample of PAL&J interventions.

with institutional reform content from 1988 onward – alongside interventions supported by the Inter-American Development Bank and others. Most World Bank projects were considered successful. They have led to significant adjustments in the way government looks, as described in project documents:[18]

- Projects produced laws on banking, trade, and privatization in the early 1990s, and established regulatory, procurement, and concessions agencies.
- The late 1990s saw new civil service laws, privatization decrees, downsizing, the creation of PFM (Public Financial Management) information systems, the formalization of civil service payment systems, and wage bill controls.
- Projects in the early 2000s bought laws on civil service and procurement, PFM, competition, and external audit. A treasury single account and multiyear budget was introduced; information technology (IT) capabilities improved; the audit court was revamped; and new strategies, procurement mechanisms, and results-based management systems were adopted.
- Between 2004 and 2008, the government revamped its civil service laws again and introduced anticorruption and transparency regulations, an anticorruption agency, participatory budgeting, and merit-based hiring and performance-based compensation mechanisms.
- Privatization continued under various operations throughout the period.

QoG scores dropped for Honduras in this time, however, and GDP per capita grew at about 2 percent per annum, much less than the average for other lower-middle-income countries. A coup in 2009 reflected on broad governance problems in the country. The large set of reforms, introduced at a cost exceeding $700 million, may have made the Honduran government look better but apparently fell short of making the government good enough to register in external indicators or to stave off political upheaval.

Mixed Results and the Context and Time of Reform

Experts on Honduras may take issue with this analysis, pointing to the impact of context and time on reform results. They might suggest that reforms have faltered because they transpired when Honduras transitioned

---

[18] The author analyzed more than 20 documents to identify achievements. A list is available from the author on request.

to democracy, for instance, which complicated progress. They may also argue that Honduras began reforms later than some neighbors and that these interventions take time to have an impact. They would be right in noting that context and time are important influences on government effectiveness and reform. How these influences matter, however, is, not always clear.

Literature identifies many contextual factors influencing the effectiveness or quality of governments.[19] Countries typically perform better on indicators used to assess this if they have stronger economies, reasonable records of growth, stable and entrenched democracies, and diverse sources of government revenue. These characteristics are evident in some improver group countries, like Poland and Serbia. They help to explain why a number of Eastern European countries seem to have experienced more success with institutional reforms than others.[20] Most developing country contexts do not enjoy such characteristics, however. This is a basic reason why such countries tend to have lower scores on prominent governance indicators. Noting this, some observers question the validity of these indicators in countries like Honduras, Afghanistan, and Burundi.[21] There is also good reason to temper expectations that such countries could or should adopt the kinds of reforms identified as necessary or "right" by development organizations. Modern civil service and PFM systems, liberalized financial systems, and the like have emerged as relevant in contexts very different to those commonly found in developing countries and may not be practically possible in these poorer contexts.

This has not stopped the aggressive transfer of modern reform agendas to developing countries, however. The list of interventions in Honduras stands as evidence. Countries like Honduras, Afghanistan, and Burundi are introducing reform types that developed countries adopted only in recent decades. Examples include modern internal audit, fiscal rules, privatization, multiyear budgeting, and meritocratic and performance-based civil service regimes.[22] Interestingly, contextual factors that trigger such reforms seem quite different from those that characterize more effective governments (from which the reforms are arguably sourced and where they have proven to be functional and effective). For instance, a number of countries in the improver group emerged recently from crisis and are poor and dependent on the external donor community. They include Afghanistan, Burundi,

---

[19] Andrews 2008, 2011, 2012; Kurtz and Schrank, 2007; Lee and Whitford 2009; Moloney 2009.
[20] World Bank 2008.
[21] Andrews 2008.
[22] Andrews 2008, 2012a; Grindle, 2004.

Mozambique, Niger, and Rwanda, which have all improved governance scores from low base levels in the 1990s. Instability and dependence seem to have been key contextual factors instigating the adoption of reforms in such countries. The question is whether these countries have contexts in which such reforms can be implemented and influential.

Studies suggest this is not the case.[23] Poorer countries that are coming out of conflict, beset with fragile economic and political orders, and highly dependent on donors tend to struggle in implementing reforms. They have a high rate of reform adoption to attract outside support but enjoy low levels of reform success. Some theorists might caution against making such conclusions too early in an institutional change process, however. It is generally agreed that new institutions take time to be fully implemented and influential.[24] This argument is taken for granted in the development domain and leads to calls for realistic expectations about the pace of reform in areas as varied as PFM,[25] decentralization,[26] and health.[27] It is possible that countries coming out of conflict may just take longer to see the results of deep institutional change than others.

Given such argument, one might expect that countries with more institutional reforms in the 1980s and 1990s saw the most progress on governance indicators in the 2000s. This expectation is not supported by basic statistical analysis, however. The average improver group country actually had fewer early World Bank projects with institutional reform content than the average decliner (even though differences are not statistically significant).[28] Countries like Argentina, Honduras, Bolivia, Senegal, Sri Lanka, Thailand, and Togo all experienced declines in QoG scores between 1998 and 2008 despite starting reforms early on. Surprisingly, the average improver group country actually had higher project numbers since 2000 than the average decliner (although, again, the difference was not statistically significant).[29] Countries like Afghanistan, Georgia, Azerbaijan, Burundi, Serbia, and Rwanda fit into this group. They have seen improved scores on governance indicators even after starting World Bank–sponsored institutional reforms relatively late.

---

[23] Andrews 2012.

[24] North 1990.

[25] de Renzio and Dorotinsky 2007.

[26] Faletti 2010.

[27] World Bank 2009.

[28] Improving group countries averaged about twenty projects in this time, while declining group countries had an average of about thirty projects.

[29] Improving group countries averaged about twenty projects in this time, while declining group countries had an average of about nineteen projects.

This evidence suggests that recent activity has a bigger influence on government effectiveness scores than past activity. It is hardly a complete assessment of the issue, however, considering only World Bank projects and lacking contextual controls. Unfortunately, there is limited work examining this issue with more rigor. A recent study that stands out in this respect assessed the impact reforms have had on the quality of PFM systems in developing countries.[30] After accounting for broad donor engagement and controlling for contextual factors, it found that early starters did perform differently. Countries that had engaged in reforms for longer did not have better results, however, or higher levels of implementation or diffusion of reforms. By contrast, the additional time had just yielded better-looking budget documents and laws and stronger central agencies. The study identifies these as the "simpler reform areas" and notes that additional time did not lead to gains in "the messier, and more difficult, challenges" of reform implementation.[31] The implication is that time helps countries perfect the form of new institutions but does not facilitate greater implementation, functionality, or influence. The authors present this as a reason why reforms seem to have a "very small impact" after even decades of engagement.[32]

A NEW PERSPECTIVE ON THIS PUZZLING EVIDENCE

The evidence presented here is hardly final or conclusive, but it is puzzling. Institutional reforms in development do seem to have mixed results that often disappoint. These results are not explained by conventional arguments. Reforms are being pursued even after disappointing results from prior, satisfactorily completed interventions. Reforms are being adopted in countries with obviously problematic contexts. Reforms often do not seem to yield more functional or effective governments, even with time.

This section attempts to explain such puzzling evidence. It presents short narratives of selected countries' experiences to suggest that reforms may often be introduced as signals to improve short-term external perceptions of government effectiveness, with little focus on fostering better long-term results. The signaling game means that countries commit to best practice reforms but seldom succeed in implementing them (especially when contexts are prohibitive). The response to poor implementation is to resume signaling, often promising better versions of the same failed reforms, instead

---

[30] de Renzio, Andrews, and Mills 2011.
[31] de Renzio, Andrews, and Mills 2011, 20.
[32] de Renzio, Andrews, and Mills 2011, 21.

of asking how the prior intervention could be made more influential. Over time, countries get better at producing the externally visible forms associated with these promises, but a gap exists between form and function.

The signaling stories emerge using a historical narrative that tracks the way reform activity was perceived in determining selected countries' WGI scores.[33] Evidence was accessed through publications that inform data used in creating these scores, including Economic Intelligence Unit (EIU), Bertelsmann Transformation Index (BTI), and International Monetary Fund (IMF) reports. A more developed narrative recounts Argentina's journey, and shorter discussions tell of experiences in Bolivia, Benin, Niger, Afghanistan, Rwanda, and Georgia.

A View on Argentina's Reforms

Externally supported reforms began in Argentina in the late 1980s. The country had a legacy of instability and a government described as inefficient. In the early 1990s, Carlos Menem's administration partnered with international organizations to address this, promoting solutions like privatization, liberalization, deregulation, and public sector modernization. There were no fewer than thirty-two World Bank projects with this content in the early 1990s, generally implemented satisfactorily.[34] Results were immediate, with Argentina "widely hailed as a case of successful market reform."[35] Foreign direct investment poured in and economic growth ensued.[36] Government was perceived as being effective, reflected in a 1996 WGI government effectiveness score of 0.32, second only to Chile in Latin America. Such performance was strongly attributed to the reform initiatives. Michel Camdessus, then managing director of the IMF, noted in 1996 that "Argentina's determined adjustment and reform efforts were rewarded with strong capital inflows, a sharp recovery and average real economic growth of more than $7\frac{1}{2}$ percent per year."[37]

---

[33] For methodological issues, see Büthe 2002; Faletti and Lynch 2009.

[34] Based on the author's analysis, twenty-eight projects were rated satisfactory or better; two were rated unsatisfactory.

[35] The 2010 Bertelsmann Transformation Index (BTI) Report for Argentina notes that "rigorous implementation of prescribed policies" led to Argentina becoming "the poster child of the neoliberal adjustment policies under the Washington Consensus." See http://www.bertelsmann-transformation-index.de/96.0.html?L=1.

[36] Inflows were 1.29 percent of GDP in 1990 and 2.6 percent of GDP in 1996.

[37] Taken from a May 27, 1996, address by Mr. Michel Camdessus, managing director of the IMF, at the Academy of Economic Science, Buenos Aires, Argentina, http://www.imf.org/external/np/sec/mds/1996/mds9611.htm.

The record began unraveling at this point, however. Economic and political instability returned via international financial crashes and growing
domestic political infighting. Recession came quickly, but perceptions of
government effectiveness fell even faster. Government effectiveness scores
dropped to 0.18 in 1998 and −0.39 in 2002, with various observers linking such decline to weak implementation of the 1990s reform agenda.
Government had halted pension privatization and labor deregulation, for
instance, canceled other privatization efforts, and violated new fiscal rules.
The IMF's Anne Krueger described Argentina as the model of a country
that "tried little, failed much" and identified the problem as "a reluctance
to follow-through, to confront the structural changes."[38] BTI commentary
noted, "Consistent, coherent reforms are not discernable. Tentative initiatives never got off the starting blocks. [One] doubts whether reforms of the
1990s increased efficiency at all."[39]

The comments suggest that 1990s reforms took the form of ambitious
signals that garnered short-term external support but could not be implemented in the medium term given instability that was part and parcel
of Argentina's context. Interestingly, the signals started again under the
new Kirchner administration in 2003. A number of reform engagements
emphasized transparency and renewed attention to building institutions
in the economy, as well as formalized, rule-based public management. A
2004 law, for example, introduced new rules to discipline the state. Efforts
also focused on re-creating regulatory frameworks to benefit foreign firms
whose 1990s privatization deals had been cancelled in 2002. The IMF's
Anne Krueger responded positively to these new signals, noting that "[t]he
Argentina government has committed itself to implementing wide-ranging
structural reforms."[40] BTI commentary at the time was similar: "The government is committed to democracy and a market economy . . . with some
Keynesian accents."[41] Such endorsements helped government effectiveness
scores recover to −0.13 in 2004 and −0.06 in 2006. The sad story of 1990s
reform was forgotten, replaced by new signals of better practice.

The sentiment changed again in late 2006 and beyond, however. The
"Keynesian accents" in Argentina's policies became a cause for concern,
with IMF, BTI, and EIU documents explicitly calling for less government
engagement in the economy. By 2009, the analyses are overwhelmingly negative, noting that the new Kirchner administration had not become more

---

[38] Krueger 2004a.
[39] See BTI Report for Argentina in 2010, http://www.bertelsmann-transformation-index.de.
[40] Krueger 2004b.
[41] See BTI Report for Argentina in 2006, http://www.bertelsmann-transformation-index.de.

"consistent," advocating policies that clashed with the messages offered to external players in reforms between 2003 and 2005. The 2010 BTI report laments that "[m]any reforms... were not carried through. [President] Cristina Kirchner neither upheld her promise to strengthen political institutions nor did she provide for a sound economic framework."[42]

Commentators noted a range of problems with reforms. Surpluses were down and arrears were growing in the provinces, for instance – surely not an example of the "fiscal responsibility" promised in the 2004 law. The nationalization of pensions was also seen to signal a preference for more intervention rather than less, which an EIU report noted would "erode confidence further in the government's respect for stable rules of the game."[43] Reflecting this sentiment, Argentina's government effectiveness scores dropped to −0.18 in 2008 and to −0.42 in 2009 – an even lower level than in 2002. As in the 1990s, reform signals had spurred perceptions of government effectiveness between 2002 and 2006. Failure to abide fully by these commitments hurt perceptions thereafter, however – as they did after the 1990s reforms.

Reform Signaling in Bolivia, Benin, Niger, Afghanistan, Rwanda, and Georgia

Bolivia and Benin offer similar stories. Both countries adopted significant institutional reforms in the 1990s and early 2000s. These emphasized smaller and more formal government and market-friendly rules of the game. This was remarkable given that both countries had legacies of very different governance structures – involving military rule in Bolivia and Marxist-Leninist government in Benin. They received credit for these reforms in early government effectiveness scores that were relatively high for their regions. Benin scored approximately zero in 1996 and seventh best in Africa; Bolivia was at −0.06 in 1998 and ninth best in Latin America. Scores declined for both countries for most of the 2000s, however, to −0.5 for Benin and −0.8 for Bolivia in 2008. Benin is now seventeenth in Africa, and Bolivia is eighteenth in Latin America (lower than even Cuba).

The declining scores are explained in large part by observed problems with reforms. Bolivia's civil service and PFM reforms were undermined in the late 1990s by what observers note as the stubborn influence of politicization and informality.[44] Benin's early downsizing reforms were also found to be

---

[42] See BTI Report for Argentina in 2010, http://www.bertelsmann-transformation-index.de.
[43] Economic Intelligence Unit (EIU) Report for Argentina, January 2009, www.eiu.com.
[44] See BTI Report for Bolivia in 2006, http://www.bertelsmann-transformation-index.de; Montes 2003; World Bank 2000b.

less than effective. Many civil servants had simply been moved onto contract for a period and returned to the payroll in later years.[45] A civil service law introduced to much acclaim in the late 1990s was never passed by Benin's parliament, either, raising questions about the commitment to reform.[46] Privatization experiences were also criticized in both countries. EIU and BTI reports point to failed hydrocarbon privatization in Bolivia as evidence of reform backtracking. BTI assessments note that "partial privatization" in Benin led to government-influenced oligopolies operating in the port authority and cotton sector.[47]

Initially rising and then declining government effectiveness scores in Argentina, Bolivia, and Benin can therefore be traced back to these countries' reform agendas. All three countries were first rewarded for signaling the intent to pass far-reaching reforms, only to face penalties when failing to implement and sustain the signaled reforms. This is an unfolding story in Niger, Afghanistan, Rwanda, and Georgia as well.

Niger and Afghanistan registered two of the highest improvements in government effectiveness scores between 1998 and 2008. Both were coming off extremely low bases, with generally accepted weak governments and especially unstable political and economic conditions. Both saw improved government effectiveness scores until 2004. Better scores were largely attributed to a raft of announced reforms that signaled acceptance of an externally driven reform approach. Both saw government effectiveness scores drop after 2004, however. BTI reports note that Niger's government ratings suffered because it did not always have "success in implementing announced reforms."[48] It cites specific examples, including expanded government spending in 2004 (which contravened rules agreed to with the IMF), inconsistent regulatory reforms, and the abandonment of plans to privatize electricity generation and fuel distribution companies. The list of poorly implemented reforms is much longer in Afghanistan. It includes privatization (where a law was passed in 2005 but had not been acted on by 2010), and public finance and civil service reform (where 2005 laws have been largely ineffective and systems are run by foreigners). Reflecting on such issues, the 2010 BTI report states, "The government of Afghanistan remains weak. It has failed to implement important reforms."[49]

---

[45] IMF 2003.
[46] See BTI Report for Benin in 2006, http://www.bertelsmann-transformation-index.de.
[47] See BTI Reports for Bolivia and Benin in 2010, http://www.bertelsmann-transformation-index.de.
[48] See BTI Report for Niger, 2006, http://www.bertelsmann-transformation-index.de.
[49] See BTI Report for Afghanistan, 2006, http://www.bertelsmann-transformation-index.de.

The stories in Rwanda and Georgia are more nuanced. Both countries have seen major improvements in government effectiveness scores since 2002, when they accelerated reform agendas. Both countries have been acknowledged as the World Bank's *Doing Business* Most Improved Business Reformer in the world at least once since 2007, and both have seen significant upticks in foreign capital inflows – much like Argentina in the mid-1990s. Government effectiveness scores have recently hit a plateau in both countries, however, with analysts questioning reform implementation and the sustainability of reform ideals given political tensions – much like Argentina in the late 1990s.[50] Key issues in both contexts are the growing expression of authoritarian control in government and high levels of politicization. The 2010 BTI report claims, for instance, that Rwandan reforms have been a façade behind which the government has exercised raw power.[51] Political influence in both countries is noted in perceptions of the way civil servants are hired and privatization awards made. Politics is also seen as distorting activities of the judiciary and a range of other areas in which reform has progressed well technically. Implementation weaknesses are noted as well, especially in Georgia. The 2010 BTI report refers to "a certain gap between legal norm and every-day practice" and notes that "Georgia's positive ranking mainly refers to legislative reforms. When it comes to assessing the implementation of legal norms in practice, the picture is different."[52]

Viewing Reforms as Signals Helps Explain Puzzling Evidence

These brief stories provide a textured perspective on the chapter's overall narrative. They tell of impressive-looking reforms that countries adopt to win outsiders over in the short term, but which prove difficult to fully implement later on. There are undoubtedly other versions of this narrative, but the one provided here helps make sense of the puzzling evidence shown earlier. The idea of reforms as signals helps one understand why different countries pursue the same international best practice reforms regardless of fit, for instance, and why reforms often fail on implementation. Additionally, it yields some explanation of why countries keep on with government reforms that do not help improve governments. The intention is to make government look better, not necessarily to make government better. Building

---

[50] See BTI Reports for Rwanda and Georgia in 2010, http://www.bertelsmanntrans-formation-index.de, and Economic Intelligence Unit (EIU) Reports for Rwanda and Georgia, July 2010, www.eiu.com.

[51] See BTI Report for Rwanda in 2010, http://www.bertelsmann-transformation-index.de.

[52] See BTI Report for Georgia in 2010, http://www.bertelsmann-transformation-index.de.

on this book's leading metaphor, one should think of a carpenter paying more attention to what his pegs look like than to whether they fill the holes in his wall or floor, because prizes are given for form and not function.

The book suggests that this idea of reforms as signals is central to understanding why many institutional reforms do not make governments better. These reforms are chosen to earn governments in developing countries short-term credit from outsiders on whom they depend. This credit is often reflected through scores on measures like the WGIs, which influence how much financial and political support developing countries receive. Unfortunately, there are reasons to believe that reforms focused on impressing outsiders in the short run often do not foster real improvements in the longer run. The following four chapters discuss these reasons. Chapter 3 argues that reformers focused on short-term signaling do not ensure that contexts are ready and open to change, for instance. This problem is compounded by the tendency to choose impressive looking but demanding interventions when adopting reforms as signals (discussed in Chapter 4). Such tendencies result in reform pegs that are the wrong shape and size for reform contexts and do not get fitted or implemented, subsequently failing to influence the behavior of most agents and improve governments (as addressed in Chapters 5 and 6).

While these issues are discussed, readers should remember that there are positive reform experiences in development – where interventions are not introduced as signals. Chapters 7 through 10 examine what these reforms look like. This discussion notes that a focus on solving problems can counter the tendency to use reforms as signals. The problem focus demands attention to context and leads a process of finding and fitting contextually appropriate solutions. This approach has facilitated more functional reforms in many countries in the past and offers an alternative to reforms as signals and square peg reforms in round hole governments.

THREE

Overlooking the Change Context

IF IT WEREN'T FOR CONTEXT

In 1997, the International Monetary Fund (IMF) and World Bank helped Indonesia create a Commercial Court and revamp its bankruptcy laws. The reforms were considered necessary given poor legal solutions to insolvency problems that emerged during the East Asian financial crisis. Unfortunately, the reforms proved a disappointment. Firms did not use the laws or court to resolve contractual failures related to bankruptcy.[1] The reasons for this, it turns out, were not new. Similar legal mechanisms had failed in the past because of what observers describe as "traditional problems of institutional weakness and failure to enforce new laws."[2] It seems that reform "occurred without fully appreciating" this context and introduced an "alien institution in unpropitious domestic soil" that was bound to fail.[3] In short, reformers ignored reality and found that, when ignored, reality bites.

This is not an isolated case. Prior chapters argued that many institutional reforms do not produce better governments. Chapter 2 suggested that failures often result from reforms adopted as "signals." The current chapter argues that this approach commonly leads reform designers to overlook important aspects of the context in which interventions are planned. This undermines the potential of reforms to effect change, sometimes even relegating interventions to what one observer of Indonesia's experience calls "window dressing."[4] To build on the book's leading metaphor, these reforms are like pegs a carpenter produces without looking at the hole he is trying

[1] Halliday and Carruthers 2007; Linnan 2000; Tomasic 2001.
[2] Lindsey and Taylor 2000, 3.
[3] Ibid., 3.
[4] Ibid., 3.

to fill. No matter how well crafted they are, pegs created in this way are unlikely to fit.

The opening section broaches this topic through two case studies of efforts to harden Argentina's budget constraint after 1990 and reduce corruption in post-1994 Malawi. These studies trace the process of reform and show that multiple efforts to reshape rules and behavior failed – ostensibly because of stubborn contextual constraints. The second section presents a theoretical argument to explain this. It introduces the idea of "inter-institutional" contexts in which multiple institutional logics interact to shape the potential for change. This potential is influenced by disruption, the level of dominance one logic has over others, the presence of viable alternative logics, and the degree to which agents push for change. The section argues that external reform designers commonly discount the influence of such factors when crafting interventions, or fail to observe those elements that are informal. This leads to cases of reforms not fitting into the targeted setting – because the setting either is not ripe for change or does not accommodate the change imposed on it.

The arguments are validated with reference to the cases from Argentina and Malawi. This is a common approach in work adopting historical narratives, in which theory is explained through the process tracing exercise.[5] A conclusion summarizes this theory and raises questions about structuring reforms to better consider context.

WHEN CONTEXT IS OVERLOOKED, "HISTORY REPEATS ITSELF"
IN REFORMS

Context affects many institutional reforms. It manifests in historical narratives emerging through the details in project documents from reform experiences. Initial design reports often reflect on opportunities for change. Annual updates often recount evidence of initial change – like the adoption of a new law. Later evaluations often note disappointing results and blame contextual factors for this – like weak political will and low capacity. Two such stories pertain to fiscal reform in Argentina and anticorruption interventions in Malawi. These stories are told here using evidence from documents produced by external agencies and secondary observers.[6]

---

[5] Büthe 2002; Faletti and Lynch 2009.
[6] Twenty years of development organization documents were analyzed, showing perspectives on reforms at different points in time. They are complemented by government, academic, and media documents. Combining such documents allows a rich and multifaceted view

Introducing Hard Budget Constraints in Argentina

Argentina faced a hyperinflation crisis in 1989. A locally devised monetary policy solution called Convertibility is arguably the most written about policy product of this event. Fiscal policy solutions were also center stage, however, given arguments that the country's public finance regime produced "incentives favoring spending without incentives to raise revenues."[7] The problem was considered particularly severe for entities outside the federal government, including public enterprises, the social security system, and provinces.[8] They routinely overspent and were bailed out by public sector banks or through discretionary executive orders the nation's presidents used to muster support.[9] This manifest as a soft budget constraint problem; spending units expected to be rescued if they ran out of funds and thus had no incentive to manage resources responsibly.[10]

Government worked with the IMF, World Bank, and Inter-American Development Bank to harden this constraint throughout the 1990s. Interventions established rules that formalized the link between expenditure and revenues. These included 1991's formula-based agreements on intergovernmental revenue sharing, 1992's Law of Public Financial Management and Performance Control, the introduction of numeric rules to constrain spending through regulations in 1996, and 1998's Fiscal Convertibility Law.[11] The latter legislation formalized limits on the size of deficits and the rate of spending growth, established a Countercyclical Fund, and introduced penalties for violators of the new rules. Such steps led the World Bank to declare success as early as 1993. The interventions were described as a set of "difficult-to-reverse reforms in the fiscal framework, institutions, and policies."[12] New laws were provided as evidence of institutional change, and decreased federal spending and employment showed that such institutions were reshaping behavior.[13]

The external view on reforms changed significantly between 1995 and 2001, however. A succession of international financial crises sent shock waves through Argentina and exposed many weaknesses in the 1990s reform

---

into the process of reform. Documents are cited throughout the text, and a full listing of sources, identified according to time, is available from the author.
[7] World Bank 1993a, 4.
[8] Ibid.
[9] Gibson 1997.
[10] The term "soft budget constraint" was coined by Kornai (1979, 1980, 1986).
[11] Bonvecchi 2010; World Bank 1995.
[12] World Bank 1993a, xi.
[13] World Bank 1995.

agenda. By 2000, the country was in dire straits because of public debt to GDP ratios that exceeded 50 percent. These ratios had grown progressively throughout the 1990s – from 29.2 percent to 41.4 percent during the booming economic years between 1993 and 1998.[14] This was driven largely by increased spending and hiring in the provinces, where cheap loans from public sector banks were still available and often kept off the books. Many observers also note that the president still used executive orders to channel money to provincial governors in the period.[15] Additionally, the newly introduced fiscal rules were often violated as soon as they were introduced.[16] When combined, these experiences indicate that the post-reform budget constraint was softer than observers in the World Bank and IMF had thought. This contributed to major crisis in 2002, when Economy Minister Jorge Remes Lenicov stated, "We are in collapse. We are broke."[17]

Lenicov was part of the team President Eduardo Duhalde set in place to restore stability in early 2002. Duhalde was one of the provincial governors implicated with spending extravagantly during the 1990s.[18] Nestor Kirchner, his replacement in March 2003, had the same reputation. Nevertheless, both men found themselves working on new mechanisms to once again try and harden the budget constraint. As in 1990, the IMF made fiscal reform a central plank of its post-crisis stability program, calling for new laws to formalize revenue sharing and for new fiscal rules.[19] Accordingly, President Kirchner hurriedly sent a new Fiscal Responsibility Law (FRL) to Congress in June 2004 – days before IMF staffers began a third review of its September 2003 agreement to provide financial support for the country. Like prior laws in 1992 and 1998, the FRL formalized budget processes, linked expenditure and GDP growth, set limits on deficits, instituted a borrowing constraint for provinces, and mandated contributions to a countercyclical fund.[20]

Unfortunately, fiscal rules central to the FRL were broken from the start. Spending grew by more than GDP in 2005, for instance, and continued growing like this in following years.[21] Procedural rules designed to enhance accountability of the executive to Congress were also never operationalized.

---

[14] Mussa 2002, 14.
[15] Benton 2009; Gibson and Calvo 2000.
[16] Braun and Gadano 2007; Levitsky and Murillo 2008.
[17] Blustein 2006, 186.
[18] Becker 2002; Benton 2009.
[19] Braun and Gadano (2007, 15) note that "the IMF gave primary importance to the approval of new fiscal legislation that included rules."
[20] Braun and Gadano 2007.
[21] Ibid.

Discretionary engagements between provinces and the presidency have also continued unabated. Observing this, Miguel Braun titles a 2006 paper written for the World Bank on fiscal reform in the country "Why History Repeats Itself."[22]

Combating Corruption in Malawi

Malawi's elections in May 1994 signaled the end of a thirty-year rule by Hastings Banda. This rule had been absolute since 1971, when Banda was declared president for life. The period, known as one of great repression and control, began to unravel in the late 1980s.[23] Various stabilization and restructuring initiatives were supported by external donors in this time.[24] Most were considered less than successful, and the Banda administration was frequently blamed for failure.[25] Reports note that rigid hierarchical leadership, lack of accountability, and general disrespect of law undermined governance.[26]

The 1994 election heralded a change, however, with a new president, constitution, and apparent commitment to change. External donors initiated various institutional reforms, including renewed efforts to deregulate, liberalize, and privatize. There was also a novel emphasis on curbing corruption, which initial diagnostics explained was rampant because of weak formal rules of the game and the perverse incentives these rules created; public officials could pursue private interests unabated.[27] Based on this diagnosis, donors supported reforms that introduced a new law – the Corrupt Practices Act of 1995 – and an agency – the Anti-Corruption Bureau (ACB) – to enforce it.[28]

Reports between 1996 and 2000 suggest that reforms were working well. They note that the president and minister of finance referenced anticorruption in prominent speeches and personally engaged with donors on the issue, acting as "champions."[29] They also cite visible action on the part of the ACB, which handled 8,335 complaints in its early years and launched 2,672 investigations.[30] Such achievements were called into question in

---

[22] Braun 2006.
[23] World Bank 1985, 1990a, 1990b.
[24] World Bank 1990a, 1990b.
[25] World Bank 1993b, 2000c.
[26] World Bank 2000c, 1–2.
[27] World Bank 1998a, v.
[28] Donors included the World Bank, DANIDA, Japan, and DFID.
[29] World Bank 1998a.
[30] Rothstein 2005, 5.

2000, however, when the "87 million kwacha scandal" erupted. More than US$2 million of donor funds earmarked for new schools wound up in government pockets instead, including (allegedly) the nation's then-president, Bakili Muluzi.[31] International agencies stopped funding as a result, and various observers started looking more closely at the anticorruption initiative.[32]

On close investigation, the new laws and anticorruption entities appeared to have had little influence. Although the ACB investigated thousands of charges, prosecutions were initiated in less than one hundred cases, and only a few of these were concluded in court.[33] Most action was taken against junior officials or members of past regimes, even though corruption was commonly associated with senior members of the sitting administration. Senior officials did not face increased attention even after the 2001 scandal, when corruption actually seemed to worsen. This is reflected in declining Transparency International scores. These fell from a high of 4.1 (of 10) in 1998 to 3.2 in 2001, 2.9 in 2002, 2.8 in 2003, and 2.7 in 2006.[34] Scores declined during the first post–Banda government (led by Muluzi) and continued falling during the next (under President wa Mutharika, who took office in 2004).

Reform results were obviously disappointing, reflecting an institutional landscape that had not changed much. For instance, the ACB was meant to be an independent body, but its head was directly appointed by the president – even when this office was considered the apex of corruption before and after reform. Furthermore, the ACB lacked the legal authority to prosecute the cases it investigated. The director of public prosecutions (DPP) – acting under control of the president – enjoyed this authority before and after reform.[35] It is also interesting to note that government increased funding to the DPP in the 1990s and 2000s, but never supported the ACB properly.[36] The ACB was always heavily dependent on donor funding, indicating limited internal legitimacy and support. It existed as a new entity in name, but did not really challenge preexisting institutional mechanisms.

Faced with the challenge of a flailing anticorruption initiative, the government rewrote aspects of the law in 2004 and worked with donors to launch a new reform in 2009. This introduced new laws and mechanisms

---

[31] See the 2007 Global Integrity report, http://report.globalintegrity.org/Malawi/2007/notebook.

[32] Ibid.

[33] Rothstein 2005, 5.

[34] These statistics are not strictly comparable over time given shifting methods and samples. They are, however, commonly compared over time to provide a picture of change patterns.

[35] Kamanga 2008; World Bank 1998a.

[36] Norad 2010.

and aimed to strengthen the ACB. A 2010 evaluation suggests that these reforms were still having a limited effect, however. New processes were identified but not implemented,[37] the ACB remained poorly staffed and funded,[38] and it still lacked the authority necessary to prosecute cases.[39] In explaining such limits, the evaluation notes that the anticorruption reforms have been "[a]ffected by a political context where politics and institutions are highly personalized and a political culture which tends to discourage impartiality."[40] The report argues that such contextual factors undermined the impact of impartial, formal anticorruption laws, and law enforcers. This resonates with comments made more than a decade before, which suggested that 1990s reforms should address contextual "reasons why the formal rules governing behaviour in the public sector have broken down, and why informality – of which corruption is one manifestation – has taken over."[41]

It appears that these contextual realities were not addressed, however, either in 1994 or in 2009. In both instances, reforms focused instead on introducing new and improved formal rules and rule makers. The result is history repeating itself, as it did in Argentina, with contextual limits emerging again and again to thwart change.

HOW INSTITUTIONAL CONTEXTS IMPACT INSTITUTIONAL REFORMS

The institutional reform experiences of Malawi and Argentina are not peculiar. They are examples of the many interventions described as failures in earlier chapters. Such failure often results from the impact of stubborn contextual constraints that are not effectively considered in most reform designs. Isabelle Werenfels points to this in arguing that Algerian privatization was undermined by "a country-specific complex interplay of . . . forces [that] decisively affect the path of any institutional transformation."[42] Andrew Wilder writes similarly about governance reform in Pakistan, where donors consistently push for change "without investing sufficiently in understanding the social, cultural and political contexts within which the civil service functions."[43]

---

[37] Norad 2010, 6.
[38] Ibid., 6.
[39] Ibid., 6.
[40] World Bank 1998a, v.
[41] http://www1.worldbank.org/publicsector/anticorrupt/MalawiGCA.pdf.
[42] Werenfels 2002, 3.
[43] Wilder 2009, 33.

Werenfels's and Wilder's comments – and the introductory stories from Argentina and Malawi – raise two important questions. What should external actors like donors know about the context in which institutional reform takes place? Why do these external actors underinvest in understanding such things? This section addresses both questions, arguing first that complex institutional structures always exist in multiples, creating a context that shapes possibilities for institutional reform. It then posits that external agents either choose to ignore much of this contextual reality or cannot "see" it because they are outside the system. These agents focus only on what they do see, which undermines their ability to identify change opportunities and constraints and explains why reforms face recurring limits. Discussion of the Argentina and Malawi cases illustrates the arguments.

Complex Institutional Structures Always Exist

"Institutions" entered the language and practice of development largely because Douglass North linked them to growth. North showed that all social groups have rules of the game, even though these rules differ in size and shape across contexts and through time.[44] This basic observation is an important starting point for thinking about context: institutions always exist, in all contexts, in many different forms. There are no such things as clean slates on which to write scripts for change.

Regulative mechanisms are the most commonly studied "rules" in new institutional economics.[45] These include laws and shaming practices that are often established, monitored, and enforced by third parties. They promise reward or punishment in response to different behavioral choices, constraining behavior through extrinsic means. These regulative devices differ from normative mechanisms emphasized by new institutional sociologists. These include norms and values and communicate what is considered socially acceptable.[46] They manifest in behaviors one would call "appropriate" and influence agents intrinsically by evoking feelings of honor or shame with compliant and resistant actions. A third kind of institutional manifestation is what anthropologists call cultural-cognitive mechanisms. These manifest in ideologies and scripts[47] reflected in symbols of group affiliation and belief, like religion, nationality, or language. They create frames through which agents interpret the world, structuring the way information is received,

---

[44] North 1989, 1319.
[45] Scott 2008.
[46] Ibid.
[47] Denzau and North 1994; Knight 1997; Scott 2008; Streit, Mummert, and Kiwit 1997.

processed, and given meaning.[48] Such frames bias agents to make specific choices, regardless of the incentives created by regulative and normative mechanisms.

Many authors refer to individual regulative, normative, and cultural-cognitive mechanisms as institutions. For instance, World Bank studies discussing "institutional context" typically provide lists of laws and other regulations.[49] By contrast, Richard Scott does not call any one of these mechanisms an institution in itself.[50] Rather, he refers to all three as "elements" of institutional structures, arguing, "Institutions are comprised of regulative, normative *and* cultural-cognitive elements that, together with associated activities and resources, provide stability and meaning to life."[51] A law on its own is not an institution. Neither is a norm, nor is a cultural-cognitive script. An institution emerges as a mix of all three.

Various scholars have embraced Scott's approach to thinking about institutions,[52] positing that the three elements (with supporting practices and resources) combine to form rules of the game. Other variants of such multidimensional constructs are evident across the literature as well. Greenwood and Hinings speak of "interpretive schemes," for instance, which comprise "values, norms, beliefs and rationalizations," that "provide both a logic and a propellant" for action.[53] A broad set of authors refers to "institutional logics" in describing such amalgam structures. These comprise material practices and rules that emerge from and reinforce entrenched assumptions, values, and beliefs.[54] The idea of "logics" has been used to examine a wide set of topics in particular fields of social engagement – "clusters of organizations and occupations whose boundaries, identities and interactions are defined and stabilized by shared institutional logics."[55] Fields of interest include central and local bureaucracy,[56] education,[57]

---

[48] Rosenbaum (2001, 892) describes this from an economist's perspective, noting that models "comprise agents' beliefs as to how their environment is structured in terms of causal relationships, tendencies and propensities."

[49] See, for example, World Bank 2008.

[50] Scott 2008.

[51] Ibid.

[52] The approach is open to critique with some but has been widely used in organizational research (Bruton and Ahlstrom 2003; Busenitz et al. 2000; Hirsch and Lounsbury 1997; Kostova 1997).

[53] Greenwood and Hinings 1993, 1056.

[54] Friedland and Alford 1991; Jackall 1988; Thornton and Ocasio 1999, 804.

[55] This definition comes from Scott (2001, 83), building on DiMaggio and Powell (1983, 148).

[56] Greenwood and Hinings 1993; Meyer and Hammerschmid 2006.

[57] Bacharach and Mundell 1993.

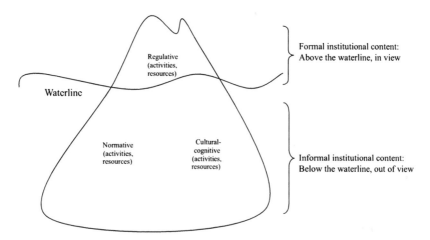

Figure 3.1. Institutional structures as icebergs.

dispute resolution,[58] entrepreneurship,[59] anticorruption,[60] and budget-ing.[61]

This way of thinking sees rules of the game working through the *interaction* of multiple institutional elements. Meyer and Hammerschmid argue, for instance, that Austria's traditional public sector logic comprised procedures and laws that supported norms underpinned by a *Rechtsstaat* understanding of the state as being primarily law based.[62] The role of cultural-cognitive and normative mechanisms like the *Rechtsstaat* tradition and its associated norms is central in this conception of an institution. These mechanisms give durability to the institutional structure and form a foundation for other elements. Evincing this thought, authors have referenced the importance of "widely shared assumptions and values"[63] underpinning institutional structures, often presenting these elements as "master principles"[64] and "taken-for-granted, resilient social prescriptions."[65]

Figure 3.1 illustrates the institutional structure implied in such work. It shows the institution – or logic – as an iceberg.[66] Normative and cultural-cognitive mechanisms form a base on which regulative devices operate. Together, the three elements establish a rule that shapes the way agents

[58] Purdy and Gray 2009.
[59] Busenitz et al. 2000.
[60] Misangyi, Weaver, and Elms 2008.
[61] Skoog 2000.
[62] Meyer and Hammershmid 2006; Scott 2008, 62.
[63] Jones, Hesterly, and Borgatti 1997, 929.
[64] Friedland and Alford 1991; Haveman and Rao 1997, 1614.
[65] Greenwood et al. 2010, 521.
[66] This has parallels with Elinor Ostrom's "nested" rules (see Ostrom 1990, 51).

think, weigh decisions, and behave. It is important to note that this kind of structure incorporates both informal and formal elements – *not one or the other*. The iceberg metaphor reflects this, suggesting that a large part of any institutional logic is unseen or below the water line because it is informal – implicit, unwritten, and seldom visible.[67] The inference is that informal elements are not bad or inferior. Informality is rather a fact of institutional structure – and a fundamental one at that.[68]

Institutional Icebergs in Argentina

This approach helps us in thinking about how institutions foster weak fiscal discipline in places like Argentina. Evincing a multi-element institutional model, for instance, Janos Kornai argues that soft budget constraints are facilitated by the interaction of the prevailing political and legal order, moral norms, and the information structure.[69] Gun Eriksson Skoog examines how such elements contributed to "a logic of the soft budget constraint" in Tanzanian parastatals.[70] One can identify such logic in pre-1990 Argentina by drawing on studies describing politics at the time and in prior decades. These reference the influence of cultural-cognitive scripts that framed governance in the language of *Caudillismo*, for example.[71] Accordingly, many citizens understood politics as involving dependence on strong personalities who required discretion to get things done – a foundation for soft budget constraints. Citizens were also seen to accept political corruption and discretion as "an inescapable fact of life."[72]

Studies infer further that it was considered appropriate for political representatives to adjust or violate procedures and rules to maintain power and distribute resources to supporters.[73] Patronage was accepted and expected, especially between national legislators and provincial party leaders. Informal political rules meant that legislators who failed to look after provincial party bosses would likely see short careers.[74] It was also accepted practice for presidents to use discretionary funds in gaining the support of provincial governors. Formal regulative mechanisms allowed this patronage to flow through a variety of vehicles – like provincial banks and presidential

---

[67] This definition draws on Helmke and Levitsky (2003).
[68] O'Neil 2007.
[69] Kornai 1986.
[70] Skoog 2000, 15.
[71] Ostiguy 2009.
[72] Fillol 1961, 8.
[73] Benton 2009; Levitsky and Murillo 2008; Webb 2002.
[74] Levitsky and Murillo 2008.

executive orders.[75] Beyond this, complex, vague, and ambiguous formal procedures made it difficult to identify and enforce responsibility for spending or results. When combined, these mechanisms created an institutional iceberg that facilitated soft budget constraints.

Institutional Icebergs in Malawi

One can similarly examine Malawi's corruption problem as a product of pre-existing institutional logics. Misangyi, Weaver, and Elms take this approach in identifying a "logic of corruption" in postwar Bosnia and Hezegovina.[76] They reference organizational behavior theory in arguing that corruption results from the interplay of regulative, normative, and cognitive mechanisms. There have traditionally been many cognitive mechanisms supporting such logic in Malawi. For instance, the language of unchallenged patrimonalism dominated political discourse for more than thirty years prior to 1994. Decades of calling the president by names like *Nkhoswe No. 1* (the patriarch of all) embedded an understanding that leaders were to be respected, not questioned.[77]

Further, the local Chichewa word for corruption, *katangale*, framed such behavior in an ambiguous, culturally sensitive way.[78] Its redistributive connotations derive from a link to the notion of "sharing" (*kugawa*) and promoted the idea that if others benefit from *katangale*, it is acceptable and morally right. This was reinforced by norms that deemed it appropriate and expected to provide for one's kin – and extended kin – from the resources gained in office.[79] These norms were buttressed by informal regulative mechanisms like the implicit threat of witchcraft, ostracism, and gossip. At the highest levels of state, regulations like the 1966 constitution gave the president wide-ranging powers and limited his exposure to criticism or investigation.[80] They formalized the informal authority granted him by norms and cultural-cognitive scripts, reinforcing a logic of corruption.

Multiple Institutional Structures Always Exist

Although short, these descriptions reveal the complexity of fiscal profligacy and corruption problems in Argentina and Malawi, respectively. The

---

[75] Benton 2009; Webb 2002; World Bank 1993a.
[76] Misangyi, Weaver, and Elms 2008.
[77] Elder respect is embedded in local language ("*kulemekeza*," "*ulemu kwa bwana*"). Anders 2002; Van Dijk 1999.
[78] Anders 2002; Moto 2001.
[79] Anders 2002.
[80] Chirambo 2009; Kamanga 2008.

institutions supporting such behaviors involved more than laws (or the lack of laws, as many economists might argue). They comprised rule-like logics that shaped how agents understood their world, what they deemed appropriate, what they were willing to enforce, and how they planned to do so. These logics had arguably become embedded over many decades prior to 1990s reforms.

Theory would suggest that logics favoring soft budget constraints and corruption were not the only institutional structures at play in these countries, however. Research relates the idea of "interinstitutional" contexts that comprise multiple institutional structures.[81] Studies show that these exist across domains, varying between the marketplace, state, corporation, profession, religious community, and family.[82] Agents split their lives across these domains and thus continually face multiple logics. For example, doctors in religious hospitals have their perceptions, choices, and behavior shaped by rules of the market, state, medical profession and religious order. Institutional structures can vary within domains as well, and in fields and organizations. Meyer and Hammerschmid explain that Austrian civil servants are influenced by a traditional public sector logic emphasizing process and a new managerial logic stressing results.[83] Purdy and Gray find two logics shaping behavior in state dispute resolution offices in the United States.[84] A judicial logic emphasizes clearing caseloads, whereas a public policy logic focuses agents on facilitating better-quality decisions.

In all cases, logics comprise multiple elements, all of which have some cognitive basis, normative expression, and regulative form. As such, they all resemble icebergs like that suggested in Figure 3.1. They combine as institutional contexts that one could compare with a sea of icebergs. Some institutions in this sea may be more prominent than others, and some may be more closely related – even clashing at times.

Researchers look for such characteristics when describing institutional contexts. Studies note particularly whether and to what degree some logics dominate their context, how competitive alternative logics are, and if logics seem to coexist or clash. The Austrian study, for instance, not only describes the traditional public sector logic as dominant but also sees the new managerial logic as competitive.[85] Greenwood and Hinings explain that British municipalities conform to either of two competing logics, one favoring

---

[81] Friedland and Alford 1991.
[82] Ibid.
[83] Meyer and Hammerschmid 2006.
[84] Purdy and Gray 2009, 360–361.
[85] Meyer and Hammerschmid 2006.

"corporate bureaucracy" and the other "professional bureaucracy."[86] Purdy and Gray find the judicial logic coexisting with the public policy logic in dispute resolution practices.[87] In all examples, agents must navigate these contexts and determine the patterns of dominance, competition, and coexistence.

Multiple Structures in Argentina

Institutional contexts are notoriously difficult to navigate, however. This is certainly true in the case of fiscal politics in Argentina, but even here one sees signs of multiple institutional logics at play. These manifest in the 1960s, for instance, through "the conflict between imported democratic ideas and the local tradition of personalistic leadership."[88] Ostiguy points to a related tension between groups predisposed to supporting personalistic governance and those cognitively inclined to impersonal authority and a procedural approach to governance.[89] He identifies political factions reflecting these extremes in Peronist and anti-Peronist parties from the 1970s onward. One can easily see how an understanding of governance as impersonal and procedural could underpin a "hard budget constraint logic" and an appreciation for spending discipline in public organizations.

Such an understanding was supported by norms and values that emphasized formal, legally mediated models of government. "Professionalism" was accepted and expected according to such norms, as was fiscal probity. A group of 1980s Peronists evinced such norms in calling themselves the *Renovadores* (Renovators) and cultivating a procedurally oriented, liberal democratic image that earned the nickname "suit and tie Peronism."[90] The logic of structured constraint was further reflected in laws intended to rationalize the way government operated. Such regulative devices were regularly touted (from the 1930s) as a way of disciplining the system of intergovernmental transfers, for example. The 1988 *Ley de Coparticipiones* was meant to do just this. Its passage indicated the growing preference for harder budget constraints. This logic was competing with that of the soft budget constraint. The latter was still seen to dominate, however, reflected in departures from the *Ley de Coparticipiones* in 1989 and substantial revisions to it in the early 1990s.[91]

[86] Greenwood and Hinings 1993.
[87] Purdy and Gray 2009, 360–361.
[88] Pendel 1968, 260.
[89] Ostiguy 2009, 7–8.
[90] Ibid., 7–8.
[91] Webb 2002.

Multiple Structures in Malawi

The logic of corruption was also arguably dominant in Malawi at the time of reforms in 1994.[92] Nonetheless, a competing alternative "logic of anticorruption" was present. It is reflected in cultural messages carried through the 1980s by musicians like Wambali Mkandawire.[93] Songs like *Kayuni Njuwi* and *Katoto* bore important messages in favor of democracy and against corruption and repression. Their popularity suggests a cognitive resonance of such messages, which were also emerging in religious communities at the time.[94] The most prominent manifestation of this was a Lenten letter criticizing the state's control and corruption, which was read in all Catholic churches on March 8, 1992.[95]

This emerging message was reinforced by growth in a number of domestic nongovernmental organizations (NGOs) and the creation (in 1991) of political movements including the United Democratic Front and Alliance for Democracy. The emergence of such organizations suggests that it was becoming more acceptable to stand against the state's corruption and challenge the ultimate elder, *Nkhoswe No. 1*. Such norms were growing in the expanding charismatic community as well, where churches were mobilizing the youth and teaching that *katangale* was unacceptable.[96] These norms were supported by formal regulative mechanisms like the Malawi Public Service Regulations of 1978 and 1991. Although problematic in many senses, such devices reflected a strong logic of anticorruption. Their influence was limited, however, given the dominant logic of corruption and authoritarian rule.

Context Shapes Change Opportunities

One wonders how institutional change happens in places like Argentina and Malawi, where dominant institutional logics prevail. Explanations of such change vary, but most authors posit that opportunities are created – or limited – by the interplay of extant institutional structures or logics. Some approaches describe an equilibrium-seeking dynamic where institutions shift between logics.[97] Others suggest that change is driven more by political contests that may or may not bring stability, depending on whether there

---

[92] Chisinga 2003.
[93] Chirambo 2009.
[94] Van Dijk 1999.
[95] Cullen 1994.
[96] Anders 2002; Van Dijk 1999.
[97] Greenwood and Hinings 1993.

is consensus on a logic or mix of logics. Both perspectives emphasize the importance of preexisting institutional orders, interruptions to these orders, and power plays involving agents. Both perspectives also suggest that change is often limited.

Studies commonly examine change in contexts where one structure dominates the institutional order, like Argentina in 1990 and Malawi in 1994. This dominant structure could be a singular logic or a stable amalgam of coexisting logics. Such structures typically undergo limited change, or what Bartunek and Moch call first-order change, where adjustments are "consistent with already-present schemata."[98] In essence, changes reinforce the dominant preexisting logic rather than replacing it. This is a key element of path dependence theory, which posits that future institutions typically reflect those of the past. Cognitive and normative foundations of dominant mechanisms become entrenched in new scripts and symbols over time, for example, and embed themselves through repeated behavioral patterns of expanding sets of agents. Regulative mechanisms are fine-tuned to reflect such logic as well. These changes reinforce power relationships and capability mechanisms, locking in the dominant logic. This logic can appear irreversible when many agents invest heavily in it over long periods. These investments become like sunk costs and decrease the willingness or ability to switch to alternative institutional structures, even though these continue to exist.

Unless the context faces disruption. This could take the form of an exogenous shock like global economic crisis or destabilizing endogenous jolts like demographic adjustments. These can be one-off events or gradually emerging disturbances. They create change opportunities if prevailing institutions cannot facilitate the resolution of emerging problems.[99] In such situations, agents are confronted by weaknesses and contradictions in their preexisting rules.[100] Faced with failing rules of the game, agents may look for second-order change – replacing a preexisting logic with another alternative.[101]

Disruptions do not always foster radical change, however. The degree of change depends on the severity of disruption, how much it tests the legitimacy of extant dominant logics, whether viable alternatives exist, and whether agents are in place to struggle for and facilitate transition. Different conditions yield different scenarios, shown in Figure 3.2.[102]

---

[98] Bartunek and Moch 1987, 486.
[99] Greenwood, Suddaby, and Hinings 2002; Tolbert and Zucker 1983.
[100] Seo and Creed 2002.
[101] Bartunek and Moch 1987, 486.
[102] Ideas about shifts, layering, and conversion are drawn from Thelen (2003).

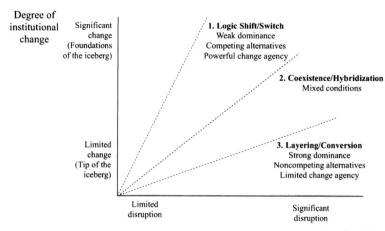

Figure 3.2. How contextual factors shape opportunities for institutional change.

One possibility (shown as scenario 1) is dramatic shifts in logics – or switches. These are possible when faced with disruption, but only where the legitimacy of preexisting institutional orders is tenuous (a condition one could call weak dominance) and alternative logics are present and competitive, supported by agents capable of challenging the old order.[103] Where one or another condition is not met, change will be more limited. It could foster coexistence or hybridization (shown as scenario 2) where elements of an alternative institutional logic are introduced alongside elements of the prevailing dominant logic. Coexistence can cause uncertainty about rules of the game, supporting and motivating differing choices and behaviors.[104] Mixed conditions could also facilitate the emergence of a new hybrid logic altogether, however, where elements of what could be called the dominant incumbent (the institutional form that already has influence) merge with elements of new alternatives.[105] If conditions are not met, one should expect even more limited change (shown as scenario 3). This could involve a limited version of layering, where visible elements of alternative logics are introduced "on top of" less visible norms and cognitive scripts of incumbent structures. This layering could lead to more significant change if new

[103] Bacharach and Mundell 1993.

[104] Scott 2008, 62.

[105] The word "incumbent" most commonly refers to people holding political or clerical office, where the holder is assumed to have an advantage over any challenger for that office. The word has also been used to describe organizations or firms holding a prominent role in their industry or sector. The current usage refers similarly to rules of the game that enjoy an advantage because they are already in place.

elements are actually implemented and reinforced over time as additional layers of similar change. Conversion is another option, where the preexisting logic is preserved but power is moved from one group to another. Incumbent structures are redirected to serve the interests of different agents and agendas in such situations.

These three general scenarios suggest that different conditions affect the degree to which institutional change emerges, even through disruption. In all cases, more disruption allows for more change. Change is greatest in the "logic switch" scenario given weak dominance, competing alternatives, and powerful change agents. Change is more limited in the "coexistence" and "hybridization" scenarios given mixed conditions. Change is most limited in the "layering" or "conversion" scenarios, where conditions limit the potential for short-term adjustment. As argued, layering could lead to deeper change – over time – if reinforced incrementally by follow-up reforms, with each layer expanding the room for change.

Most authors would argue that these last two limited-change scenarios are a more likely outcome of institutional adjustment when a dominant logic is in place, even in the face of significant disruption. This is partly because informal dimensions of incumbent logics change slowly, if at all. Mauro Guillen notes such in stating that logics are "deeply rooted in collective understandings and cultural practice, and resilient in the face of changing circumstance."[106] As a result, one is likely to find informal elements of incumbent logics holding on even when regulative mechanisms appear to change.

How Context Affected Change in Argentina

As argued, Argentina's fiscal arena was dominated by a soft budget constraint logic in the 1980s – built on embedded models of discretionary, personalistic political leadership. In 1989, however, the country was in the grips of a major fiscal crisis that had disrupted many aspects of society. Internal and external commentators blamed this crisis on the prevailing logic. They questioned the legitimacy of the incumbent soft budget constraint by referring to the way decades of overspending had led to debilitating debt.

An alternative hard budget constraint logic was also present, reflected in movements that favored disciplined and impersonal political structures. This logic had gained momentum with the resumption of multiparty democracy in 1983 and was bolstered by reforms introduced under a series of IMF and World Bank adjustment operations. This alternative logic was also supported by new laws that were being introduced to formalize fiscal

---

[106] Guillen 2003, 20.

management. The logic was also championed by agents close to power, such as the *Renovadores*, who stood in favor of such an alternative within the Peronist party for much of the 1980s. After his 1989 election, President Carlos Menem also appeared to be a powerful advocate for harder budget constraints, which were explicitly advocated by his Harvard-trained Minister of Finance Domingo Cavallo.

Apparent success with ambitious externally supported reforms throughout the 1990s seemed to confirm a shift from soft to hard budget logics. Numerous new laws were passed that introduced fiscal rules and formal budget procedures. There were also apparent changes in behavior, including large-scale privatization and lower federal spending and employment. Unfortunately, however, experience at the end of the decade suggested that this change was limited. As discussed in the first section of this chapter, provincial governments increased expenditure and hiring throughout the decade. New laws and fiscal rules were routinely changed and violated, and overall government debt grew unabated – all manifestations of a soft budget constraint logic. Apparent champions of change like President Menem were still acting in ways that represented this soft budget logic as well, regularly trying to adjust new laws, including the constitution. Menem also continued to use selective incentives and discretionary executive orders to funnel money to provinces.[107] Future presidents like Eduardo Duhalde and Nestor Kirchner were commonly on the receiving end of such efforts.[108] These and other governors also managed their campaigns and administrations in ways reflecting embedded personality-based politics (*Caudillismo*), which was conducive to a soft budget constraint logic.

As the story unfolds, one must question the degree to which the crisis in 1989 did create an opportunity for second-order change in Argentina's fiscal institutions. Informal foundations of the dominant soft budget constraint logic were extremely entrenched in the political landscape. Apparent champions of change like Menem were themselves heavily influenced by such logics – before, during, and after his presidency.[109] Pierre Ostiguy notes that such influence was painfully evident before reforms, given the profligacy Menem advocated throughout his 1988 election campaign.[110] Allyson Benton argues that such a style continued into his presidency, demonstrated by constant efforts to soften budget rules and provide cheap budget support

---

[107] Benton 2009.
[108] Becker (2002) points out that Duhalde and Kirchner ran large deficits and expanded the payroll when governor.
[109] Bonvecchi 2010.
[110] Ostiguy 2009.

to provinces.[111] This resembles a limited-change scenario like short-term layering, illustrated in scenario 3 in Figure 3.2. The dominance of an incumbent soft budget constraint logic relegated change to new laws being introduced as a layer above established norms and cognitive scripts. Institutions looked different at the tip of the iceberg – but were not really different at its foundation. New layers were the same over time (with repeated versions of similar reforms) and showed no signs of being implemented.

Given this argument, it appears that agents in 1999 were dominated by rules of the game – and soft budget constraint logics – that prevailed in 1989. The same entrenched rules still seemed influential in 2005 – allowing history to repeat itself regardless of reforms. Reflecting on this experience in 2007, Argentine academics Miguel Braun and Nicolas Gadano comment, "In contexts... like that in Argentina, where the executive amends laws with surprising frequency and ease, it is hard to imagine that a fiscal responsibility law might significantly constrain the decision-making of those in government."[112] The observation, in essence, is that Argentina's institutional context did not provide opportunities for reform that external reform designers thought it did. A better understanding of the logics in place might have accommodated a better expectation and design.

How Context Affected Change in Malawi

A similar observation emerges from Malawi. The country seemed ripe for major change when multiparty elections were reintroduced in 1994. The election itself was a signal that the authoritarian leadership style of *President for Life* Banda was over. This signal was reinforced in 1993 when the state charged Banda with prominent murders that had occurred in 1983. Furthermore, incoming President Muluzi referenced corruption in his inauguration speech and targeted it as a focal point of his administration. Given such signals, one might have expected a lot from the 1995 anticorruption law and the new Anti-Corruption Bureau (ACB). It appeared as though a new anticorruption logic had emerged in only five years.

Unfortunately, however, the old logic of corruption proved strongly dominant. When the "87 million kwacha scandal" erupted in 2000, President Muluzi himself was implicated. It turns out that old-style Malawian corruption had continued under the new administration. On investigation, such corruption seemed to be a continuing characteristic of the entire country. This is reflected, as discussed, in the declining Transparency International

---

[111] Benton 2009.
[112] Braun and Gadano 2007, 63.

data over the period. These data show that high-level and low-level corruption had remained rampant even after the major democratic and anti-corruption reforms. Old traditions that treated certain types of *katangale* as acceptable were still significant, as was the culturally embedded understanding of government as the parent, beyond reproach and critique.[113] This disempowering perspective was spread deep and wide, even in 2003 and 2009, when 70 percent and 61 percent, respectively, of Afrobarometer survey respondents agreed that citizens are "children" for whom government should care.[114]

Given these kinds of entrenched understandings, Gerhard Anders describes Malawi's corruption problem as "embedded" in a social setting where multiple rules operate, complicating the lives of public officials.[115] He opines that old rules dominate new ones even a full decade after reforms, supporting what Western observers would call a persistent logic of corruption and unquestioned top-down leadership. The persistence of this logic can help explain why Malawi's government never effectively financed the ACB.[116] It was accepted in principle but has never been considered sufficiently appropriate or legitimate to merit the expenditure of Malawi's own money. Donors had to keep the ACB alive as a result, given that institutions "not empowered or regenerated by resources would eventually be abandoned and forgotten."[117] The influence of this stubborn logic can also shed light on the failure of Malawi's government to give ACB officials any prosecutorial authority. This authority resides traditionally with the Department of Public Prosecutions, which is itself controlled by the presidency under the entrenched rules of the game. These entrenched rules also help explain why the ACB leadership has never enjoyed its own independence from the executive – even though external parties repeatedly call for such – and has a dismal record of prosecuting senior members of sitting administrations.[118] The rationale is simple: although the ACB may be considered necessary, it still needs to be controlled by the "parent" who ultimately decides who shares, how, and when. There is no space for an independent ACB that monitors and controls government and stops sharing altogether.

Once again, reform appears to have been limited by stubborn institutional logics that dominated the context and did not accommodate proposed

---

[113] Anders 2002.
[114] www.Afrobarometer.org.
[115] Anders 2002.
[116] Norad 2010.
[117] Sewell 1992, 3.
[118] Norad 2010.

change. It would seem that the reforms facilitated low degrees of change, shown as scenario 3 in Figure 3.2. In a sense, the reforms involve layering – where new regulatory structures now sit on top of a difficult-to-change set of norms and cultural-cognitive scripts. In this interpretation, reform has done little more than create a set of regulatory mechanisms that do not function – much as existed before the 1990s and is common in neopatrimonial states.[119] The situation could also reflect simple conversion – where power has shifted between parties without a change in the dominant logic. This is a plausible explanation for the period up to at least 2003. The Muluzi administration pursued corruption in much the same way as the prior Banda administration. It used reforms to signal support for a new anticorruption logic but continued operating according to the entrenched logic of corruption.

External Reformers Commonly Overlook Context

There is reason to believe that many reform designers will discount the influence of this kind of contextual complexity on reform. The very idea of institutional reform assumes "that institutions can be purposefully created or re-created by rational agents."[120] This is an intoxicating assumption for those working in development, who may consider themselves the "rational agents" capable of manipulating the way developing countries work. This thinking is implicit in the "cargo cult" concept discussed by some postcolonial theorists.[121] This refers to a belief "that development is something that flies in from the outside" to overwhelm and improve the inefficient ways of developing countries.[122] All that is needed to effect change is the superior outside idea and influence.

Such thinking is reflected in Peter Evans's description of how reforms work in development: "International organizations, local policy makers, and private consultants combine to enforce the presumption that the most advanced countries have already discovered the one best institutional blueprint for development and that its applicability transcends national cultures and circumstances."[123] Such thought runs through many discussions of institutional reform in development and the mechanisms and indicators used to assess governments in developing countries. Reforms are typically

---

[119] O'Neil 2007.
[120] Ingraham, Moynihan, and Andrews 2008, 67.
[121] Said 1978; Spivak 1990.
[122] Hanlon 2004a, 605.
[123] Evans 2004, 33.

presented in overwhelmingly positive ways, as initiatives where "the right institutional framework [can] unlock a nation's wealth potential."[124] Constructs like the World Governance Indicators give the same message, promoting a confidence in outside ideas as powerful, generic solutions. This confidence helps explain the finding in Chapter 1 that reform designers advocate more and more reform – even when evidence suggests that many reforms produce disappointing results. Contexts in which reform does not work are disparaged as having weak leadership but not given more attention.[125] The assumption is that superior externally sourced solutions will eventually prevail if local leaders allow them to.

This idea of a cargo cult does not hold across all development, however. Many external agents do see the importance of local context in the change process. The continued emphasis on country "ownership" in development is one indication of this. Reform strategies and handbooks produced by development organizations also routinely cite the influence of context on reform.[126] Contextual factors are seldom detailed, defined, or deciphered in such references, however. This is partly because of an inability to see and map context. There is something to be said for the fact that a large part of any institutional logic is informal and difficult to see. One cannot expect external reform designers to identify informal institutional elements falling below the iceberg's waterline given the limited engagement they enjoy in target countries. Reform projects in organizations like the IMF and World Bank are designed with limited budgets in periods ranging from six to eighteen months, often by "experts" with limited country experience who fly in and out of the reforming context every six months. Their government counterparts are often in narrow technical agencies at the head of economic agencies like the Ministry of Finance.

It is questionable how much these agents can speak to the country's political and cultural contexts, partly because these contexts usually stretch beyond their view and reach, and also because many institutional elements are invisible even to those affected by them. This is particularly the case for most dominant structures, which are taken for granted and hence enjoy low visibility. Furthermore, reform engagements typically focus on the solutions and not the problems, with pressure to finalize program documents for specific, ambitious, and linear reform programs in short periods and in a language of development that requires sanitized communication. This constrains discussion about contextual problems or the cultural-cognitive

---

[124] Yeager 1999, 113.
[125] Andrews 2012a; Evans 2004; Hanlon 2004a.
[126] World Bank 2000a, 2008.

and normative roots of such. As Peter Evans says, "Arenas that are less accessible and less transparent . . . are ignored, almost of necessity."[127]

Evidence of Overlooked Context in Argentina and Malawi

A cargo cult mentality is apparent in the stories of both reforms analyzed in this chapter. In Argentina, it took the shape of a push for fiscal rules. The IMF and Inter-American Development Bank introduced Argentina's authorities to such, presented as a best practice solution emerging from countries like Chile and New Zealand.[128] Reform designers detail the technicalities of this reform,[129] describing the "cargo," if you will, but provide little discussion about whether and how it could fit into Argentina's context. The implied belief was that the "cargo" would make a difference, regardless of its landing zone. This belief prevailed in government, too, where the promise of a solution undermined public or parliamentary discussion about what really caused the problems of fiscal profligacy.[130]

The cargo cult in Malawi aimed similarly to establish an anticorruption commission at the center of reform. Such commissions were in vogue at the time, with prominent examples in places like Hong Kong and across Anglophone Africa.[131] Malawi took the cargo from Hong Kong and Botswana, with the ACB's business strategy drawing "heavily" from both.[132] There was limited engagement about the issue in parliament, business, and civil society, and no apparent discussion with church groups that had been centrally involved in pushing for democratic change prior to 1994.

This mentality is arguably also evident when considering the multiple attempts to revive Argentina's fiscal rules and Malawi's anticorruption commission. Governments were held responsible for repeated failures in both cases, suggesting that they should simply have done a better job with the cargo received. IMF leadership blamed Argentina as the country that "tried little, failed much" in the 1990s, given "a reluctance to follow-through."[133] President Kirchner was subsequently held personally responsible when 2004's Fiscal Responsibility Law fell short of providing the rules IMF experts demanded.[134] Similarly, commentators criticized Bakili Muluzi

---

[127] Evans 2004, 34.
[128] Braun and Gadano 2007.
[129] Kopits 2001; Kopits and Symanksy 1998.
[130] Braun and Gadano 2007, 64.
[131] Doig, Watt, and Williams 2005; Heilbrunn 2004.
[132] World Bank 1998a, 21.
[133] Krueger 2004.
[134] Braun and Gadano 2007.

in post-Banda Malawi, claiming that he exhibited tendencies of his predecessor – trying to stay in power and use resources for his own ends.[135] His
successor, Bingu wa Mutharika, was then singled out as the reason reforms
stalled. Commentators frequently lament that the country would be further
ahead "[i]f only Malawians were luckier with their leaders."[136]

Such references indicate that external commentators paid some attention
to context in these two cases. However, commentators saw only what was
obvious, the "bad" politicians and political squabbles of the day. In so doing,
they ignore the idea that social and political behavior is a product of embedded rules of the game and tensions between them. The contextual references
that matter are thus systemic and historical, not personalistic and contemporary. Accordingly, the tendency of Presidents Menem and Kirchner to
bypass formal laws is less interesting than the way Argentina's rules of the
game embed a predisposition for strong leaders who repeatedly challenge
and flout procedure.[137] Similarly, the "Big Man" behavior of President wa
Mutharika deserved less attention than the way Malawi's institutions allow
such leadership to repeat itself over successive administrations, even after
major disruptions.

Evidence suggests that these foundational institutional elements were
routinely ignored whenever external entities examined the context in
Argentina and Malawi. Beyond references to politics, contextual analyses
involve nothing more than a discussion of laws and organizational entities
prevailing in specific areas. The IMF's recent 2008 "Accounting and Auditing
Report" for Argentina,[138] for instance, includes a seven-page description of
the "Institutional Framework for Corporate Sector Accounting and Auditing," which shows numbers and types of formally registered entities in the
country and discusses the legal requirements for accounting and auditing. There is no discussion of the informal mechanisms at play, including business norms or cultural-cognitive scripts that structure thinking
about appropriate levels of disclosure and other important concepts. Similar documents were produced in Argentina throughout the period analyzed,
including the 1990 and 1996 World Bank studies on Provincial Government
Finances, the 1993 Policy Research Working Paper about effects of tax reform

---

[135] See www.bbc.co.uk/2/hi/africa/3586807.stm.
[136] Taken from a 2011 article in the *Malawi Democrat* by Greg Mills of South Africa's
Brenthurst Foundation, http://www.malawidemocrat.com/politics/long-fingers-in-the-
warm-heart-of-africa/.
[137] Ostiguy 2009.
[138] The Report on Observation of Standards and Codes, http://www.worldbank.org/ifa/rosc_
aa_arg_2008.pdf.

on Argentina's revenues, the 1996 public sector assessment of Cordoba, and a 1988 assessment of the convertibility plan.[139]

One can find similar studies in the case of Malawi. A five-page summary of the Public Financial Management institutional framework was sponsored by the European Commission in 2007 and examines the institutional context.[140] It provides a comprehensive summary of the laws in place and the organizational entities in government responsible for enforcing and implementing them. There is no discussion of the informal social, political, and bureaucratic mechanisms other authors have described as vital to explaining public financial management institutions.[141] The World Bank's 1993 public sector management review does similarly, as do the 1994 civil service pay and employment study and the 2003 financial accountability assessment.[142] The most interesting example comes from a 1998 World Bank report, which alludes to the fact that corruption has deep roots in complex political and social relationships but admits, humbly, an "inability" to "map" the nature or extent of such.[143] The authors exhibit less humility in providing a raft or highly specific reform ideas intended to strengthen laws and the anticorruption agency.

Even though they could not "see" the informal mechanics of Malawi's corruption problem clearly, these reform designers proposed specific solutions based on formalizing rules and rule-makers. In their study on Bosnia, Misangyi, Weaver, and Elms criticize this kind of approach, focused as it is on "explicit, formal regulative structures in explaining and combating corruption."[144] They argue that the approach "has had limited success in remedying corruption because it neglects the role that normative and cognitive structures play in the development, perpetuation, and remediation of corruption."[145]

GETTING SERIOUS ABOUT CONTEXT

The Argentina and Malawi cases tell of stories where external reform designers overlooked contextual factors that ultimately limited the space for change. Context was even overlooked when reforms were redone, resulting

---

[139] These studies and reports are available in the World Bank's online publication database.
[140] See www.crownagents.com/Core/DownloadDoc.aspx?documentID=4272.
[141] Andrews 2011a.
[142] These individual studies and reports are available in the World Bank's online publication database.
[143] World Bank 1998a, 6.
[144] Ibid.
[145] Misangyi, Weaver, and Elms 2008, 750.

in similar limits a second time around. This is what commentators call "history repeating itself." It is a common phenomenon in development. Consider, again, Andrew Wilder's account of recurring failure in Pakistan's civil service reforms.[146] Citing a former finance secretary, he notes that external agencies working in Pakistan treat civil service reform as "a technical exercise" in which "problems are reduced to boxes and then solutions are found to fit into the boxes." The finance secretary concludes, "The political and cultural contexts are lost in these exercises," which is a problem because of the "inherently political nature of civil service reform." Consider also Indonesia's insolvency law, which suffered premature failure because it was never "socialized" into the context.[147] Bemoaning such results, Melbourne University's Roman Tomasic notes that "multilateral agency expectations and timeframes may not always be in accord with local realities."[148]

In all of these situations, reforms ran into trouble when they encountered a cluttered institutional context comprising multiple logics – iceberg-like structures combining regulative, normative, and cultural-cognitive mechanisms. Contexts with strongly dominant logics and weak alternatives failed to accommodate the intended institutional change, even though there was disruption that many may have thought always facilitates adjustments. The problem was that contexts actually provided limited space for change. These conditions were much like those in the left column of Table 3.1, which shows "small-hole conditions" that limit the size of a potential reform peg. When external agents overlook contextual conditions, they assume that all situations have large holes, shown at the right, and accommodate a high degree of change. Unfortunately, this is often not the case, and small-hole conditions undermine reform attempts.

There are various ways in which reforms would be improved if context were better considered in design. One could imagine that the selection of where and when to do reform would be sharpened, for example. Fewer institutional reforms would be initiated in contexts with small-hole conditions – where governments and societies may not be ready for change. A greater sense of context also could help to inform expectations of reform and guide processes of implementation and oversight. Reform designers aware of the importance of context could factor in regular assessments of the factors named in Table 3.1, for instance, monitoring context and not just progress with technical content in reforms. Finally, one could imagine a sense of context assisting in defining reform content itself. Reforms

---

[146] Wilder 2009, 27
[147] Linnan 2000.
[148] Tomasic 2001, 5.

Table 3.1. *How contextual factors "Size the Hole" in which reform pegs are to fit*

Contextual factor	Small-hole conditions, conducive to low degree of change	Large-hole conditions, conducive to high degree of change
Severity of disruption	Disruption limited in size and duration; does not foster deep reflection on status quo or manifestation of contradictions and inconsistencies in incumbent institutions	Disruption is significant, enduring, and causes deep reflection on status quo and manifestation of contradictions and inconsistencies in incumbent institutions
Strength of dominant logic	Deeply embedded incumbents (strong dominance)	Tenuous incumbents (weak dominance)
Evidence of alternative logics	Alternatives not present or not competitive	Present and competitive alternative logics
Activity of change agents	Agents not present or incapable of challenging old order, introducing new logic	Agents present and capable of challenging the old order, introducing new logic

initiated in large-hole settings would be fashioned to support viable alternative logics that have emerged in such contexts, for instance. Reforms initiated in small-hole conditions could be shaped to increase the size of the reform space itself – introducing alternative ideas, gathering potential change agents, or helping interpret disruptions as sources of change.

Indonesian insolvency reforms discussed in the introduction to this chapter might have focused on strengthening informal dispute resolution mechanisms instead of creating more formal laws, for example.[149] Informal mechanisms were ostensibly a more viable and accepted mechanism given the context, and their medium-term use could have bought time for government to properly develop a more legitimate court system. Similarly, Malawi's anticorruption activities could have stressed the role of agencies promoting the new anticorruption logic (churches, for instance) rather than betting on change in the traditional conservator of the old corruption logic (the executive). External agencies like the IMF similarly could have required that Argentina's legislature actively debate the causes of fiscal profligacy instead of just rubber-stamping reforms proposed by the executive as "signals."

An awareness of context could also help external reform designers ensure that their interventions do not undermine change opportunities that exist or could be expanded. This comment draws on a sizeable literature that sees

[149] Linnan 2000.

the international aid community impacting negatively on the politics of development through its reform interventions.[150] Some argue, for instance, that loans from international organizations can contribute to and reinforce dominant logics of soft budget constraints.[151] Others suggest that external funding for reforms can strengthen a logic of corruption by adding to sources of cheap rent.[152] Some consider these perspectives controversial, but they should rather be seen as obvious. The theory of institutional change behind Table 3.1 demonstrates clearly that external engagements can shift a situation from potentially large-hole to small-hole conditions. For instance, loans can stabilize an otherwise-disrupted context, reinforce a dominant logic that would instead be tenuous and vulnerable to change, or support agents who are unlikely to change the status quo. A mix of these effects was arguably evident in Argentina and Malawi, where donors tempered the severity of disruptions and ultimately facilitated layering or conversion instead of more extensive institutional change.

This argument suggests that external reform designers should better account for context than they have in the past. Think, perhaps, of project preparation processes that allow one to assess the size of the hole in which reform pegs are intended to fit. This, arguably, is the role political economy analysis is slated to play in project design. Such analysis is surely a good thing, and it is positive to see increasing numbers of reforms informed by perspectives on politics. There are some high-quality analyses emerging in this tradition,[153] but many emphasize contemporary politics only, ignoring the historically embedded logics that may be driving behavior. There is also a tendency to focus on political figures or parties and not the systemic structural mechanisms in which such actors are embedded. One wonders how political economy studies could actually comment on such mechanisms in even the best-case scenario given their hidden, taken-for-granted nature. Studies can speak only about what is seen, so they should be expected to overlook "below-the-waterline" content in this institutional icebergs driving behavior.

The value of external contextual assessments is also questionable because of its inevitable external bias, which can reinforce an ignorance of the real context. In discussing this point, Kate Kenny notes that external agencies are increasingly recognizing the importance of considering context when designing reforms. She points to a widely held belief that "despite the many

---

[150] Bräutigam and Knack 2004; Easterly 2002.
[151] Skoog 2000.
[152] de Renzio and Hanlon 2008; Hanlon 2004b; Kolstad, Fritz, and O'Neil 2008.
[153] Including de Renzio and Hanlon 2008; Hanlon 2004b; Kolstad, Fritz, and O'Neil 2008.

differences" it is fully possible for external reform designers to come to know and understand "the Other."[154] Often, she notes, this understanding is slated to be "achieved through the project methodology." Methods of doing this are never neutral, however, and Kenny speaks of a bias toward having "binomial" representations in development. There are experts (in the aid agencies) and non-experts (in the countries), for instance, and good politicians (who support external reforms) and problematic politicians (who do not). Kenny argues that analyses fostering such views "ensure that organization members [in external entities] remain blind to their inherent assumptions."[155]

Given such problems, this book argues that written studies by outsiders are probably not the best entry point for addressing concerns about context. Chapter 7 suggests a different course of action. Reforms should focus on the disruptive problems that emerge in particular countries, and designs should allow contextual complexities to reveal themselves while addressing these problems. This requires an approach to institutional reform that acknowledges its endogenous nature and seeks to develop and implement designs actively through a problem-driven incremental process in the context, with local agents occupying the driving seat. This is proposed as the only way in which contextual factors can be effectively accounted for in institutional reforms. Even when context is accounted for, however, institutional reforms may yield limited results – especially if they still emphasize "reforms as signals." The next chapter argues that such reforms do not only overlook context, but they also overspecify externally sourced best practices as generic solutions and oversimplify what these solutions require to work.

---

[154] Kenny 2008, 64.
[155] Ibid., 73.

FOUR

Reforms as Overspecified *and* Oversimplified Solutions

REFORM IS A COMPLICATED THING

A massive earthquake devastated Haiti on Tuesday, January 12, 2010. Many buildings in the capital of Port-au-Prince collapsed and shanty villages simply disappeared, leaving twenty million to twenty-five million cubic yards of debris. The building collapses exceeded most recent earthquake events. This prompted questions about how structures were erected. Numerous commentators claimed that Haiti had no building codes.[1] Donors have been clamoring to provide new internationally approved codes ever since, as rules of the game for builders. On closer reflection, however, one finds that there were codes for Haitians to use in the past, and reforms were designed to strengthen such.[2] The country lacked enforcement inspectors, builders trained to adhere to codes, and residents in shantytowns who cared enough or could afford to demand compliance with these formal rules. It is unlikely that new codes alone will address these gaps in institutional content.

An institutional reform based on the belief that new, world-class codes alone will solve Haiti's building problem is oversimplified. It is, however, a good example of what institutional reforms in development commonly look like, especially when they are what Chapter 2 calls reforms as signals. Such reforms commonly prescribe externally sourced best practices as paths toward better government and development. These solutions require a lot

---

[1] Problems with Haiti Building Standards Outlined. *CNN World*. January 13, 2010, http:// articles.cnn.com/2010-01-13/world/haiti.construction_1_building-code-haiti-earthquake?_s=PM:WORLD.

[2] Builders could use codes from France, Canada, or the United States. The Organization for American States initiated a project to introduce new hurricane-resistant codes in 2007. The *Online Building Safety Journal* noted that the problem was about weak enforcement, poor-quality materials, and other factors that would not be rectified by a new code, http://bsj.iccsafe.org/april/features/haitip2.html.

of specific content to work, however, including regulative, normative, and cultural-cognitive mechanisms. Visible regulations, for instance, need supporting capacity and unseen norms of appropriateness to work. Reforms frequently address only visible elements, however, and ignore other content or assume it will materialize. This is like a carpenter attempting to replicate the most detailed peg in the world without considering the original craftsman's mindset or ensuring he has the peculiar tools used to make signature markings.

This chapter argues that institutional reforms frequently fail because of this problem. They overspecify what reforms should involve – demanding international best practices – but oversimplify the content it takes to produce such. The argument emerges through a specific study of efforts to create and strengthen the accounting profession and practice in Africa. International organizations have promoted such interventions for decades, with the World Bank sponsoring reforms under a theme called "Standards and Reporting." Although the reforms intend to influence the private sector, external agencies work with governments as primary counterparts. This is because governments determine the institutional mechanisms affecting firms' accounting and reporting requirements in most countries.

A first section introduces readers to this area, noting that reforms have been pursued without yielding improved accounting systems in many countries. Section 2 uses institutional theory on isomorphism to explain such situation. Building on the idea in Chapter 2 of reforms as signals, the section argues that best practice interventions are pursued to gain short-term legitimacy. These reforms demand high content, however, which is lacking in many developing countries. Reforms do not provide for much of this content, either, which undermines the potential of these "solutions" to effect positive change. In ignoring the complexity of institutions, these interventions thus limit their own success.

THE PROBLEM OF OVERSPECIFIED, OVERSIMPLIFIED REFORM

Prior chapters showed that institutional reforms have become a staple of development. Many countries do not see positive results after reforms are completed, however. This holds when considering accounting reforms in Africa. International organizations have spearheaded initiatives to strengthen African accounting since the 1980s. The belief is that better accounting practices will stimulate the development of African markets and facilitate the engagement of African firms in the global economy.

Such belief has spawned more than eighty projects and grants supporting accounting reforms by the World Bank alone in more than thirty-five

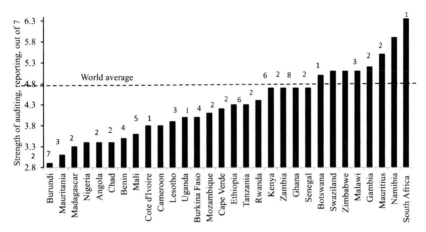

Figure 4.1. Auditing and reporting quality and reform numbers in select African countries. *Notes and source:* Scores reflect business perceptions of the "strength of auditing and reporting standards." Numbers indicate World Bank projects with an accounting and reporting component.

African countries.[3] The quality of accounting and reporting remains low in most of the targeted countries, however. This is evident in Figure 4.1, which shows the World Economic Forum's 2010 country scores for "strength of auditing and reporting standards." The measure captures firm responses to the question "In your country, how would you assess financial auditing and reporting standards regarding company financial performance?" It is arguably the most applied question of its type, capturing views of businesspeople who "gain their perception of accounting and auditing as they see it practiced in their respective organizations."[4] The scores in Figure 4.1 show weighted averages of answers ranging from 1 (extremely weak) to 7 (extremely strong) for 30 African countries of a sample of 139. The figure also shows, above the bars, numbers of World Bank accounting interventions since 1987.

Scores leave 22 of the 30 African countries lower than the full 139-country population mean of 4.77. Eight of these 22 were in the lowest global decile, registering scores at or below 3.5. Another 6 fell in the bottom quartile, scoring at or below 4. Only 8 scored above the full sample mean, including 2 countries – Namibia and South Africa – that were in the top decile. Interestingly, the top-performing countries had significantly less external

[3] As identified through a search of World Bank projects, including the theme "financial standards and reporting" and information collected from the World Bank's financial management sector.

[4] Malagueño et al. (2010) consider this a measure of the subjective value businesspeople in the formal sector see in national accounting and reporting practices.

World Bank assistance in accounting reform than those at the bottom. The 8 countries with scores higher than global means averaged just over one project or grant each, whereas the 22 falling below global means had more than three interventions. The 8 lowest-percentile countries had at least two reform engagements, with an average of three.

Figure 4.1 suggests that most African countries have weak auditing and reporting practices, regardless of reforms intended to strengthen them. Countries with the weakest practices seem to have had the most reforms (at least through the World Bank). As prior chapters showed with other reforms, this data illustrates that accounting interventions have failed to improve functionality in many countries.

EXPLAINING THE FAILURE OF COMPLEX REFORMS

One has to wonder why reforms to accounting systems do not work and how international organizations can consistently pursue accounting interventions that yield limited gains for many developing countries. The questions could be asked with regard to other reform types as well. For instance, many developing countries have liberalized their banking rules in the past three decades without seeing stronger financial sectors. Sub-Saharan Africa's financial sector may, in fact, have weakened in the liberalization era: "Excluding the top 15 countries, the ratio of private sector bank credit to GDP declined by about 50 percent, on average, from 17.2 percent to 8.7 during this period."[5]

This section uses institutional theory to reflect on these disappointing results. Such theory informs the argument that international organizations support reforms based on best practice that require specific and high content to yield functional results. This content is lacking in many African countries, but reforms only address such deficiency in respect of more formal content elements – providing laws, training facilities, and the like. The continued lack of informal institutional content – appropriate norms and cultural-cognitive scripts in particular – undermines the influence of these reforms.

A Bias toward High-Content Best Practice Reforms

Ashworth, Boyne, and Delbridge identify two extreme reasons why organizations change their institutions.[6] At one extreme, they identify a

---

[5] Karikari 2010, 2.
[6] Ashworth, Boyne, and Delbridge 2007, 165.

"rational" reason for such change, whereby new rules are needed to ensure continued or improved functionality. Change is motivated by the pursuit of improved performance, often in the face of a threat. Matthew Dull's "reform as problem solving" fits such approach, presenting reforms as "innovations prompted by disparities between existing conditions and preferred states."[7]

At the other extreme, organizations pursue change to get "greater legitimacy" rather than better performance.[8] Called isomorphism, this approach emerged from DiMaggio and Powell's observation that organizations exist within fields – "those organizations that, in aggregate, constitute a recognized area of institutional life" – and face pressure to conform to externally defined "belief systems and related practices that predominate" such fields.[9] These belief systems often manifest in best practices. Organizations that do not yield to isomorphic pressures to adopt these best practices face losing legitimacy and external support.

Isomorphism is commonly seen as explaining change in contexts where entities are highly dependent on external constituencies in which more appropriate best practices are highly defined.[10] Dependent entities adopt such forms through a mixture of coercion, mimesis, and normative transfer. Coercive pressures involve one or more organizations exerting power and influence over another to force the adoption of preferred structures or institutions, often through political and legal means or by controlling resource access. Mimetic pressures center on the influence of best or good practice on the choices an organization makes, and the tendency of many organizations to emulate practices that appear desirable or accepted. Normative pressures relate to the influence of communities of professionals (or other externally legitimated groups) on thinking about which structures or practices are better than others.

Organizations that do not respond to such forces and fail to adopt the legitimated best practice mechanisms are "open to claims of being negligent, irrational or even unnecessary."[11] Such claims imply a loss of external legitimacy that is particularly problematic for some organizations – especially those that are dependent on their external environment for political support and resources, are internally uncertain about their own means and ends, and occupy fields in which established professional or quasi-professional

---

[7] Dull 2006, 190.
[8] Ashworth, Boyne, and Delbridge 2007, 165.
[9] DiMaggio and Powell 1983, 148.
[10] DiMaggio and Powell 1983; Frumkin and Galaskiewicz 2004.
[11] Townley 1997, 261.

groups have identified certain process and practice norms as best practice.[12] It is reasonable to expect that such organizations will, motivated by survival, adopt these externally defined best practices to gain external legitimacy.

Because such characteristics are common to most developing countries, isomorphism is well suited to thinking about institutional reform in these contexts.[13] Developing countries depend on – and are influenced by – external international organizations and the global economic and political environment they represent. African countries gain financial support from organizations like the World Bank on condition of reform, for example. Reforms can also enhance the legitimacy of African firms in world markets, especially when endorsed by global bodies like the International Federation of Chartered Accountants (IFAC).

One would not expect international organizations like IFAC and the World Bank to endorse and approve all varieties of institutional reform, however. They will support interventions that seek to establish institutional forms that have been deemed best practice in the global economic and political environment. These are chosen because they confer legitimacy on the international organization proposing reform and on the reforming country itself. They also provide a replicable reform product in which international organizations can specialize – cementing the role such entities play in international development's institutional reform market.

Given such thinking, one would expect accounting reforms to focus on improving country-level compliance with "international accounting standards."[14] This kind of best practice comes out of developed, Western countries where various institutional elements facilitate functionality. This content can be expressed in terms of Scott's three elements and supporting mechanisms, discussed in Chapter 3[15]:

- Regulative mechanisms are important because they shape behavior through threat of sanction. These include laws requiring firms to adopt international accounting standards.
- Norms make desired behaviors socially appropriate and acceptable, causing agents to intrinsically "decide" in favor of specific actions. For instance, norms of standardization and professionalization are key to international accounting regimes.

---

[12] Andrews 2011a; Dacin, Goodstein, and Scott 2002; DiMaggio and Powell 1983; Meyer and Rowan 1977.
[13] Andrews 2011a.
[14] Sadler 2001; Sian 2006, 2007; Uche 2002.
[15] Scott's (2008, 48) schematic is used here, as detailed in Chapter 3.

- Cultural-cognitive mechanisms are needed to structure the information that agents receive and how they interpret it. In order to facilitate thinking that supports the best practice international standards, for example, firms and accountants need places to learn about generally accepted accounting practices.
- Finally, these mechanisms are "given life" through supporting activities and resources. Organizations enforce laws, activities reflect norms, and trainers are paid to instruct new accountants.

As discussed in Chapter 3, theory suggests that these elements impact behavior when interacting to create one complete structure. This is ostensibly what international organizations observe when identifying best practices in developed countries – and why they prescribe such as institutional reforms in development. The point that needs to be noted, however, is that such prescriptions are for solutions that require specific and high content – in the form of peculiar regulative, normative, and cultural-cognitive elements as well as supporting activities and resources. Richard Rose points to such high-content requirements for best practice reforms in his warning about the relevance of such in developing countries:[16]

There are differences . . . in the resources required by best practice programmes. A best practice social security system will cost a lot of money; a high-quality university system requires able staff as well as money; and a programme for minority rights requires the honest and effective administration of laws. An ample supply of laws, money and personnel is taken for granted in countries credited with best practices. But this cannot be assumed of governments in developing and especially low income countries.

The Best Practice Bias in African Accounting Reforms
One gets a good view into the thinking of international accounting reform designers when looking at Accounting and Auditing Reports of Observation of Standards and Codes (ROSCs), produced by the World Bank and International Monetary Fund (IMF). These are documents used to assess the quality and reform needs of a country's accounting and auditing system.[17] Written by experts using a common and consistent methodology, ROSCs provide a wide and consistent window on the way international organizations conceive of institutional reforms. Twenty studies in Africa are listed in Table 4.1. Multiple researchers analyzed these documents to address

---

[16] Rose 2003, 17.
[17] ROSCs are available at http://www.worldbank.org/ifa/rosc_aa.html, which also describes the analytical method.

Table 4.1. *African accounting and auditing ROSCs published since 2003, with dates*

Benin (2009)	Ethiopia (2007)	Mauritius (2003)	Sierra Leone (2006)
Botswana (2006)	Ghana (2004)	Mozambique (2008)	South Africa (2003)
Burundi (2007)	Kenya (2001)	Nigeria (2004)	Tanzania (2005)
Congo (DRC) (2010)	Madagascar (2008)	Rwanda (2008)	Uganda (2005)
Cote d'Ivoire (2009)	Malawi (2007)	Senegal (2005)	Zambia (2007)

Source: All ROSCs are accessible through http://www.worldbank.org/ifa/rosc_aa.html.

issues raised in this chapter, starting with the idea that reforms exhibit a best practice bias.[18]

Evidence from these ROSCs does suggest a biased focus on best practice accounting standards. There are more than 2,000 references to such international standards in the twenty ROSCs analyzed, averaging 102 references per ROSC or 3.6 per ROSC page.[19] These standards are most commonly referenced as benchmarks against which country systems are compared and as guides for reform recommendations. These applications are apparent when one reviews how standards are discussed in the preface, executive summary, and introductory sections. Such sections allude to standards as "internationally accepted good practices" with which countries should comply with. Twelve of these sections speak additionally of standards as a "guide" to policy reform.

Various explanations are given as to why international standards matter so much. Standards are presented as necessary to control risk for firm and financial sector failure in seventeen ROSCs, for example. Fourteen ROSCs note further that standards will help countries to attract foreign investment. Ten ROSCs cite benefits of adopting standards in fledgling banking sectors and stock markets.[20] The narrowness and outward focus of these functional gains are important to note and suggest an isomorphic influence on reasons why reforms focus on international standards. The emphasis is on gaining legitimacy from parties outside the countries. Only three ROSCs allude to examples of firm failures in the African country being assessed when arguing that international standards will help alleviate risk for

[18] The content of each document was analyzed by two people, one of whom was always the author. Coding, scoring, and other analysis required agreement of both parties.
[19] References were identified in a content search. Identifiers were ISA (International Standards on Auditing), IAS (International Accounting Standards), and IFRS (International Financial Reporting Standards).
[20] Another five ROSCs note that international standards are important in privatization and anticorruption programs.

such failure, for example. By contrast, fourteen ROSCs sell the idea using examples of broader international financial crisis. This suggests what could be called a "functional mimicry" rationale for reform: developed countries learned through crisis that international standards are necessary, and African countries should copy their responses. The ROSCs imply normative pressures as well, suggesting that international standards have become the legitimate language of international investors and global banking and equity markets.[21]

The message seems to be that African economies will lack legitimacy if they do not comply with these norms, and may be excluded from international engagements as a result. This message is obviously relevant to formal, internationally active corporate entities in Africa. These comprise small portions of most of the countries in the ROSC sample, however, where most economic activity is informal and localized. The ROSCs provide little information as to how this broader set of actors will benefit from adopting international accounting standards, even though this is ostensibly the focus of reform recommendations.

Evidence shows further that such best practice institutional reforms require specific and high content to function. This content is reflected in the common focal points of ROSC analyses (given that ROSCs assess compliance against international standards). Two researchers worked together to identify these focal points across all twenty ROSCs, categorizing such as regulative, normative, or cultural-cognitive elements. For instance, ROSCs assessed whether countries had laws requiring firms, banks, and other economic entities to account, report, and undergo audits according to specified processes and using international standards. Normative elements were also identified, including standardized requirements for accounting practitioners to join internationally accredited professional bodies and hold internationally accredited qualifications. These and other requirements are shown in Table 4.2, which illustrates the content ROSCs typically examine as "benchmark" characteristics of an accounting system that complies with international standards. The text in this table is thick and difficult to navigate, reflecting how demanding reforms like this are.

Characteristics not in italics reflect formal content, assessed with reference to written laws and regulations. Characteristics *in italics* represent more informal content, which was only indirectly reflected in ROSC discussions

---

[21] The Nigerian ROSC notes that international accounting standards are required because "Nigeria is making efforts to attract foreign investments into the economy" and "international investors require comparable financial information from countries competing for foreign investments." The summary statement is absolute in this regard: "This requires that Nigerian corporate sector comply with globally acceptable standards and codes."

Table 4.2. *Specific, demanding content required for international standard accounting*

Regulative mechanisms

1. Laws requiring accounting, auditing, and reporting. Laws require economic entities to account, report, and audit according to specified processes, using updated international standards.
2. Laws regulating the accounting and auditing profession. Laws regulate the accounting and auditing profession, creating professional bodies, stipulating rules for entry, codes of behavior, and standard-setting responsibilities.
3. Regulation of compliance with accounting, auditing, and reporting law. Entities exist to regulate economic entities' compliance with accounting, reporting, and auditing requirements. They have effective sanctions, a track record of applying such, and information and capacity to facilitate regulation.
4. Regulation of accounting profession. Entities exist to regulate the accounting and auditing profession with clear responsibility, international legitimacy, sanctioning authority, and experience and capacity to regulate.

Normative mechanisms

5. Formal accounting, auditing, and professional standards. Entities exist to set standards, which are in place and comply with international requirements for accounting, auditing, ethical behavior of practitioners, and entry and accreditation.
6. *Norms of accounting and auditing practitioners. It is widely appropriate for accounting and auditing practitioners to: be members of internationally accredited professional bodies; hold internationally accredited qualifications; and adhere to internationally determined ethical requirements, standards of practice, and norms of professional responsibility and independence.*
7. *Accounting, reporting, and auditing norms in business community. It is widely appropriate for economic entities to hire professional accountants, comply with international standards, disclose financial information fully, use standardized financial information in decision making, and adhere to international norms of professional responsibility and independence.*

Cultural-cognitive mechanisms

8. Formal information, education, training, and guidance. Economic entities are informed about international standards. There are widely available, internationally accredited educational opportunities for practitioners, with ongoing educational opportunities and regularly produced guidelines to ensure updated compliance.
9. *Cognitive capacities of accounting and auditing practitioners. Accounting and auditing practitioners know what information and practices are required to ensure compliance with international standards, understand how to interpret and apply these in the local context, and have the awareness of (and skills to) produce reliable financial information products.*
10. *Cognitive capacities of business community. Firms are aware of their responsibilities to provide reliable financial information, know what information is required to facilitate compliance with international standards, and understand the value of transparent and standardized financial information.*

Source and notes: Characteristics of national accounting and auditing systems compliant with international standards, given analysis by author and fellow researchers.

of practice and perceptions of accounting and auditing quality. These discussions note how likely it is for accountants to be members of professional associations, for example, regardless of laws that may require such.

ROSCs present these ten characteristics as necessary in accounting systems reflecting international standards. Laws in such systems require accounting according to international standards, for example; norms make it appropriate to use such standards in reporting and auditing; and educational opportunities train practitioners to account, report, and audit using international standards. The characteristics are also demanding – or high content – breaking down into multiple dimensions. This kind of system requires a complex set of business norms identified in characteristic seven from Table 4.2, for example, that make it appropriate for economic entities to (i) hire professional accountants, (ii) comply with international standards, (iii) fully disclose financial information, (iv) use standardized financial information in decision making, and (v) adhere to international norms of professional responsibility. Detailed demands in these and the other nine characteristic areas add up to fifty institutional requirements for establishing international accounting standards.

These fifty regulations, norms, and cultural-cognitive mechanisms make an internationally standardized accounting system demanding. The extent of such demand can be illustrated in contrasting the documentation associated with existing accounting codes in developing countries with International Financial Reporting Standards (IFRS) documentation. For instance, Mozambique's accounting and reporting requirements have been guided by the 72-page Plano Geral de Contabilidade (Standardized Chart of Accounts) or PGC.[22] This is half the size of the "IFRS in Your Pocket Guide" bought out by the accounting firm Deloitte (which is 134 pages long).[23] It is significantly smaller than Deloitte's full "Guide to IFRS Reporting," which goes on for 2,918 pages. This is, in fact, shorter than the full IFRS documentation, which implies the need for rules, norms, and ways of thinking that are more than forty times the content traditionally evident in countries like Mozambique.

Reforms Do Not Provide *All* of the Pieces for Best Practice Interventions

Developing countries like Mozambique are unlikely to satisfy the specific and high-content requirements of institutional reforms that introduce

---

[22] Mozambique ROSC, 9, http://www.worldbank.org/ifa/rosc_aa_moz.pdf.
[23] Deloitte IAS plus Web site, http://www.iasplus.com/dttpubs/pubs.htm.

best practices like international accounting standards. This is because such reforms come from very different contexts where they have emerged through endogenous processes over long periods of time. Modern accounting practices in the United States emerged gradually in the nineteenth and twentieth centuries, for example, as the country advanced economically and the nature of business practices got more complicated.[24] Laws that support accounting by international standards are fairly new even in many developed countries and will probably be lacking in most African countries.[25]

Normative structures – and underpinning value systems – are also likely to be absent in many African countries. Accounting formalization, professionalization, standardization, and disclosure were accepted as appropriate in many developed countries only after economies had grown to levels that required such behaviors.[26] Such norms are not as evident in less-developed economic settings, especially where family-based business is common and transactions are informal and localized. Similarly, cultural-cognitive mechanisms supporting modern accounting systems – including graduate-level chartered accounting knowledge – emerged in developed countries only when demand for such services was growing. Limited demand in developing countries is likely to lead to a lack of such content. One would expect deficiencies in supporting activities and resources as well.

The degree to which a developing country lacks requisite content will depend on its own historical, economic, and political profile. Anglophone countries are more likely to have content in place, given that international standards exhibit a strong bias toward British accounting traditions and practice.[27] Countries that are less developed and economically sophisticated will probably be more lacking in content.[28]

As with all institutions, the content required for introducing best practice institutions is both formal and informal. Formal content is visible, like a codified law, written standard, or university accounting program. Informal content, by contrast, is implicit and seldom visible.[29] Examples include ideologies and unwritten customs. Whereas regulatory elements can be informal, unseen content dominates normative and cultural-cognitive elements. Both are influenced by values and reflected in social structures. Although informal, they are key to political and economic power relationships in

---

[24] Andrews 2008.
[25] Ibid.
[26] Gray 1988; Salter and Niswander 1995; Ueno and Sekaran 1992.
[27] Zeghal and Mhedhbi 2006, 378.
[28] de Renzio, Andrews, and Mills 2010.
[29] Helmke and Levitsky 2003.

place in any group. Informal mechanisms often determine the influence that formal dimensions enjoy and the avenues that exist for change – and hence reform – given that "[o]nly practices or organizational forms that 'make sense' [in the context of informal mechanisms] are adopted."[30]

Chapter 3 advanced an argument that international organizations will struggle with informal institutional content, however. This plays out in the way one expects these organizations to represent the best practice institutions they transfer to developing countries. It is hard to "see" the informal content required to make these institutions work, especially when one has only an external vantage point (as international organizations often do). As a result, reforms will tend to emphasize formal content only, focusing on the parts of the best practice that can be "observe[d]."[31] Formal dimensions also offer more immediate gains in terms of legitimacy, being quickly visible to external audiences. Mary Shirley alludes to this in explaining why international organizations often focus on legal changes that "can be instituted rapidly and be easily used as benchmarks for dispersing funds and assessing outcomes."[32] Because of such thinking, one would expect reforms sponsored by these organizations to introduce formal accounting laws, enforcement agencies, written standards, and educational programs. Informal content like unwritten norms supporting disclosure or professionalization will be ignored or assumed to exist.

Evidence of Content Gaps That Reforms Do Not Fill

ROSCs were analyzed to assess whether and to what degree the content shown in Table 4.2 was apparent in each country. Evidence supports the argument that many African countries lack content elements. This evidence was collected from each country ROSC for detailed dimensions of all ten content areas. Two researchers identified specific information in each ROSC to score the content in relevant dimensions as present ($=1$), absent ($=0$), or without basis for judgment ($=$ no score).[33] A total was then calculated for each characteristic, noting how much content was present. These totals were prorated out of 5 in all cases. The averages for all twenty countries are shown in Table 4.3, with Burundi and South Africa scores provided as the lowest and highest examples. The table also shows how many of the countries totaled 2 or below out of 5 in each of the ten content areas.

---

[30] Guillen 2003, 21.
[31] Frandale and Paauwe 2007, 369.
[32] Shirley 2005, 17
[33] Records are available from the author.

Table 4.3. *How much African systems satisfy requirements for international accounting*

Key content area	Average (prorated out of 5)	Burundi (prorated out of 5)	South Africa (prorated out of 5)	Number of countries (out of 20) 2 or less
Regulative mechanisms				
1. Laws requiring accounting, auditing, and reporting	3.5	3	5	0
2. Laws regulating the accounting and auditing profession	3.75	3	5	2
3. Regulation of compliance with accounting, auditing, and reporting laws	2	2	3.5	10
4. Regulation of accounting profession	2.25	2	5	6
Normative mechanisms				
5. Formal accounting, auditing, and profession standards	2.75	2	5	8
6. *Norms of accounting and auditing practitioners*	*0.6*	*0*	*3.5*	*17*
7. *Accounting, reporting, and auditing norms in business community*	*0.6*	*0*	*3.5*	*17*
Cultural-cognitive mechanisms				
8. Formal information, education, training, and guidance	2.5	2	5	10
9. *Cognitive capacities of accounting and auditing practitioners*	*0.6*	*0*	*3.6*	*17*
10. *Cognitive capacities of business community*	*0.5*	*0*	*2.5*	*17*

Source: Author's analysis, based on the data in accounting and auditing ROSCs.

Table 4.3 shows that most of the countries actually scored reasonably well on the content areas in the regulative element. Laws were the strongest content items across all twenty countries. Supporting practices and resources, in the form of regulatory agencies enforcing laws, were not as consistently present, however. These agencies were practically absent in a diverse set of six to ten countries that includes Burundi, Uganda, Sierra Leone, Mozambique, and Benin.

A similar small-sized group of countries also had limited content with regard to characteristic five "formal accounting, auditing and profession standards." Most countries scored fairly well in this formal dimension of the normative institutional element, however. This stands in contrast to the weak scores for informal dimensions of the elements "norms of accounting and auditing practitioners" and "accounting, reporting and auditing norms in business community." Seventeen of the twenty countries scored 2 or below on these dimensions, with ROSC evidence pointing to a deficiency of such content. These ROSCs commonly indicate, for example, that businesses do not consider it widely appropriate to adopt international standards and disclose their financial transactions fully when accounting and reporting. Twelve of the ROSCs note that most firms are family owned, with business norms that do not support professionalization and standardization.

Informal dimensions are weaker in the cultural-cognitive element as well. Half of the countries had reasonable formal content in this element, given the presence of educational opportunities, information about international accounting standards, and the like. However, evidence suggests limited informal cognitive capacities in the community of accounting and auditing practitioners and in business more broadly. ROSCs noted, for example, that although accountant practitioners commonly know that they need to apply international standards, they often do not know how to deal with complex practice requirements in these standards or how to apply such in the local context. ROSCs also commonly cite a poor understanding of the role accountants and auditors play and the importance of audit independence. They also note that many businesspeople do not know what to do with standardized, complex financial information and hence typically ignore such when making decisions.

This kind of informal institutional content seems especially deficient across the African countries. Combined scores in the four informal content areas (areas 6, 7, 9, and 10) yield an average of 2.3 of 20 (with a high total of 13.1 in South Africa making up for most of the evidence in favor of such content). The basic picture is simple: norms and informal ways of seeing and thinking about business and financial transactions do not satisfy the requirements of accounting systems compliant with international standards. Content deficiencies in more formal areas – laws, regulatory agencies, formal standards, and educational opportunities – are less severe. Combined totals in the six formal content areas (areas 1, 2, 3, 4, 5, and 8) yield an average of 16 of 30. Although there is an obvious content gap here, it is not as large as the one that exists with informal characteristics. The formal deficiencies are also more targeted, with between six and ten countries having total scores lower than 2 in these areas. Informal content gaps are pervasive, however, with seventeen of twenty countries having fewer than two of five content items in all four of these areas.

This is not the impression one would get if considering only the ROSC recommendation sections. The content in these sections shows that international organizations focus reforms predominantly on introducing formal content. Fourteen of the ROSCs introduced recommendations using exactly the same statement that endorsed a focus on formal dimensions. Ostensibly reflecting opinions of local professionals interviewed, the statement held that "[i]nterviewees in general view that the precondition for improvements in the quality of corporate financial reporting is the establishment of a strong regulatory regime with effective enforcement mechanisms for ensuring compliance with accounting and auditing standards."[34]

This perspective was further reflected in patterns of recommendations. Two researchers categorized each ROSC's recommendations in the ten content areas shown in Table 4.3. There were 279 recommendations across all twenty countries, averaging 14 per country and ranging from 5 (in South Africa) to 24 (in Madagascar). As Table 4.4 illustrates, 86 percent of these recommendations (241 of the 279) emphasized improvements in the six formal content areas. Improvements were most commonly slated for the formal regulatory regime – including enforcement mechanisms. More than half of all recommendations (146 of the 279) proposed various ways of strengthening laws and the bodies regulating firms and accounting and auditing practitioners. A further 49 recommendations focused on improving formal educational opportunities, whereas 46 targeted changes to the formal accounting, auditing, and reporting standards.

These recommendations appear relevant in most cases, given that formal content is needed to establish institutions that facilitate accounting by international standards. The formal proposals overwhelm recommendations to address informal content deficiencies, however. Only thirty-eight such recommendations were identified over twenty countries and from 279 reform ideas. Twenty-one of these focused on informal aspects of cognition, and the remaining seventeen addressed informal norms.[35] Summary analysis in Table 4.4 shows these to be the weakest content areas in

---

[34] This statement was repeated, verbatim, in various ROSCs. It is copied here from the Tanzania ROSC, para. 40.

[35] Recommendations were vague, aiming to sensitize users about the value of modern accounting.

Table 4.4. *How reform recommendations exhibit a bias toward formal elements*

Key content area	Average (ex 5)	Countries < 2 (ex 20)	Recommendations (ex 279)
Regulative mechanisms			
1. Laws requiring accounting, auditing, and reporting	3.5	0	21 (formal)
2. Laws regulating the accounting and auditing professions	3.75	2	18 (formal)
3. Regulation of compliance with accounting, auditing, and reporting laws	2	10	57 (formal)
4. Regulation of accounting profession	2.25	6	50 (formal)
Normative mechanisms			
5. Formal accounting, auditing, and profession standards	2.75	8	46 (formal)
6. Norms of accounting and auditing practitioners	0.6	17	11 (informal)
7. Accounting, reporting and auditing norms in business community	0.6	17	6 (informal)
Cultural-cognitive mechanisms			
8. Formal information, education, training, and guidance	2.5	10	49 (formal)
9. Cognitive capacities of accounting and auditing practitioners	0.6	17	13 (informal)
10. Cognitive capacities of business community	0.5	17	8 (informal)

Source: Author's analysis, based on data in accounting and auditing ROSCs.

African countries – with the lowest country averages and the highest number of countries scoring less than 2 of 5. These informal content areas are the biggest gaps for reform to fill. The evidence suggests, however, that reform recommendations are seldom identified to fill these gaps.

Unfilled Gaps and Failed Reforms

One could expect limits to this approach where informal content does not exist. Reforms may lead to changes in formal elements in such settings but will not address deficiencies in informal content. These deficiencies will likely undermine the legitimacy of new formal elements, failing to establish functional best practice. Laws requiring high levels of information disclosure will not enjoy support in countries where business norms foster

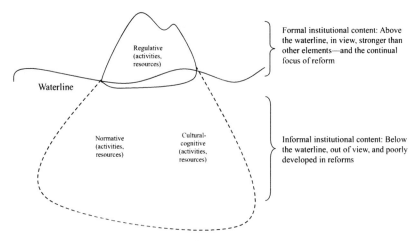

Figure 4.2. Reforms foster new institutions as foundation-less icebergs – the sinking kind.

relational connections and transaction secrecy, for instance. Reforms may even foster dysfunctional practice in such situations, given that formal and informal institutional mechanisms "support and motivate differing choices and behaviors."[36] This can destabilize the rules of the game completely, creating confusion as to which element should drive behavior. Brokers often emerge in such situations to help individuals navigate between the different elements, leading to suboptimal behavioral patterns. Firms may choose to remain small so as not to reach a fiscal size at which formal financial reports are mandatory, for example. Professional accountants may help firms work around tax and disclosure rules using creative accounting practices.

Using a metaphor from Chapter 3, one could characterize these reforms as creating new institutions that resemble iceberg tips with no foundation – as in Figure 4.2. The tip may appear intact above the water line, but it is only a matter of time until it sinks, given a lack of norms and cultural-cognitive fundamentals.

Although it is a simple metaphor, the idea of a sinking iceberg tip is of vital importance: *If reforms introduce rules of the game that require a lot of content, but then do not provide such, the reforms guarantee their own failure.* The idea also requires urgent attention in development, given the expected predilection for visible best practice reforms in this context. Given this predilection, one would expect international organizations to respond to such situations by suggesting even more formal reform – perhaps stronger

[36] Scott 2008, 62.

laws or more capable enforcement mechanisms. Unfortunately, the repeated prescription of more formal reform will not close gaps in informal content, which will undermine the functionality of new institutions. At the same time, the focus on more and more formal best practice interventions will crowd out efforts to introduce reforms with less-demanding, more fitted content; that could actually enhance functionality.

Evidence of Unfilled Gaps and Failed Reforms

The evidence thus far suggests that international organizations do appear to focus on best practices that demand specific and high content in the reform agendas. Additionally, developing countries do lack much of the content required to ensure that these practices are introduced functionally. Furthermore, international organizations do emphasize formal content in their reforms and thus leave major gaps in terms of the absent informal content. The remaining question is whether evidence supports the argument that such reforms become iceberg tips that ultimately sink. In terms of the current study, the question is simple: Does the double bias toward best practice international standards and the formal content of externally influenced reforms lead to a continued lack of informal content and undermine the functionality of new accounting institutions in African countries?

ROSCs do not provide information on the functionality or usefulness of African accounting systems, frustrating the analysis of this question. ROSCs do provide information about the way gaps in informal content impact the uptake of more formal reform elements, however. ROSC content was analyzed to search for evidence of such effects. Words and phrases suggesting the limited influence of a formal mechanism were identified, including "noncompliance," and the surrounding sections were evaluated to note any discussion of deficient informal content. This search yielded evidence supporting the fourth hypothesis, although future research is needed to tell the full story. For instance, the ROSCs averaged twelve references to "noncompliance" or "compliance gaps" related to informal-content deficiencies.[37] The most common reference linked noncompliance to a pervasive lack of "understanding" about the importance of accounting, the role of financial information, or the fundamentals of professionalism in business. In theoretical parlance, this relates to informal cultural-cognitive frameworks. A second type of reference noted the weak incentives for businesses to adopt new standards or comply with laws, given entrenched traditions of secrecy

---

[37] An additional seventeen references were made, on average, per ROSC, that described noncompliance or linked noncompliance to deficient formal content.

and the dominant role of familial relationships in commercial engagements. These informal influences made it inappropriate to share information that should be disclosed in an international standards system. A third example involved observations that, given established business norms, many economic agents were simply unwilling to pay the fees for professional accountants, and practicing accountants saw little reason to join or support professional bodies. Norms driving demand for professionalism were lacking, and this led to deficient support for new formal mechanisms – like laws, regulatory bodies, and educational mechanisms.[38]

Given such evidence, it is valid to argue that the continued lack of informal content will undermine formal institutional reforms required by international organizations. This could thwart the functionality of accounting systems in African countries altogether, given the potential displacement effects of a narrow best practice reform focus like the one in evidence. Instead of asking what businesses currently do and where and how this can be improved, reforms are likely to continue demanding high content best practices that cannot be effectively introduced.

GETTING MORE FLEXIBLE – AND SPECIFIC – ABOUT CONTENT

The evidence indicates that externally influenced accounting reforms in Africa overspecify solutions and oversimplify what it takes to adopt and implement them. The over-specification comes through pressure to adopt particular international best practices. The oversimplification arises from a tendency to introduce only the formal aspects of such practices through reforms. The result is a steady stream of reforms with limited influence. Accounting systems in many countries remain weak because best practice international standards demand more – and different – content than is available, and reforms do not fill the content gaps.

This is a valid way of thinking about past failures to establish building standards in Haiti. Reforms sponsored by various donors introduced specific laws and formal codes. The additional content required for these standards to work – norms, cultural-cognitive mechanisms, and regulatory devices – was not part of reforms, however, and is still lacking. The explanation also holds for reforms emphasizing business and financial deregulation:

---

[38] Many practitioners do not consider professional training necessary and do not provide membership fees for professional bodies. The lack of support results in a deficient set of formal products like training events.

Table 4.5. *Being more specific about the content needed in best practice accounting reforms*

Key content area	Content demands of best practice reform	Content evident in reform context	Content gap
Regulative mechanisms	20 requirements	11.5 of 20	High: 42.5% of the content is still required
Normative mechanisms	15 requirements	3.95 of 15	Excessive: 76% of the content is still required
Cultural-cognitive mechanisms	15 requirements	3.6 of 15	Excessive: 76% of the content is still required

Source: Author's analysis, based on data in accounting and auditing ROSCs.

- Numerous studies show that deregulation fosters entrepreneurship when significant institutional content is in place; businesses consider it appropriate to provide information to the market, entrepreneurs can access needed factors of production, and consumers and investors have alternative means to hold entrepreneurs accountable.[39] This content is seldom included in reforms fostering deregulation, however, which undermines success.
- Specific content is similarly required, but often ignored, when countries liberalize their financial sectors. Reforms often fail to establish norms of information sharing or government supervision mechanisms. This can lead to excessive risk taking by newly private banks.[40] Noting the lack of such content in many reforms, Obstfeld warns, "Taken all alone, financial openness is not a panacea – and it could be poison."[41]

On the face of it, this problem calls for better understanding and specification of the content required to introduce best practice reforms into new contexts. Table 4.5 provides a simple mechanism to facilitate this. The first two columns require reform designers to reconcile the content requirements of specific best practices with content realities in the focal context. The final column allows for the identification of reform needs – filling gaps between the first two sets of responses. If used for the accounting reforms

[39] Busenitz et al. 2000; Kostova 1997.
[40] Martinez Peria and Schmukler 2001.
[41] Obstfeld 2009, 104.

discussed in this chapter, such a tool would show that the content gap was high in terms of regulative mechanisms, but even higher – and excessive – with regard to normative and cultural-cognitive mechanisms (given data in Table 4.3).

In the language of Richard Rose, such approach could lead reform designers to reassess the relevance of best practices in targeted contexts.[42] This would be an especially wise approach where best practices prove too difficult to theorize in the manner required. This situation arises where designers struggle to identify the capacities and normative and cultural-cognitive content required to make a best practice work. In the case of accounting systems, for instance, there are valid questions regarding whether any expert knows how to get countries to become more transparent. It would also be particularly wise where too many gaps exist between content demands and content in evidence, such that a country or an organization lacks too much regulative capacity or cognitive and normative foundation to make a best practice function.

Observers noting such situations have at times called for an approach to reform based on the "basics" instead of best practice. In the area of public financial management, for example, Alan Schick advocates introducing standardized controls before performance-based reforms.[43] The approach sounds attractive, but even the basics are a version of best practice that has its own content demand; standardized controls require highly specific political and social norms and cognitive mechanisms, for instance, that are often lacking in developing countries.

In many developing countries, the search for reform content requires going beyond best practice or "basics first."[44] A more flexible approach to reform is needed, emphasizing an incremental search for solutions to problems that local agents care about. ROSCs allude to this kind of solution emerging in Africa. Fifteen ROSCs note that international banks, listed companies, large mining firms, and big trading enterprises all account and report in compliance with international standards, regardless of content deficiencies in the local accounting and auditing context. This compliance has very little to do with institutional requirements or incentives in the countries themselves. Companies are complying because it is required for their ongoing business interests. In every case, the accounting, reporting, and auditing was done by international firms (like Deloitte). These international firms provided professionals with requisite formal and informal attributes

---

[42] Rose 2003, 26.
[43] Schick 1998.
[44] Andrews 2006.

needed to facilitate modern accounting. The firms also self-regulated to a great extent and offered in-house training, mentoring, and the like. They overcame glaring accounting system deficiencies in countries like Nigeria, the Democratic Republic of Congo, Rwanda, and Mozambique.

Some ROSCs refer to these global accounting firms in a negative way, suggesting that engaging such entities could undermine the development of local accounting institutions. Another perspective would see these entities as global carriers who ensure that Africa's internationally active companies can converse and engage in the global language of business. Literature suggests that these global carriers will play an important role in facilitating the development of trade and market capitalization processes in developing countries for many years to come, filling gaps in local accounting institutions. These firms have played this role in countries like Japan and South Korea. They provide "important sites where accounting practices emerge, become standardized and regulated, where accounting rules and standards are translated into practice, and where professional identities are mediated, formed and transformed."[45] In this light, Anne Loft argues that accounting is going "beyond the state" and that the key agents of its future development are likely not going to be the bodies or professional associations within countries but those entities that cross boundaries.[46]

International development organizations are likely to balk at the idea of allowing accounting systems to emerge endogenously through non-state agents. What systems will develop in the short and medium terms, as these international agents work their way toward new mechanisms? Which local agents would be engaged in promoting local systems, and what would they consider "appropriate"? This kind of flexible approach to defining reform is, however, vital if institutional reformers are serious about breaking out of a focus on overspecified best practices.

A more flexible approach could allow countries to build domestic systems that are less specific and demanding and more locally functional than the best practice models currently imposed on them. Chapter 7 argues that this approach will emerge if problems are made the focal point of reforms. This requires moving from an isomorphic focus on coercion and mimicry to "reform as problem solving."[47] Chapter 8 posits that flexible approaches will emerge if reforms emphasize processes of finding and fitting solutions to problems. Examples of such processes are evident as well, including decentralization in Rwanda and anticorruption reforms in Indonesia. In

[45] Cooper and Robson 2006, 417.
[46] Loft 2007.
[47] Dull 2006, 190.

both cases, reforms facilitated processes through which relevant – and viable – reforms could emerge gradually, over time, in response to new needs. The reforms involved agents who knew the contexts and could fashion content that fitted such. Chapter 5 discusses such agents – and the way in which reforms typically do not facilitate their engagement.

FIVE

Limited Engagement, Limited Change

THE ILLUSORY PROMISE OF "CHAMPIONS"

A Harvard teaching case tells the story of industrial reforms in Suzhou, China.[1] These involved significant institutional change, given the goal of importing Singaporean "software" into a new industrial park. This software would bring new rules, procedures, work ethic, and business orientation to Suzhou. This idea emerged from the highest levels of government, championed by premiers in China and Singapore. Such support engendered an expectation of guaranteed success, especially given beliefs that top-down commands elicit responses in supposedly hierarchical countries like China. Such success was not forthcoming, however. Those charged with implementing the project at regional and local government levels accepted the industrial park idea, but not the proposed "Singaporean feel." Many implementing agents did not, therefore, support the proposed top-down change. Instead, local agents in Suzhou initiated their own China-only industrial park project as a rival to the Singapore-China model.

High-level champions – or heroes – are commonly considered central to the success or failure of institutional reforms in development. They are assumed to play a number of vital roles in the change process. This includes identifying where change is needed and providing new ideas, political will, authority, and motivation required for implementation. Others are assumed to follow these authorized and influential operators, implementing new institutions by edict.[2] This chapter challenges these assumptions. It posits that institutional change is not something that individual champions achieve by themselves. Change requires the coordinated interaction of many

[1] Harvard Kennedy School 2007.
[2] Nutt 1986.

capabilities that are seldom found in isolated individuals or narrow groups. Craftsmen require others to provide wood to make pegs, to inform them about the size and shape of holes needing filling, and to ultimately help in shaping pegs to fit these holes. Agents provide these capabilities only if they support the task or change at hand, however, which they are unlikely to do simply because superiors require it. As a result, institutional reforms require broad engagement. Limited engagement leads to limited change, which is one reason why institutional reforms often fail to make governments better in developing countries.

This argument emerges through three sections. The first section introduces the problem of limited reform engagement in a discussion of public financial management reforms in Mozambique. These reforms look successful when one considers work by a narrow set of politicians and technocrats. Unfortunately, they appear less successful with regard to implementation by broader, more deconcentrated sets of agents. The second section provides a theoretical perspective on this problem. It argues that multiple leaders or institutional entrepreneurs are required to facilitate reforms and that distributed agents beyond these leaders are also needed to actually implement change. Reforms typically focus on solitary reform champions or heroes and not distributed agents, however, which undermines the diffusion and implementation of change. This is partly because reforms are introduced as signals. This focus creates pressure to get change accepted by influential individuals and draws attention away from ensuring that it is accepted by the hard-to-reach, more mundane agents that ultimately are responsible for implementation. Experience from Mozambique is used to illustrate this discussion. It leads to a conclusion that reformers should look for ways to foster more inclusive reform processes.

THE PROBLEM OF LIMITED REFORM ENGAGEMENT

Located on the southeastern coast of Africa, Mozambique is a large nation with multiple provinces, more than a hundred district governments, and many municipalities. A variety of ethnic groups inhabit this land, speaking different languages and following different religions. They also took different sides in a civil war that ended in 1992. These and other historical, geographical, and economic divides make the country difficult to govern. Reforms intended to improve governance have been numerous as a result, with a particular focus on strengthening the public financial management (PFM) system. Since 1989, the World Bank alone has launched ten projects with content aimed at improving public expenditure, financial management, and procurement. More than fifteen other donors routinely support such interventions as well.

Public financial management reforms have been championed at the highest levels of government since at least the late 1990s. Presidential attention has been high, as has the engagement of successive ministers of finance. These champions have ensured that PFM has been front and center in national reform and development plans. This support also manifests in the influential vehicles created for reform. Political and technical backing has been available for officials in key Ministry of Finance departments like Treasury and the Budget Office. Cadres of consultants were ever present in these locales for much of the 2000s as a result. Beyond this, a concentrated agency called Unidade Técnica de Reforma da Administração (UTRAFE) was created to lead reforms in 2001. Headed by a former deputy minister of finance, UTRAFE was established "to drive and coordinate the execution of the entire program of reforms in the financial administration of the state."[3] In many senses it was the organizational arm of the ultimate champion, the minister of finance.

Reforms driven by these agents have delivered many things. These include new budgeting and financial management laws, modernized internal and external audit agencies, and an information technology (IT)–based integrated financial management information system (IFMIS) called e-SISTAFE that formalizes all aspects of money management. This system provides a formal mechanism through which agents can budget, transact, disburse, and report. It is a major reason Mozambique recorded one of the highest overall average Public Expenditure and Financial Accountability (PEFA) scores in Africa. This score comes from a multidonor PEFA assessment donor agencies created to test whether countries comply with "existing good international practices."[4] Mozambique scores a B average on this test, better than expected from a large, distributed nation that happens to be the sixth poorest on earth.

The PEFA assessment raises some concerns, however. Scores are higher on some dimensions than on others. For instance, the country scores an A on the dimension evaluating whether cash flows are forecast and monitored. It scores a D on the dimension assessing the transparency and frequency of cash payments. Overall, one gets the picture of a system in which a few agents forecast and monitor cash flows perfectly while most others spend cash in ways that fall outside the forecasts and go unmonitored. A similar

[3] According to the dispatch of March 21, 2001.
[4] PEFA 2006, 5.

observation can be made about intergovernmental allocations. Mozambique scores an A for the rules used to distribute money to subnational governments. The quality of information about revenues and expenditures in these subnational entities is given a D rating. Again, a few agents are making great rules, but with limited information from the many agents that have to live by such rules – who do not report on what they receive or spend.

In this case, one can actually identify the agents responsible for both A and D scores. New laws and processes that helped the country reach its highest scores were produced by rule makers in concentrated units in the Ministry of Finance (like the Budget and Treasury departments). Poor scores resulted when deconcentrated budget holders were involved; in line ministries, state-owned enterprises, districts, and provinces. These deconcentrated agents are responsible for implementing the rules of the game developed by concentrated Ministry of Finance agents. They do not implement these rules well, however.

This was further apparent in feedback from government officials at a 2009 budget reform workshop.[5] Thirty officials were asked to rate the post-reform quality of laws introduced by central departments and the *implementation of these laws* by different sets of deconcentrated agents. They gave laws an average rating of 8.3 of 10, compared with 7.3, 6.5, and 5.6 for *implementation* by central government agencies, provinces, and districts. The implementation gap was between 1 and 2.7.

PEFA data show a similar gap between laws created by concentrated agents and implementation by deconcentrated agents. These data cover sixty-four PFM process areas, running from budget formulation to audit and legislative oversight.[6] Countries receive a score for these dimensions, between A and D (where A reflects compliance with good international practice and D is far from compliance). Most of the sixty-four dimensions (thirty-eight, or 60 percent) reflect reform actions that require deconcentrated agent involvement.[7] Countries struggle to get a C or higher on these dimensions without active engagement of agents like line ministries, provinces, and districts. Mozambique's average score on these dimensions was 2.15 of 4 – approximately a C. The other twenty-six dimensions (or 40 percent) relate to reform actions that can be done by concentrated groups in areas like

---

[5] Held in Maputo in December 2009.
[6] The full PEFA set has seventy-three dimensions, but nine were dropped because they relate to outcomes or to donor processes.
[7] Dimensions were coded as deconcentrated if a C could not be achieved without the involvement of a deconcentrated set of actors. Three coders identified thirty-eight such dimensions, with an intercoder reliability of 0.978 (calculated using Fleiss' kappa and Krippendorff's alpha). See Andrews 2011a.

the central Ministry of Finance budget office or Treasury. The average score on these was 2.93 – approximately a B. The difference was 0.77 – nearly a full symbol. Once again, the evidence points to reforms working when they engage narrow sets of concentrated agents. By contrast, reforms falter when they require engagement by broader groups of deconcentrated agents.

AGENCY AND INSTITUTIONAL REFORM

This finding is not exclusive to Mozambique. Reforms often progress well when under the control of champions in concentrated agencies directly involved in designing the change. Reforms falter when deconcentrated agents must implement what these agencies design. Geoff Dixon provides an example in the story of Thailand's 1990s PFM reforms.[8] These reforms were driven by donors and the powerful Bureau of the Budget (BoB). This bureau led significant changes in law and introduced new systems and procedures. Unfortunately, progress was muted in the line ministries. These entities achieved little from a reform in which they were not directly engaged and which they perceived as a vehicle the BoB was using to expand its dominance. Carlos Montes tells a similar story of civil service reforms in Bolivia in 1993 and in 1999. Both interventions had high-level political support and led to the introduction of new laws and strategies to improve the public administration. Both produced disappointing results, however, because of poor engagement with implementing agencies. Civil servants resisted reforms because they clashed with incumbent norms of patronage and entrenched political pressures. Montes notes that these pressures were not considered in reform design, and reforms were ultimately rejected by agents charged with implementation: "Project management was too centralized and as a result the participating agencies did not 'buy' into the modernization."[9]

In these and other cases, reforms faltered even though they had champions at the helm in highly effective concentrated ministries. In ensuring that a champion was present, these reforms had not disregarded the importance of leadership altogether. Having a champion was not enough, however, which raises important questions: What kind of agency engagement is needed to make institutional reforms work? Why do reformers continue to focus on champions even if they are insufficient? This section addresses both questions, in three parts. It first identifies the need for leadership by multiple parties in reform processes, rather than high-profile individual leaders. It

[8] Dixon 2005.
[9] Montes 2003, 10.

then notes that distributed agents are also required to facilitate change. Finally, it argues that pressures of doing reforms as signals often impede efforts to build broad sets of entrepreneurs and distributed agents.

Multiagent Leadership Fosters Change (Not Solitary Leaders)

New institutionalist studies do not speak of champions, heroes, or leaders when reflecting on the agents involved in making change happen. They refer instead to "institutional entrepreneurs." These are the agents "who have an interest in particular institutional arrangements and who leverage resources to create new institutions or to transform existing ones."[10] Agents qualify as institutional entrepreneurs when they break with dominant institutional logics *and* institutionalize alternative rules, practices, or logics.[11] Such entrepreneurs must have a certain detachment from the incumbent institutions. This gives them the freedom to see the need for change and to conceive alternatives to incumbents. At the same time, they must be engaged enough in the institutional context to know about field-level contradictions, alternatives, and problems that might facilitate periods of change (as discussed in Chapter 3).[12] Their engagement also needs to ensure sufficient authority, leverage, and power to turn ideas for change into reality.

The picture of a "supermuscular" entrepreneur doing all this is questionable, however. Few agents can provide both the ideas required for change and the power and resources to get these implemented. Such concern relates to what authors call the paradox of embedded agency.[13] This paradox emerges from arguments that many "preconscious" and "shared" institutional devices shape thoughts and actions before agents even begin thinking in a given situation.[14] This raises an important question about the role agents can play in effecting change: If institutionalized rules of the game have a preconscious and shared influence on agents, how can agents even imagine changing these rules and subsequently get others to adopt and implement them?

This is an important paradox to consider, because it challenges the assumption that agents can facilitate institutional change at all. At an extreme, the paradox assumes that all agents become embedded in the institutional fields they inhabit, and this constrains their ability to perceive the need for change or to appreciate opportunities for novelty.

---

[10] Maguire, Hardy, and Lawrence 2004, 657.
[11] Dacin, Goodstein, and Scott 2002.
[12] Giddens 1984; Grannovetter 1985.
[13] Seo and Creed 2002.
[14] DiMaggio 1988, 3.

Recent studies question the rigidity of such assumption, however,[15] noting that agents are not all embedded to the same degree in any given field.[16] These studies argue that agents at the periphery of social networks are less embedded than others. They are less influenced and beholden to extant rules as a result and benefit less from such. This low embeddedness makes such agents more open to criticizing incumbents and entertaining change.

This argument allows one to understand how some peripheral agents might imagine changing established rules of the game in any setting. It does, not, however, solve the paradox of embeddedness. Peripheral agents may have the incentive and cognitive capacity to imagine and advocate for change, but they lack the power to effect such. This power resides with those at the center of social networks – often called elites and "resource rich" agents.[17] They are more embedded in extant institutional systems, heavily exposed to normative processes,[18] committed to reinforcing existing mechanisms,[19] and espousing interests supported by and aligned with incumbent rules of the game.[20] As a result, they are less capable of perceiving weaknesses in these incumbents or of imagining the need for or content of alternatives.

According to theory, institutional change occurs when something creates a bridge between these highly embedded agents with power and low embedded agents with new ideas. This bridge could be direct or indirect. Greenwood and Suddaby point to the former in explaining changes that saw Canada's largest accounting firms offer management consulting services.[21] These firms were central actors in the country's narrow accounting field, where consulting was considered anathema. They adopted such services after learning that *clients* considered the accounting product less then complete without such. A direct bridge to peripherally located clients gave these centrally located entities the perspective of a low embedded agent, even though they still enjoyed the power of an elite. The authors summarize: "When low embeddedness is combined with a motivation to change, central actors become institutional entrepreneurs."[22]

---

[15] Garud and Karnøe 2003.
[16] Greenwood and Suddaby 2006.
[17] Ibid., 29.
[18] DiMaggio and Powell 1983.
[19] Tushman and Anderson 1986.
[20] Greenwood and Suddaby 2006, 29.
[21] Ibid.
[22] Ibid., 29.

Whether direct or indirect, such bridges connect different agents and their capabilities in a manner that facilitates change. These agents can be organizations or individuals whose interactions generate transitions from one rule of the game to another. Different agents have different functional roles in their networks given different social positions and capabilities. Some provide power, and others bring awareness of problems. Some supply ideas or resources, whereas others act as connectors or bridgers. Change comes out of their connections, not from these isolated capabilities. This makes it appropriate to speak of institutional entrepreneurship instead of institutional entrepreneurs. Using more common language, one might say that multiagent leadership fosters change, not solitary leaders. It is unlikely that institutional reforms will progress far where such multiagent leadership is not in place.

Multiagent Leadership in Mozambique

Champions appear at the helm of all of Mozambique's PFM reforms, typically in the guise of a minister of finance. Other agents have consistently contributed to multiagent leadership groups responsible for the progress seen to date, however. For instance, reform ideas in the 1990s often came from consultants in organizations like the World Bank and the Swedish government, who formed bridges to a larger set of global reform ideas.[23] Senior finance and planning ministry officials were responsible for authorizing interventions based on such ideas, however.[24] They did so partly because the country lacked basic systems when the civil war ended in 1992.[25] They also faced conditions linking reforms to continued external support, which the government sorely needed and individual officials relied on (to employ consultants, e.g.).[26]

These early engagements spawned new mechanisms like 1997's Budget Framework Law. Additional donors engaged in reforms after this, aligning with different units in the Ministry of Finance. The Accounting Directorate worked with the Swedes, for instance; the Budget Directorate with the British; and Treasury engaged the European Commission. Most donors established a local presence during this time, and officials in the different units combined with external consultants and donor officials to foster reforms. These interactions fed into 2002's creation of a new public finance

---

[23] de Renzio 2011.
[24] Fozzard 2002, 36.
[25] Sulemane 2006.
[26] de Renzio 2011, 33.

law and a novel entity (UTRAFE) to "ensure better coordination and integration of the various strands of budget reform."[27]

UTRAFE was formed under the leadership of a former deputy minister of finance who had been engaged in the 1990s reforms. He assembled a staff of influential ministry insiders, bright Mozambican graduates, and international consultants. UTRAFE also centralized external support by coordinating donor funding into one Common Fund. This concentrated interactions in the PFM field and helped UTRAFE lead the design and technical adoption of what Paolo de Renzio calls "the mother of all reforms," an integrated financial management information system (IFMIS) called e-SISTAFE.[28]

e-SISTAFE was a largely endogenous intervention that reflects the changing nature of institutional entrepreneurship and reform leadership in Mozambique. Many of the reform ideas now came from within UTRAFE, for instance, given that international consultants resided within the organization. These consultants facilitated visits by Mozambican decision makers to other countries as well, where these officials were able to see alternative PFM systems and institutional regimes firsthand. The ambitious reform was authorized by central players like the minister of finance, who delegated such to UTRAFE. Funding still came from donors, but it was motivated less by conditions demanding change than it had been in the 1990s. By contrast, financing was seen as support to the government's own program. More than $70 million was spent through UTRAFE between 2004 and 2008, which was about double the amount spent on all PFM reforms in the 1990s. This money allowed the concentrated but still multiagent group of reform leaders to pursue new interventions, including multiyear and program budgeting.

Deconcentrated or Distributed Agents Must Also Be Engaged

Given this discussion, Mozambique's reforms seem to have been led by groups of concentrated agents from central agencies in the Ministry of Finance and donor organizations in the capital city. Reform documents informing such discussion seldom refer to the role of more deconcentrated agents – in sector ministries, provinces, or districts – in the reform process. Such agents are not given much attention in the literature on institutional change, either. As Andrea Whittle and colleagues note, this literature

---

[27] de Renzio 2011, 14.
[28] Ibid., 26.

ascribes "agentic qualities . . . only to the 'exceptional' individuals and organizations, namely, institutional entrepreneurs, renegades and outsiders."[29]
Whittle and colleagues comment further that "this omission is problematic
because an institutional template that is not enacted by all members of an
organizational field would invariably fail to become an institution at all."[30]
Jin, Kim, and Srivastava point to a similar bias in institutional literature on
diffusion. They contrast the common focus on diffusion between organizations with the dearth of studies emphasizing intraorganizational diffusion –
where innovations are implemented *within* the targeted context.[31] Combining these perspectives, one can say that institutional theorists have not given
sufficient attention to the processes that move innovations from adoption
by a few special agents to implementation by a majority of such.[32]

Whittle and colleagues suggest that this omission can be addressed by
introducing the idea of distributed agency into mainstream institutional
research. It is a concept that widens the lens through which agency is viewed
when examining institutional change, implying "the involvement, interaction and conjoint activity of multiple actors" in change.[33] If institutional
entrepreneurship relates to the work of a few agents in facilitating institutional change, distributed agency reveals "the more mundane and less
prominent, but nevertheless essential, activities of 'others' in the institutional work associated with emergent institution-building."[34] These others
need to be considered because they are also subject to questions of institutional embeddedness. If institutionalized rules of the game have a preconscious and shared influence on these agents, why should they be expected
to change simply because some entrepreneurs say so?

Issues related to agent embeddedness often make it difficult for distributed agents to implement reforms designed by central agents. Reforms
can demand behavior that jars with political rules of the game distributed
agents face, for instance, or can require capacities that distributed agents
lack and cannot acquire. Given such issues, it is critical to engage distributed
agents early in the reform process as designers, not just as late-stage adopters.
Such engagements are the best way of ensuring these implementers accept,
understand, and use the reforms.[35]

---

[29] Whittle, Suhomlinova, and Mueller 2011, 552.
[30] Ibid., 552.
[31] Jin, Kim, and Srivastava 1998.
[32] Tolbert and Zucker 1983.
[33] Whittle, Suhomlinova, and Mueller 2011, 553.
[34] Ibid., 553.
[35] Jin, Kim, and Srivastava 1998, 231.

Greenwood, Suddaby, and Hinings' model of institutional change is help-ful in thinking about when and what this engagement should be.[36] They suggest that institutional adjustment typically emerges from a process that begins with jolts (as argued in Chapter 3) but passes through a series of stages they call deinstitutionalization, preinstitutionalization, theorization, diffusion, and reinstitutionalization:

- Deinstitutionalization involves the growing awareness of problems and consensus that change is needed. Institutional entrepreneurs facilitate the discussion, but consensus requires broader engagement with dis-tributed agents. These agents need to be convinced of the need to change.
- Preinstitutionalization refers to the stage when groups begin inno-vating, "seeking technically viable solutions to locally perceived prob-lems."[37] Again, this may be led by narrow groups of entrepreneurs. The importance of innovations being technically viable makes it vital that implementing agents be engaged in the search process, however. These agents are frequently distributed.
- Theorization is the process by which proposed new institutions are explained to the broader community. It involves specifying the fail-ure that requires change and justifying the choice of solution.[38] This requires an ongoing dialogue between entrepreneurs and distributed agents, from which emerges a compelling message about change. Greenwood and colleagues note: "Diffusion occurs only if new ideas are compellingly presented as more appropriate than existing practices."[39]
- Diffusion follows theorization and allows innovations to become "objectified." This entails a process through which increasing num-bers of distributed agents implement the new institution. The increased implementation (and positive results) fosters broad consensus about the pragmatic value of the intervention.[40]
- Reinstitutionalization occurs as the density of adoption increases. New institutions are seen as legitimate and even taken for granted across broad sets of distributed agents.

There are key roles for institutional entrepreneurs in the change process discussed, but the engagement of broader sets of distributed agents is vital.

---

[36] Greenwood, Suddaby, and Hinings 2002.
[37] Ibid., 60.
[38] Tolbert and Zucker 1996, 183.
[39] Greenwood, Suddaby, and Hinings 2002, 60.
[40] Suchman 1995.

Actually, distributed agents *dominate* the agenda beyond preinstitutional-ization. A change strategy is required to reach these agents and ensure their buy-in, fostering diffusion and reinstitutionalization. There likely will be limited buy-in and diffusion where narrow groups identify, define, and then demand institutional reform.

This point is reinforced in research showing that higher levels of decision centrality in institutional change processes yield lower rates of intraorga-nizational diffusion.[41] By contrast, higher rates of participation in change decisions often produce greater rates of diffusion. Such effect is amplified where the organization or field undergoing change is large, deconcentrated, and informal; and where distributed agents co-inhabit multiple other fields that foster heterogeneous interests and cognitions in those targeted for change. Diffusion is extremely difficult under such conditions and is fur-ther undermined by an overly centralized approach to change. One finds that many agents in the heterogeneous, deconcentrated group will not implement the adopted changes under such conditions. They cannot be forced to do so and will not do so voluntarily because they do not share the understanding that change is needed or that the prescribed solutions are appropriate.

Mozambique's Distributed Agents and Diffusion Problem

Although Mozambique's PFM reforms were effectively designed by groups of institutional entrepreneurs, the country has had a diffusion problem. Evidence already provided shows that new laws introduced by reform leaders have not been fully implemented. Evidence illustrates that implementation gets worse as one moves from central to provincial to local government. Reasons for this are varied, but one emerged from discussions on reform at a 2009 workshop.[42] Three groups of officials were asked about the quality of the laws, and gave different answers. Representatives of central agencies responsible for introducing the new laws scored such as 8.8 of 10 (on average). A group of provincial government officials rated the laws as 8.1.[43] District and sector ministry officials gave the laws an even lower rating of 7.3. When asked why they rated laws nearly two points below the ratings of their central government colleagues, the last group noted that they could not implement various new legal requirements – either because of deficient capacity or different local political and governing realities. They had not

---

[41] Jin, Kim, and Srivastava 1998.
[42] Held in Maputo in December 2009.
[43] There were eight officials from the provinces, also at the 2009 workshop.

been asked about these issues when reforms were designed and had become quite frustrated and bitter about the imposed nature of the changes.

This story is not new in Mozambique, where distributed or deconcentrated agents have not been engaged in reforms and frequently fail to implement them properly as well. For instance, Adrian Fozzard criticized a 1997 expenditure reform strategy because it had "little to say about line Ministries' budgeting processes, accounting structures or budget execution procedures."[44] A high-level official recently criticized one of the reforms emerging from this strategy, the medium-term budgeting framework (CFMP), saying that it "does not have much influence over the budget process because it is not seen as credible."[45] The credibility gap was worst with distributed agents who had contributed to an underlying planning exercise believing that their ideas would result in changes to policy and budget allocations through CFMP. Unfortunately, however, they "never saw their proposals discussed . . . [or]concretised in the annual budget."[46] In 2010, de Renzio quoted a technician as saying that distributed entities – in central, provincial, and local governments – are "not interested in the CFMP as a planning tool."[47]

The lack of effective engagement with distributed agents was also a problem with the program classification mechanisms introduced in 2008. The reform involved central agents in the Ministry of Finance attempting to link activities of governmental units and objectives in the government's centrally devised five-year plan.[48] The bulk of the work demanded complex computer programming in the budget department and UTRAFE. There was little to no engagement with implementing sectors. As a result, "many sectors saw the initiative as yet another centrally-driven reform they had to comply with without having been involved enough in its design."[49] The reform has not, to date, proved very useful.

This problem also manifested in the way e-SISTAFE emerged. Created to facilitate the computerized implementation of the SISTAFE law, it is described as the "Rolls Royce of financial management systems."[50] Its use by distributed agents is limited, however, with only 23 percent of expenditures covered by this system in 2008.[51] In reflecting on such, de Renzio comments

---

[44] Fozzard 2002, 28.
[45] de Renzio 2011, 29.
[46] Cabral and Fernandez 2003, 26.
[47] de Renzio 2011, 25.
[48] Ibid., 19.
[49] Ibid., 20.
[50] Ibid., 27.
[51] Cavanagh and Gustaffsson 2009.

that it originated in the narrow engagement between the IMF, UTRAFE, and Brazilian consultants: "Some interviewees repeatedly stated that the IMF was insisting on the Brazilian model, given that many of the key officials involved were Brazilian themselves. Once the model was adopted, further choices were made that have been questioned in terms of their adequacy."[52] Given such sentiment, agents in distributed agencies perceived that "[t]he system was designed mostly to respond to the needs of the Ministry of Finance, without adequately taking into account the needs of sector users, who are key in ensuring that the system works effectively."[53] Many distributed agents, especially in the health and education sectors, actually used other systems for most of their PFM work until recently, citing e-SISTAFE's failures to deal with problems they faced.

These anecdotes underscore the argument that PFM reforms in Mozambique have been too centralized. There has not been enough distributed engagement to facilitate the selection of feasible reforms or to theorize the reforms that have emerged or to ensure diffusion of these reforms. The limited engagement is further illustrated in data about communications in the reform process collected from officials at the 2009 workshop already mentioned.[54] These officials were asked to identify key players needed for successful reform. More than 230 organizations and individuals were identified: 17 percent were in the Ministry of Finance and UTRAFE, and 73 percent were distributed across government[55] in line ministries, provinces, and districts. Officials then gave impressions about who talked with whom about reform and who drove the discussions. They noted that 70 percent of the discussion involved the 17 percent of agents from the Ministry of Finance and UTRAFE, who were seen as initiators more than half of the time. Sectoral, provincial, and local officials initiated fewer than 17 percent of the reform engagements. The many distributed agents needed to make reform work were hardly engaged in thinking about and designing such interventions.

The Narrow Emphasis on Champions

The focus on special concentrated groups of agents and not on distributed or deconcentrated agents is obviously a problem in the context of

---

[52] de Renzio 2011, 29.
[53] Ibid.
[54] Held in Maputo in December 2009.
[55] There were forty-three in the Ministry of Finance itself, fifty-nine in other central ministries and agencies, sixty-one at the provincial level, and forty-three in district and local government.

Mozambique's PFM reforms. As noted earlier, it is also a problem that other observers have seen in other countries and reform experiences. Thailand's PFM reforms stressed the role of narrow specialists in the Bureau of the Budget, which undermined reform engagement in line ministries who ultimately balked at the reform.[56] Bolivia's civil service reforms were similarly initiated, conceptualized, and shaped by exclusive groups in concentrated units of ministries in La Paz.[57] They failed to gain traction in the ministries, cities, and districts beyond these units, however, where past practices like patronage continued.[58]

One can argue that external influence was part of the reason for narrow and exclusive engagement in these reforms. This argument emerged from Chapter 1, which noted that World Bank project documents regularly emphasize the role central players like the Ministry of Finance plays in reforms. These agents are the legal partners in projects and the political champions considered vital to ensuring project success. Project documents rarely mention distributed agents who implement such reforms, apparently assuming that they will support change simply because ministers of finance tell them to do so.

This assumption reflects a teleological theory of change, which holds that adjustments are rational, linear, and driven by high-level leaders who enjoy extreme levels of authority or charisma. Such theory pervades development because of a tendency to see governments in these contexts as hierarchical bureaucracies operating in paternalistic cultures. Those at the top of such organizations are expected to have extensive authority given both factors. Those who implement reforms are assumed to hear and follow the voices of these leaders. The approach was neatly summarized by the management scholar Henry Mintzberg after a visit to Ghana. He speaks of the belief that "[m]anagers are important people, quite apart from others who develop product and deliver services. The more higher "up" these managers go, the more important they become."[59]

Such beliefs are problematic in most contexts, however. The assumption that officials hold authority because they are higher up in an organization presumes that formal organizational structures dominate informal mechanisms, which few observers would agree is the case.[60] Even if it does hold to some degree, the expression of authority is typically messy. A finance

---

[56] Dixon 2005.
[57] Montes and Andrews 2005.
[58] World Bank 2000b.
[59] Mintzberg 2010, 3.
[60] Andrews, McConnell, and Wescott 2008; Schick 1998.

minister leading reform seldom has authority over officials in the education sector or a far-flung district government. Different authority structures, which are often informal, will hold in these different domains. Given that all individuals coexist in multiple domains (discussed in Chapter 3), one should expect that the authorizers to whom they respond are multiple as well. It is thus unlikely that an official in one part of a government system will respond clearly or directly to one official voice in any given domain. Change is rarely implemented across broad settings by a single, narrow edict in such contexts.

Beyond the problematic assumptions about authority, reformers often also exhibit unwarranted confidence in the technical content of reforms. Reform designers seem to believe that good technical content will attract support from rational, public value–oriented leaders. This presumes that such leaders are bent on producing broad-based public value, however, and that such prescriptions provide feasible avenues to do such. It also assumes these leaders understand, appreciate, and support the cognitive and normative underpinnings of proposed institutional reforms. There are problems with these assumptions as well. First, various observers argue that aid-related support piques the personal interests of those agents engaging most directly with international actors.[61] These agents could look to use the support to further their own financial, political, or administrative goals, for instance. The lure of such personal gains gives agents an incentive to masquerade as the transformational leader needed to facilitate institutional reform, even if they are not up to the task. Second, the paradox of embeddedness should engender skepticism whenever a leader claims to appreciate the importance of institutional change and have the power to enforce such by edict. Theory suggests that one should expect those in power to have a cognitive and normative limit to "seeing" the need for institutional transformation. If they do "see" such need, they may not be as powerful as one assumes.

Many external agents working on reforms in developing countries recognize these kinds of concerns. One may still expect them to engage narrowly with champions, however, given constraints on their own time and access. Most institutional reforms are supported by projects prepared over periods of six to eighteen months. Project teams are typically dominated by experts residing in Western capitals. They visit target countries periodically, on limited budgets, often only in the capital city. Government counterparts with whom they meet are often narrowly defined by the economic ministries holding legal responsibility for projects. Local agents are often, therefore,

[61] Hanlon 2004b; Kolstad, Fritz, and O'Neil 2008.

found around political champions like ministers of finance, and have Western training similar to that of external experts. How much they know about or engage with distributed agents is questionable.

External Influence and the Narrowness of Engagement in Mozambique

Whether reflecting these practical limits or assumptions about the efficacy of top-down leadership, external organizations working in Mozambique have indeed engaged narrowly in fostering the PFM reform agenda. This is apparent from evidence that emerged in the 2009 reform workshop mentioned earlier.[62] Government officials at this workshop were asked to list the donors involved in reform, and to note who in government engaged with these donors. In response to these questions, they identified twenty-five bilateral and multilateral agencies involved in reforms and noted seventy-nine instances of interaction with these external players. Of these, seventy-five were between donors and the ten representatives from central agents in the Ministry of Finance and UTRAFE. One would expect these agents to engage with donors more than others, but the extent to which they dominate the dialogue is significant. The additional twenty workshop participants from line ministries, provinces, and local governments had a cumulative four points of interaction with donors. This is 5 percent of the engagement from 76 percent of workshop attendees.

The data are obviously partial in terms of coverage of agents and of substance. Theys reflect on impressions of communication, not actual events, and it is possible that distributed agents have biased impressions about being left out. Even if one were to moderate the data in recognizing such concerns, however, it is unlikely that the communications bias would be closed. Evidence of this bias is also apparent in documentary descriptions of how reforms emerged and who has been engaged since the 1990s. Paolo de Renzio and Joseph Hanlon note that Mozambique's engagements with donors have been dominated by narrow groups in central ministries, for instance.[63] Engagements have been fragmented across government, with senior officials in different sectors monopolizing specific donor support for their own specific reform agendas. This is how PFM reform was shaped in the late 1990s, when strategies were hatched between the Washington organizations and the central planning and finance ministries.[64] Engagements were even further stovepiped than this, with different units of the Ministry

---

[62] Held in Maputo in December 2009.
[63] de Renzio and Hanlon 2009, 250.
[64] Fozzard 2002.

of Finance dominating different donors to ensure support.[65] These engagements continued even after UTRAFE was created to coordinate reforms. A
group of donors did concentrate their support through UTRAFE, however,
which became the new narrow entity tasked with interacting with donors
and managing all of government reforms.

The evidence thus suggests that external agents have worked almost
exclusively with central players when sponsoring PFM reforms. This is
surprising, given the large number of donors engaged and the fact that
many of these have enjoyed a local presence in the country for more than
a decade. A partial explanation is provided by a team Tony Killick led to
examine government-donor relations in 2005.[66] It argued that government
lacked agents with the authority or technical expertise to facilitate broader
dialogue with donors. The technical nature of donor-driven agendas and
pressure to have senior government partners who can make decisions did not
allow for broader sets of interlocutors to emerge. The message is reinforced
by Sarah Lucas from the Center for Global Development, who notes that
donors typically demand the engagement of a limited number of senior,
technically proficient officials in their projects.[67] Such demand narrows the
pool of potential interlocutors and excludes most distributed agents from
reform discussions.

Another problem relates to the motives of senior officials with whom
donors engage so narrowly. de Renzio and Hanlon suggest that these officials have an incentive to feign support for reforms and ensure they gain
external legitimacy and aid, while simultaneously satisfying local political
pressures.[68] A common view holds that these pressures center on further-
ing the "narrow 'predatory' interests" of Mozambique's leading families, its
"politic-business elite."[69] de Renzio points out that agents directly engaged
in these reform discussions have gained personally as well. They built up new
organizations (like UTRAFE) with salaries unconstrained by civil service
laws and also funneled money to senior officials in the Ministry of Finance.[70]
Although not necessarily corrupt gains, these are examples of direct interlocutors drawing personal value from donor engagements. Beyond this, top

---

[65] The Accounting Directorate worked with Sweden, Budget with the United Kingdom, and
Treasury with European Commission.
[66] Killick and Castel-Branco 2005.
[67] Lucas writes in field notes from Mozambique, as a staff member for the Center for
Global Development (CGD), http://www.cgdev.org/section/initiatives/_active/assistance/
mcamonitor/fieldreports/mozambiquefield.
[68] de Renzio and Hanlon 2009, 260.
[69] Hodges and Tibana 2004, 13.
[70] de Renzio 2011.

officials in places like the Ministry of Finance ultimately lacked the influence to push reforms onto distributed agents that donors assumed they enjoyed. Interestingly, donors have been partly responsible for undermining such authority. This is because distributed agents in sector ministries often control resources such as earmarked revenues and off-budget donor funds that are not directly under the Ministry of Finance's authority. "This not only limits the power of the finance ministry to impose reforms on sector ministries, but also means that in many cases sector ministries will have an interest in maintaining the status quo."[71]

GETTING INCLUSIVE ABOUT AGENCY

The basic message in this chapter is that institutional reform requires more than the narrow engagement of institutional entrepreneurs, no matter how impressive these may be. It also calls for the involvement of distributed agents who ultimately have to implement reforms. Unfortunately, institutional reforms are seldom this inclusive about agency. These reforms emphasize the roles of concentrated champions and heroes and ignore those who are more deconcentrated or distributed. Andrea Whittle and colleagues call this latter group the "others" responsible for "more mundane and less prominent, but nevertheless essential, activities . . . associated with emergent institution-building."[72] Their exclusion is a major reason why many externally influenced institutional reforms are poorly implemented and ultimately fail to change behavior or improve government.

A core part of the theoretical argument proposed in this chapter shows that distributed agents are required in most stages of institutional change. These stages are conceptualized in light of Greenwood, Suddaby, and Hinings' model, which posits that institutions do not change just because they are threatened by jolts or crises. Change comes only when incumbent institutional mechanisms are deinstitutionalized and agents become engaged in a process of finding, introducing, and reinstitutionalizing a new set of rules. Table 5.1 shows the stages in this process and the roles institutional entrepreneurs and distributed agents play in each stage. It is obvious that distributed agents are key players in the final stages – diffusion and reinstitutionalization – where others may prefer to use terms like implementation or roll-out. It is important to note, however, that distributed agents must be involved in earlier stages as well, or these latter stages may be compromised.

---

[71] de Renzio 2011, 35.
[72] Whittle, Suhomlinova, and Mueller 2011, 553.

Table 5.1. *How agency roles matter in the different stages of institutional reform*

Stage of institutional change	Key focal point and activities	Role for institutional entrepreneurs	Role for distributed agents
Deinstitutionalization	Growing awareness of problems, consensus that change is needed	Emerge to facilitate discussion about change	Need to be convinced of the need to change
Preinstitutionalization	Innovation to find viable solutions to local problems	Lead scanning, experimentation to find new solutions	Some agents help in scanning, experimentation to ensure solutions are viable
Theorization	Change explained, specifying failure, justifying chosen solution	Craft compelling message about change, ensure it reaches distributed agents	Some agents help craft message, others facilitate transmission
Diffusion	Change is "objectified," implemented by more distributed agents, building consensus about its value	Lend support to roll out, facilitate with storytelling about change value	Implementers of reform, sources of stories that allow objectification
Reinstitutionalization	As adoption density increases, new institutions seen as legitimate, broadly taken for granted	Consolidate stories of new institutions as taken for granted, introduce reinforcing mechanisms	Agree that new institutions are legitimate, taken for granted; fully abide by new rules, reinforcing such with new mechanisms

Source and notes: Author's summary, based on Greenwood et al.'s model of institutional change.[73]

If distributed agents responsible for implementation are not engaged in finding the solutions during preinstitutionalization, for instance, there is a risk of picking unviable solutions.

The Mozambican study shows that distributed agents are seldom involved in early stages of institutional change, however. Such agents were excluded in Mozambique on the apparent assumption that high-level champions and heroes would be able to force implementation by edict. This assumption

[73] Greenwood, Suddaby and Hinings 2002.

is often made when reforms are adopted as signals, and questions about how they actually diffuse and drive behavior are not addressed until after loans are disbursed. The assumption has been found wanting in places like Mozambique, however, and one can expect this to be the case in other cases of externally influenced reforms in development as well. Heroes often lack the influence they are assumed to have, and they often end up pursuing private gain instead of public interest. Both problems emphasize the risk external organizations take when they depend too much on champions to make reform happen. Alluding to such issues, Henry Mintzberg concludes his discussion on Ghana's leadership problems by quoting from Bertolt Brecht's play *Life in Galileo*.[74] A character in the play laments, "Unhappy is the land that has no heroes," to which another replies, "No. Unhappy is the land that need heroes."

The next chapter summarizes limits one can expect from reforms as signals. One of these relates to the idea of reduced reach in reforms. This problem results from an exclusive focus on heroes and champions. Not all externally influenced institutional reforms are so exclusive, however. Chapter 9 discusses examples of reforms where international organizations have participated in or facilitated inclusive processes of change. The engagement of multiple players in these processes has led to the shaping of endogenous solutions to contextual problems. Tying back to the book's leading metaphor, this engagement fosters group-based craftsmanship that seems vital to ensuring the fit between reform pegs and the holes these need to fill.

[74] Mintzberg 2010, 10.

SIX

Expecting Reform Limits in Development

WHAT YOU SEE IS FREQUENTLY NOT WHAT YOU GET IN REFORM

Uganda has adopted many externally supported institutional reforms since President Yoweri Museveni began engaging with the World Bank and International Monetary Fund (IMF) in 1986. The country has had visible gains from these reforms. Currently, for instance, they are credited with the best anticorruption laws in the world. The think tank Global Integrity gives these laws 99 of a possible 100 points. This legislation emerged from externally supported projects that included the formation of an Inspector General of Government (IGG), Auditor General, and Human Rights Commission.[1] Although these reforms produced impressive-looking laws and agencies, however, their impact has been limited. Corruption still festers, relegating Uganda to a lowly position of 126 in the world on the 2008 Transparency International Corruption Perceptions Index.[2] This speaks to a gap between laws and their implementation, which Global Integrity measures at 44 of 100. With this gap, Uganda has both the world's best laws and among the world's largest gaps between laws and practice. What you see from reforms, in the form of new laws and agencies, is not what you get in practice.

This book builds on the observation that many reforms look like those in Uganda. Data presented in Chapters 1 and 2 suggest that many interventions look better than they are, proving more limited than one would expect or want to admit. Essentially, every reform peg that fits a hole is matched by a number that does not – leaving a landscape of unfilled holes and random pegs that have limited use. Chapter 2 closed with a simple explanation of the many failures: countries commonly adopt reforms as signals that are

---

[1] World Bank 1998b.
[2] U4 Helpdesk, Overview of Corruption in Uganda. http://www.u4.no/helpdesk/helpdesk/query.cfm?id=191.

intended to make government look better, but not necessarily to make government function better. The last three chapters discuss implications of this, arguing that reforms as signals frequently (i) fail to factor the influence of a context into design, (ii) promote interventions that are too content specific and demanding, and (iii) enter through overly narrow sets of champions who cannot ensure implementation.

The current chapter merges these arguments into a narrative about the limits one should expect from externally influenced reform. It posits that reforms as signals will lead to change at the margins of government mechanisms in areas that are externally visible and where reform is influenced by concentrated sets of reform champions. Section 1 identifies the kind of gaps this leaves in public financial management (PFM) reforms globally, particularly in Africa. Section 2 applies institutional theory to explain this behavior, introducing the idea of decoupling to the discussion on institutional reforms in development. A third section applies ideas about decoupling to explain why gaps exist in African PFM systems after decades of reform. It shows that reforms have delivered better budgets but not better spending, improved laws but not better implementation, and stronger central bureaus but not more engaged distributed agents. In essence, what you see is not what you get.

REFORMS THAT ONLY MAKE STATES LOOK BETTER

This book argues that institutional reforms are central to development. The content of such reform is guided and evaluated using indicators like the Country Policy and Institutional Assessment (CPIA).[3] A 2008 evaluation of CPIA data and project evaluation records found that World Bank public sector reforms had a dismal record in most areas.[4] PFM reforms stood out as a positive outlier, however – projects were generally given satisfactory evaluations, and CPIAs had improved in many countries. This is seemingly good news, given that PFM often dominates the public sector reform agenda in developing countries. PFM has been a major component of 81 percent of World Bank public sector management projects, for example.

On close inspection of many countries' PFM reform records, however, one finds mixed records of improvement. This is certainly the case with reports based on the Public Expenditure and Financial Accountability (PEFA) Performance Measurement Framework. Developed by a multidonor

---

[3] PEFA 2006, 5.
[4] World Bank 2008, 28.

group, PEFA allows one to assess the degree to which PFM systems meet "existing good international practices,"[5] or what Clay Wescott calls "the immediate objectives of reform."[6] Using these data, Paolo de Renzio finds that reforms have improved the way governments budget – in what some call the upstream part of PFM – but have not improved downstream budget execution.[7]

Claims of reform success contrast with evidence of continually weak results in many countries. Take Uganda, for instance, where PFM reform in the late 1990s was regarded as a "rare success story in Africa."[8] Donors like the Global Fund endorsed the view that PFM had improved by channeling its grant funds through government systems. In 2005, however, the Global Fund suspended funding because of financial irregularities in the Ministry of Health. Internal controls and monitoring mechanisms that had appeared strong after 1990s reforms turned out to be deficient.[9] These revelations are reminiscent of a 1999 World Bank report that found that 1990s procurement reforms were less successful than most donors had thought. Government had adopted procurement reforms as slated, but on close inspection the procurement system remained one "riddled with sleaze and inefficiency."[10]

Afghanistan, Georgia, and Honduras are additional examples. All three countries have been recognized for their reform successes, given performance on indicators like PEFA. A 2008 news release from Britain's Department for International Development announced, for example, that "Afghanistan [is now] ranked higher than middle income countries."[11] A 2010 comment claimed, likewise, that "Georgia and Honduras have moved ahead of the G7"[12] in terms of the support they give to international public sector accounting standards. These sanguine perspectives contrast with other realities, however. A 2010 World Bank assessment found that Afghanistan's PFM processes do not function properly and argued that donors should still keep funds outside government systems.[13] Similarly, Georgia and Honduras produce PEFA scores like those in middle-income

---

[5] PEFA 2006, 5.
[6] Wescott 2008, 22.
[7] de Renzio 2008.
[8] Lister et al. 2006.
[9] See the news report on this issue at IRIN global, www.irinnews.org/report.aspx?reportid=58620.
[10] See IRIN news report, Uganda: Global Fund probe reveals massive graft. IRIN global, www.irinnews.org/report.aspx?reportid=58620.
[11] See http://webarchive.nationalarchives.gov.uk/+/http://www.dfid.gov.uk/news/files/afghanistan-pefa.asp.
[12] www.freebalance.com/blog/?tag=georgia.
[13] World Bank 2010a, ii.

countries for many process areas but record Cs and Ds on questions asking about the quality of budget outturns. Budget documents and processes look great in both countries, but budgets are not executed at all as they are passed.

This is also the case in Indonesia, where the IMF comments favorably on "far-reaching reforms" adopted since 2005.[14] These include a new legal framework, Treasury Single Account, government accounting system, performance budget, and medium-term expenditure framework. These reforms have earned a number of high PEFA scores. Indonesia gets A and B scores for the quality of its budget classification, comprehensiveness of budget information, adherence to a budget calendar, provision of budget circulars, and timeliness of budget approval, for instance. It gets C and D scores for budgetary outcomes, however, showing that actual spending results were significantly different from what stellar budgeting documents indicated they would be.

Against this story of mixed reform results, authors are quick to cite the need for patience and realistic, time-sensitive expectations. de Renzio comments that reforms in the weaker PFM downstream "take longer" than others.[15] This implies that, with time, developing countries will realize the expectation of achieving "good international practice" even in these downstream dimensions. Such is the apparent thinking behind de Renzio and Dorotinsky's comment that "[h]aving realistic expectations of the possible rate of PFM system improvement is critical," which leads to the recommendation that "for donors . . . longer-term, sustained commitments to PFM reform may be a critical element of success."[16] Chapter 2 indicated that reform results may not be greater over time, however, and it seems there are real questions about the validity of this expectation. A different approach would be to ask what kind of limits one should expect, even over time, from externally influenced institutional reforms in development.

WHAT REFORM LIMITS SHOULD BE EXPECTED, AND WHY?

The development community has not promoted much thinking about areas where its imposed reforms might face expectable limits. Such thought is required, however, given evidence that such limits may, in fact, be real. The IMF report on Indonesian PFM reforms suggests, for example, that Indonesia faces a common problem in translating new laws into practice.[17] Such

---

[14] Lienert 2007.
[15] de Renzio 2008, 7.
[16] Ibid., 21.
[17] Lienert 2007.

appears to be the problem with Uganda's anticorruption initiatives referenced at the start of this chapter. As already shown, Global Integrity gives
the country's laws a score of 99 of 100 but rates implementation of the laws
at only 44. Interestingly, Global Integrity shows many developing countries with legal systems rivaling the best of the developed world. Indonesia, Bangladesh, Nepal, Belarus, Colombia, the Philippines, Argentina,
Moldova, Pakistan, and Azerbaijan all have anticorruption laws that are
better than or equal to those of countries like Italy, Hungary, and even the
United States, Japan, and Canada. The difference between developed and
developing countries manifests, however, in the gap between law and practice. The gap is 9 in Italy, 12 in the United States, and 18 in Hungary. It is
28 in Indonesia, 31 in Bangladesh, 33 in Belarus, 38 in Colombia, and 51 in
Azerbaijan.[18]

This section argues that externally supported reforms should be expected
to yield such gaps and limited results. Agents and organizations are forced
to adopt parts of these reforms, given the isomorphic motivations underpinning such discussed in Chapter 4. They will commonly change only
those areas considered peripheral and visible to outsiders, however. This
ensures that they get needed legitimacy but with the lowest level of change
possible – preserving incumbent logics mentioned in Chapter 3. Where
leaders actively advocate change beyond these limits, one can expect greater
penetration of a reform agenda. This penetration is limited to the organizational areas managed by such agents, however, because they typically
do not engage with deconcentrated or distributed groups beyond such (as
discussed in Chapter 5). The following discussion presents this argument
in detail. The next section applies it to a study of PFM reforms in Africa.

Decoupling and the Limits of Isomorphic Change

Chapter 4 argued that externally influenced institutional reforms are commonly motivated by isomorphic pressures. According to such theory, externally dependent organizations and countries face pressure to adopt what
influential outsiders would call best practice reforms, through coercion,
mimicry, and normative transfer. Actors affected by such change are not
passive to such influences, however,[19] and isomorphic change is not a deter-
ministic, osmotic process through which organizations absorb environmental pressures to become that which is more appropriate and externally

---

[18] Author's calculations based on Global Integrity data.
[19] Townley 1997, 262.

legitimate. Instead, agents within these organizations manage the influence of external pressures so that change is limited to what is needed for legitimacy – but does not penetrate the organization beyond this line. Frumkin and Galaskiewicz capture this well, suggesting that isomorphic mimicry may lead to changes in outward structure, but that this "structure may be decoupled from the organizational mission."[20]

Decoupling is a critical concept new institutional theorists offer to facilitate a better understanding of change and its limits. Its central idea is that not all organizational characteristics are affected by isomorphic pressures. Some are more protected from externally influenced change than others. Theory helps to identify these areas, emphasizing the importance of visibility and core-ness in organizational attributes, and professionalism and concentration in agents.

How Visibility and Core-Ness Shape Change Possibilities

As a starting point, visibility is central to the mechanics of isomorphism. External institutional reform demands affect organizational constructs that are "comprehensible" and reflected in "appearances."[21] This is because isomorphic influence requires that external parties exerting influence, and internal parties being influenced, can describe, package, and evaluate the relevant characteristics. Imagine how hard it is to coerce someone to do something you cannot describe or evaluate. It is also difficult to identify something as best practice without visibility. External pressures are thus limited to practices outsiders can "observe . . . in other organisations."[22]

The reality is that organizations have many nonvisible processes in which isomorphic influences are limited. Aaron Wildavsky emphasized these in discussing the politics of the budgetary process. He distinguished between "formal" and "practical" budgeting, for example, saying that the latter takes place "in a twilight zone between politics and efficiency."[23] He saw the opaqueness of these processes as a limit on reform prospects: "dark" areas of an organization are simply harder to reform from outside. As a result, isomorphic influences may foster change in areas of an organization that are visible to outsiders, but these will be decoupled from more opaque dimensions where change will be limited.

Importantly, the literature suggests that organizations often keep specific processes opaque. Fogarty and Dirsmith identify processes that are "less

---

[20] Frumkin and Galaskiewicz 2004, 285.
[21] DiMaggio and Powell 1983; Wuthnow et al. 1984, 50.
[22] Frandale and Paauwe 2007, 369.
[23] Wildavsky 1992, 598.

visible to external constituents" as those that "denote an intimate relationship with the technology used by the organization to perform its tasks."[24] Kirkpatrick and Ackroyd note similarly that organizations use opaqueness to protect characteristics associated with core values.[25] This is like saying that organizations shield practices embedding "what we believe and what type of organization this is."[26]

Ashworth, Boyne, and Delbridge use the word "core" to describe processes that are likely to be opaque and protected from change.[27] In so doing, they tap into a rich vein of thought in organizational theory. Hannan and Freeman identified four "core aspects" nearly thirty years ago: the organization's de facto mission, authority structure, technology, and marketing strategy.[28] These are differentiated from more marginal structures,[29] "the detailed arrangements by which an organization makes links with its environment and tries to buffer its ... core."[30] They present these as "more plastic than the core set" of organizational characteristics: "They can be transformed because attempts at changing them involve relatively little moral and political opposition."[31] By contrast, they argue that change to the core threatens the organization, shoring up significant resistance.

Although these assertions have been tested with mixed results,[32] they provide an intuitive explanation of why isomorphic change may be limited to some organizational characteristics (at the margin) rather than others (at the core). Many organizations will limit change in its core because of the fear that "[i]f organizations attempt to integrate institutional prescriptions and their backstage processes, they may provoke conflicts both within and outside themselves and threaten their survival."[33] Organizations – and developing-country governments – thus accept changes at the visible margin, but decouple these changes from the more opaque core. This allows for the protection of incumbent institutions important to insiders while still getting legitimacy for change demanded by outsiders.

How Agency Type and Location Shape Change Possibilities

These decoupling limits can be overcome if insiders actually advocate for the externally influenced reforms and see them as more than an avenue

---

[24] Fogarty and Dirsmith 2001, 248.
[25] Kirkpatrick and Ackroyd 2003.
[26] Miles and Snow 1983.
[27] Ashworth, Boyne, and Delbridge 2007, 1870.
[28] Hannan and Freeman 1984, 156.
[29] The authors call these "peripheral."
[30] Hannan and Freeman 1984, 156.
[31] Ibid.
[32] Ashworth, Boyne, and Delbridge 2007; Barnett and Carroll 1995.
[33] Bagdadli and Paolini 2005, 2.

to gaining form-based legitimacy. These insiders may facilitate change in opaque and core areas if they see such change improving functionality. This makes it important to think about who is engaged in reform, and where they are located.

Professionalization is a staple of isomorphism literature and emerges as the basis for external normative pressure: "Much of the pressure for [normative] change stems from the increased number of professionals being employed."[34] This is because professionalized individuals bridge external communities. They thus often act as institutional entrepreneurs and transmit external ideas into organizations, holding similar ideological positions to the outsiders, viewing things through the same cognitive lens, and having similar ideas about "the most appropriate organizational design."[35] Professionalization also leads to the "filtering of personnel" whereby normative selection criteria determine entry to specific organizational positions. This ensures strong professional presence at the top of many organizations across fields, which establishes concentrations of "people with similar values and beliefs about the purpose and design" of organizations.[36]

Profession proficiency thus stimulates isomorphic change, whereas profession deficiency undermines isomorphic change by weakening normative and mimetic pressures. This is a problem for budgeting and accounting reforms, even in developed-country contexts like the United Kingdom. Mahmoud Ezzamel and colleagues found that politicians in this setting failed to embrace recent reforms because of their limited "accounting/finances background or extensive experience in the public sector."[37] The lack of professional affinity undermined change, manifesting in "a lack of interest in, or ability to comprehend" the new approaches that "may in itself [have] encourage[d] politicians to treat financial information as less relevant to their deliberations."[38] Put more plainly, because politicians did not appreciate the value of new information, they decoupled such from their decisions.

Concentration is a second, related dimension of this argument and derives from the observation that some change dimensions center more on small, concentrated cadres than others. These concentrated interventions lend themselves to stronger isomorphic influence because it is easier (i) to externally coerce smaller, more proximately located and interested groups, (ii) to facilitate access for concentrated groups to externally sourced better

---

[34] Slack and Hinings 1994, 819.
[35] Ibid., 820.
[36] DiMaggio and Powell 1983, 152.
[37] Ezzamel et al. 2007, 29–30.
[38] Ibid., 30.

practice examples, and (iii) to accommodate normative transfer within smaller groups. Where change requires engagement and cooperation of groups that are deconcentrated – professionally, geographically, and organizationally – coercive, mimetic, and normative transfer is much more complicated, and one is more likely to see variation in organizational practice and limits to externally defined change. This will be exacerbated where deconcentrated groups are not populated by professionals who appreciate the reform ideals. As discussed in Chapter 5, these distributed agents will likely yield to some aspects of change – to which they are forced through law or other authority – but will decouple the changed areas from other areas, retaining as much of their incumbent structures as possible. Drawing on Chapter 5, one would expect local budget officers in Mozambique to use new electronic systems in reporting on expenditures, but to stick with preexisting paper mechanisms for actual management and disbursement activities.

DECOUPLING AND THE LIMITS OF ISOMORPHIC CHANGE IN AFRICAN PFM

All three sets of isomorphic pressures are evident in the development community's PFM reform field. Politically vulnerable, resource-poor governments are highly dependent on donor organizations, which offer support on condition of specific types of PFM reform. The reform designs are also influenced by scripts like the PEFA mechanism, which alludes to good international practice that countries appear willing to replicate because of a dearth of local solutions to the problems they face. PFM is also an area dominated by professionals, like accountants and auditors. Many of these professionals work in donor organizations and have become central to the growing PFM field. They have contributed to the emergence of the PEFA assessment tool and standardization mechanisms like the International Public Sector Accounting Standards (IPSAS). These establish the normative legitimacy of specific practices, inferring the need for governments to adopt such.

One should expect that these reforms will be limited, however, given the underlying isomorphic motivation for change. This section proposes three potential limits to PFM reform, following the arguments about visibility, core-ness, and professional, concentrated agents: (i) Budgets will be made better than they are executed; (ii) budget laws will be better than budget practices; and (iii) central agents will accommodate more reform penetration than other agents. The section also tests these proposed limits in a study of African PFM systems.

Expecting Limits to PFM Reforms

Given the discussion, one should expect that isomorphic influence will be more limited in downstream budget execution than in upstream budget making. The idea is that upstream planning and budget preparation processes and products are more visible and marginal than downstream processes.[39] Hence the upstream processes are more susceptible to isomorphic influence. This idea has a fairly long history in institutional literature. Formal budgets and plans are often portrayed as "rituals of reason" organizations use to declare their rationality in the broader environment.[40] As a result, they produce plans and budgets because "[c]reating a myth of compliance with such rational systems can endow . . . bodies with legitimacy."[41]

The development community entrenches this mode of thought in the emphasis placed on Poverty Reduction Strategy Papers (plans) to access resources and the near-universal use of loan conditions centered on adopting more structured and rational budgets. The problem is that literature suggests potential decoupling between these more visible, ceremonial PFM dimensions and the real process of resource allocation (in the budget execution downstream). Allan Schick wrote that, in developing countries especially, "[t]he government has two budgets: the public one that is presented to the parliament and the real one that determines which bills are paid and how much is actually spent."[42] He suggests that the latter budget is revealed only in the execution process and is commonly very different from its formal partner. Pettersen tells a similar story of health budgeting in a developed country, Norway, where she finds "systematic decoupling" between budgets and actual execution – even after new budgeting and execution reforms were introduced to close such gap.[43] She discusses how the decoupling arises because of visibility and core-ness issues. On the one hand, health administrators are willing to abide by formal budget processes and even stand by formal budget products in order to gain public support. On the other hand, administrators speak of having their "real budgets" in their desks and suggest that they will not allow formal budgets to threaten their mission.

Beyond this upstream-downstream argument, it also makes sense to expect that de jure change (to laws and formal procedures) will be more susceptible to isomorphic influence than de facto change (to how systems function). This is partly because de jure devices are visible and easily used in

---

[39] This is not to say that all downstream dimensions are opaque and core.
[40] Czarniawska-Jorges and Jacobsson 1989.
[41] Ezzamel et al. 2007, 32.
[42] Schick 1998, 128.
[43] Petterson 1995.

reform as signals. Shirley alludes to the importance of short-term visibility in explaining that donors "prefer changes that can be instituted rapidly and be easily used as benchmarks."[44] She notes, "This results in a focus on de juri rather than de facto change. De facto change is often slower, and is usually only measurable after the project is ended, if at all."

Many also suggest that developing country governments may be open to adopting laws and other formal de jure changes because they perceive such as marginal and not affecting core parts of organizational life. They expect that business will continue as usual, according to the entrenched informal system they know to have de facto influence. Schick captures the issue in his description of developing country civil service systems:[45]

Many developing countries have formal management control systems that pre-scribe how government should operate. . . . On paper everything is done according to rule . . . [but] . . . Where informality flourishes . . . this is not the way many civil servants get their jobs . . . there are two coexisting civil service systems – one based on formal rules, the other on actual practices.

Supporting the argument in Chapter 3 of this book, Schick notes that these informal systems are internally appropriate, legitimate, and practically influential in many contexts, whereas formal rules and laws are seen as more ceremonial. One should expect that laws will be accommodated quite readily in such situations, where formal institutions are considered peripheral, decoupled from the informal systems actually regulating organizations. Such decoupling of law and practice is not always evident or extreme,[46] but it is commonly alluded to in developing countries. McCourt and Ramgutty-Wong reference it in the case of Mauritius, for example, where civil service hiring is formally presented as merit based and efficient, but accounts of actual bureaucratic structures suggest a different, more informal reality.[47] Marcel Fafchamps shows that practice differs from formal rules in Africa's private sector as well, with Ghanaian firms contracting through informal ties instead of legal mechanisms, even where these exist.[48]

A final expectable limit relates to problems of profession deficiency and deconcentrated agency in reform. Normative PFM models increasingly sug-gest a key role for central players in a top-down or hierarchical relational structure. The central players include budget offices, treasuries, tax agencies, and procurement and internal audit regulatory entities. These players are

[44] Shirley 2005, 17.
[45] Schick 1998, 127–128.
[46] Covaleski and Dirsmith 1988.
[47] McCourt and Ramgutty-Wong 2003.
[48] Fafchamps 1996.

often the direct counterparts in loan agreements, reform projects, and the like, small in size and populated with the most professionalized people in the system. Through their connections, these people also enjoy greater access to international best practice than others in the system. One should therefore expect more successful change when reforms are concentrated in the hands of such players. Reforms are more susceptible to coercive, mimetic, and normative isomorphic influence when these agents have influence.

Change will be more limited when deconcentrated actors are involved. Deconcentration can be geographic, professional, or organizational. The more deconcentrated a change engagement is, the greater the number of players who are not directly influenced by coercive pressures (they are not engaged in loan negotiations, e.g.), mimetic pressures (they do not get to see best practices), or normative pressures (they are not affected by the same professional influence). In a sense, then, the problem is simply one of limited isomorphic reach. This is a large PFM problem, however, as the normative model in vogue centralizes regulation but decentralizes implementation – so there is a big role for distributed line ministries, agencies, and local governments. These are the exact players one would expect isomorphic pressures not to reach.

Testing the Propositions: Is Decoupling a Part of PFM Reform Reality?

The discussion provides a simple theory about the limits one should expect with PFM reforms in development. The basic idea is that such reforms will yield lower compliance with external standards of appropriateness in downstream budget execution dimensions of the PFM system, de facto practices, and deconcentrated, profession-deficient areas of the system. Compliance will be higher where PFM system dimensions are upstream, de jure in nature, and involve concentrated professionals. These dimensions will be decoupled from the others, however. The result: what you see is not what you get from such reforms.

PEFA data have been used to test this theory. As already introduced, the PEFA framework was developed in 2003 by a group of donors prominent in the PFM field. It lists process dimensions described as "critical" to the "performance of an open and orderly PFM system" and "key . . . to achieve sound public financial management."[49] Thirty-one African countries'

---

[49] PEFA 2006, 2. Nine dimensions were dropped because they related to outcomes and donor practices. Dimensions are shown at www.pefa.org.

Table 6.1. *Average scores of different PFM dimension types*

Dimension type	Average (of 4)	Dimension type	Average (of 4)
Upstream	2.29	Downstream	1.89
de Jure	2.30	de Facto	1.97
Concentrated	2.32	Deconcentrated	1.88

Source: Derived from Andrews, 2011a.

systems had been assessed using these assessments by 2008,[50] yielding more than 1,900 measures of cross-country compliance with these critical standards.[51] Scoring an A on any measure ostensibly represents compliance with good international practice (as defined by donors). It equates with scoring 4 of 4 on a numeric measure. Scores lower than A imply decreasing degrees of compliance (with a B reflecting 3 of 4, a C being 2, and a D garnering just 1). Prior studies have already categorized PEFA dimensions as upstream (25 percent of the dimensions) or downstream (75 percent), de jure (41 percent), or de facto (59 percent), and concentrated (41 percent) or deconcentrated (59 percent).[52] Given this, the theory in question can be tested by asking simply whether upstream, de jure, and concentrated dimensions had higher scores than downstream, de facto, and deconcentrated dimensions. [53]

In showing average scores for the different PFM dimension types, Table 6.1 provides initial evidence that these differences do indeed seem apparent. Dimension types to the right are those where limits should be expected, given theory presented, and they do indeed have lower average scores. The difference is about 0.5 in all cases, suggesting that limits to reform do exist.

These differences in means do not prove that proposed isomorphic limits exist, however, especially given that means are not good measures of the average in ordinal data. One also has to wonder how other factors affect scores and if the influence of dimension type disappears when considering

---

[50] Countries included Benin, Burkina Faso, Cameroon, Central African Republic, Comoros, Congo, Cote d'Ivoire, Democratic Republic of the Congo, Ethiopia, Gabon, Ghana, Guinea, Guinea Bissau, Kenya, Lesotho, Madagascar, Malawi, Mali, Mauritania, Mauritius, Mozambique, Nigeria, Rwanda, Senegal, Sierra Leone, São Tomé, and Principe, Swaziland, Tanzania, Togo, Uganda and Zambia.

[51] There were 1,918 values. PFM Performance Reports (PFM-PRs) gave the rationale and evidence for scores. This allowed verification for the basis and quality of scores. In a verification exercise, 66 scores were recorded as legitimately missing because the PFM-PRs indicated that the dimension was not reviewed.

[52] Andrews 2011a, 2012b; see also Porter et al. 2011.

[53] The correlation is 0.33 between downstream and de facto dimensions, 0.11 between downstream and deconcentrated, and 0.48 between de facto and deconcentrated.

these other factors. Past work on the subject suggests that a variety of variables should be controlled for to account for such factors.[54] The length of reform commitment should be considered, for instance, given arguments that time facilitates reform progress. Income per capita also matters, with prior work showing that low-income countries have lower reform demand and capacity. Per capita income growth should also be included, with evidence showing that growth spawns reform. Research also suggests that a country's colonial legacy impacts reforms, with French or Belgian colonies in Africa often expected to have weaker reform results. Weaker compliance is also expected from politically fragile and resource-dependent states (especially those highly dependent on oil for revenues).

These variables were included in statistical work published in a 2011 article on PFM in Africa.[55] The method, robustness tests, and detailed statistical results of this analysis are presented in the article but deserve some brief attention here as well.[56] The score on all sixty-four PEFA dimensions across all thirty-one countries was used as the dependent variable, with downstream, de jure, and deconcentrated dimension dummies and country controls used as independent variables. These data were analyzed using a multivariate ordered logistic regression, given the ordinal nature of PEFA scores. This approach is required because PEFA scores are not continuous: an A (4) may be better than a B (3) and a B better than a C (2), but one cannot assume that there is equal distance between the symbols. One also cannot assume that explanatory variables facilitate similar moves from C to B and from B to A. Given this, regression results do not show the continuous impact of an explanatory variable like income growth on the dependent variable, PEFA scores. Instead, results show whether the explanatory variables are more likely to yield one score or symbol compared with others. They show, for instance, whether income growth is more likely to lead to lower PEFA scores or symbols (like D, or 1) compared with higher symbols (like C, B, and A, or 2, 3, and 4).

Table 6.2 simplifies these results, illustrating which of the explanatory variables impacted PEFA scores – measures of compliance with international standards – and how. All three key dimension variables have a negative impact on such compliance, as hypothesized. PEFA scores were more likely to be lower when dimensions were downstream, de facto, and deconcentrated. All three dimensions were more likely to deliver D scores than anything else. This supports the contention that reform results have been

---

[54] Including de Renzio 2008; de Renzio and Dorotinsky 2007; Wescott 2008.
[55] Andrews 2011a.
[56] Andrews 2011a.

Table 6.2. *How different factors limit progress with PFM reforms*

PEFA scores were more likely to be limited to D (instead of C, B, or A) if:	PEFA scores were more likely to be limited to D (instead of B or A) if:	PEFA scores were more likely to be limited to D, C, and B (instead of A) if:
Dimensions were: Downstream, de facto, deconcentrated	*Dimensions were:* Downstream, de facto, deconcentrated	*Dimensions were:* Downstream, deconcentrated
Countries were: Fragile, oil dependent, higher income, and low growth	*Countries were:* Fragile, oil dependent, higher income, and low growth	*Countries were:* Oil dependent and low growth

Source: Based on Andrews, 2011a.

limited in such dimension areas. The pressure to adopt reforms as signals results in decoupling and gaps between PFM form and function. Upstream budgets look good, but downstream execution is weak. De jure mechanisms are better than de facto implementation. Concentrated agents making rules perform better than deconcentrated agents that implement these rules.

One should note that these effects are evident when country factors are controlled for, suggesting that the limits hold across a varied set of circumstances, even in the presence of mitigating factors. Several mitigating factors and controls are, however, also significant. PEFA scores were typically lower in countries with low per capita economic growth, as expected. Fragile and resource-rich (oil) countries were also less likely to score higher than D, which accords with expectations as well. Interestingly, countries with a Francophone heritage and longer reform commitment did not seem to have significantly lower or higher reform results, a finding many would not have anticipated. A similar finding with respect to reform tenure was discussed in Chapter 2 of this book, however, where evidence did not suggest that time made a major difference in reform progress and system quality. Finally, many would have expected low-income countries to routinely record more D and C scores, but this was not the case. Actually, higher-income countries in the sample were more likely to produce these weak results. One should note that higher income countries in this sample are those with per capita GDPs of about $1,000 – so these are not wealthy nations. The result suggests, however, that poorer countries may be more dependent on external support than others, and thus more susceptible to isomorphic pressures that do ensure some reform gets done. One should also remember that higher scores in the lower-income countries are much more likely in upstream, de jure, and concentrated dimensions, however. These are the limited results one can expect from isomorphism, especially in capacity-deficient, low-income countries. Decoupling may be most severe in such contexts, with greater gaps between form and function given heavy pressure to do reforms as signals.

Alternative specifications of the model have been explored in various studies and do result in some changes of significance with the explanatory variables.[57] The length of reform commitment variable gains significance at low levels when the fragile measure is dropped, for example (given correlation between the two). The most important takeaway from these studies, however, is that the three key variables – representing PFM dimensions that are downstream and de facto and that involve deconcentrated agents – consistently retain their significance and signs. These results support the argument that reforms face limits in such areas, which are decoupled from other more visible, peripheral, or profession-rich areas. What you see after reform is not what you get in practice.

EXPECTING REFORMS THAT ARE ABOUT FORM, NOT FUNCTION

The central message of this chapter is that many externally influenced institutional reforms should be expected to yield limited results. This is because such reforms are commonly motivated by isomorphic pressures that are open to easy resistance. Agents can adopt such reforms in ways that garner external legitimacy – which is the goal – while still retaining much of the incumbent institutional structure ostensibly requiring change. Through this process of decoupling, organizations and governments can be made to look better after reform even if they are no better in a functional sense. What you see is not what you get.

The chapter argued that decoupling will typically result in change to visible and marginal dimensions of an organization or government given isomorphic pressure, whereas opaque and core dimensions will stay the same. This decoupling will likely be mitigated when concentrated groups of professionals work within governments. Reform concepts typically resonate with such groups, so that they advocate deeper adoption and implementation. Their reach is frequently limited, however (especially given the discussion in Chapter 5), and adoption will be shallow where they do not have direct engagement. The chapter provided evidence supporting this argument in the prominent area of African PFM reform. This evidence shows that reforms yield budgets that are made better than

[57] Andrews 2011a; de Renzio, Andrews, and Mills 2010; Porter et al. 2011.

they are executed, laws that look better than they are implemented, and strong processes involving concentrated groups of professionals that are not diffused to deconcentrated agents.

PFM is considered the better-performing of all public sector reform areas, so one will not be surprised that evidence of decoupling manifests in other domains as well. As discussed, Global Integrity data show that many developing countries are likely to have anticorruption laws that look similar to those in developed countries, for instance, but their implementation of these laws is much worse. They look better than they are, whereas wealthier countries are, invariably, almost as good as they look (even if that is not so appetizing, in the case of a country like Italy).[58] Andrews finds, similarly, that developing countries are now more likely than developed countries to boast systems that resemble international best practice.[59] These countries often have better-looking medium-term budgets, internal audit systems, fiscal rules, and even performance-based public management systems than developed countries. Although they sometimes look less impressive in terms of their management forms, however, developed countries still have much better functionality. Government services are more reliable, budgets are more meaningful, and civil servants perform at a higher level.

The gap between appearance and reality in institutional reform should be of concern to policy makers in the development community. It emerges, especially when reforms are adopted as signals, because of the problems discussed in Chapters 3 through 5. Broad and deep reform is not promoted when context is overlooked, content is overspecified as ill-fitted best practice, and narrow sets of agents are engaged in the change process. Isomorphic pressures introduced in such conditions should be expected to yield reforms with limited impact. The limits are summarized in Figure 6.1. It shows that change will be most likely in the top-right quadrant, where organizational dimensions are visible and marginal (given that these characteristics often overlap) and there are concentrated professionals engaged.

Change will be least likely in the lower-left quadrant, where dimensions are opaque and core and deconcentrated nonprofessionals are engaged. The problem is that more organizational dimensions typically fall in this "least likely change" quadrant than any other. As the figure shows, this quadrant houses 40 percent of the PEFA measures analyzed in this chapter's study. By contrast, only 11 percent of the PEFA measures are in the "most

---

[58] Italy's laws score 82 from Global Integrity, which is low for a wealthier country. Its implementation is 73; however, supporting the contention that developed nations have lower implementation gaps, not necessarily better laws.

[59] Andrews 2008.

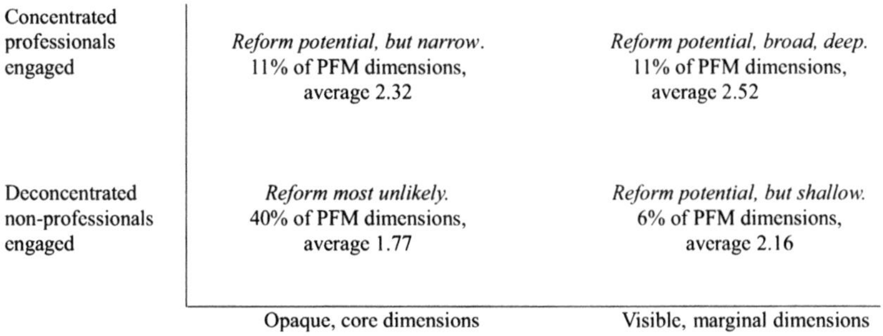

Concentrated professionals engaged	*Reform potential, but narrow.* 11% of PFM dimensions, average 2.32	*Reform potential, broad, deep.* 11% of PFM dimensions, average 2.52
Deconcentrated non-professionals engaged	*Reform most unlikely.* 40% of PFM dimensions, average 1.77	*Reform potential, but shallow.* 6% of PFM dimensions, average 2.16
	Opaque, core dimensions	Visible, marginal dimensions

Figure 6.1. The change potential of public financial management (PFM) reforms in Africa. Averages are for PEFA scores, out of 4.

likely change" quadrant. Given this summary, one should expect limits to institutional reforms in many areas, particularly where organizations or governments adopt reforms as signals.

Chapters 1 and 2 noted that there are other countries where reforms are not adopted simply as signals and are producing better results. The following three chapters discuss lessons from these examples: about ways reforms can be better structured to improve results and overcome expected limits. Chapter 7 argues that examples of more successful interventions begin with a focus on problems in the target organizations and governments. Chapter 8 discusses ways in which contextually fitted, feasible, or relevant solutions to these problems emerge through purposive muddling instead of isomorphic mimicry. Chapter 9 emphasizes the importance of engaging groups of actors, including distributed agents, in the process of identifying problems and solutions. The reforms these agents come up with may not look sophisticated or resemble international best practice, but they have the best chance of producing pegs to fit the governance holes that need filling.

SEVEN

Problem-Driven Learning Sparks Institutional Change

WHEN REFORMS SOLVE PROBLEMS...

In 2007, Norway's public financial management (PFM) system was evaluated using the multi-donor Public Expenditure and Financial Accountability (PEFA) framework discussed in Chapter 6. It is the only Organisation for Economic Co-operation and Development (OECD) country to undergo this evaluation. Scores were predictably high in most areas, supporting the view that PFM in Norway is well run. Low scores were registered in more than a fifth of the indicators, however, reflecting apparent weaknesses requiring reform. Interestingly, the Norwegian government defended practices associated with most of these low scores, arguing that they were relevant and functional given established rules of the game.[1] Weaknesses identified through the PEFA analysis were not deemed "problematic in the Norwegian context" and thus did not call for reform.[2]

The Norwegian government's response to its PEFA assessment reinforces the argument from Chapter 3 that context matters. The realities of preexisting institutions cannot be ignored in thinking about what, when, and how to do institutional change. This is a message that empowered governments like Norway can give to external parties in the international donor community. The observation suggests that institutional reform is warranted only when insiders agree that problems exist because of weaknesses in incumbent mechanisms. It is not a message the other hundred-plus developing

---

[1] These include no central collection of municipal budget information, no central regulation to publish information on resources available to local service delivery units, lack of multiyear budgeting at disaggregated level, internal audit functions being optional for agencies, and lack of a central consolidated assessment of risks in public corporations and autonomous agencies. http://blog-pfm.imf.org/pfmblog/2008/08/norways-public.html.

[2] http://blog-pfm.imf.org/pfmblog/2008/08/norways-public.html.

countries subjected to PEFA assessment can give to donors on whom they depend. It is, however, a message that donors should embrace.

Internally identified problems are regularly seen as entry points for institutional reforms in more developed countries. Observers note that Norway's modern PFM reforms were actually introduced as solutions to internally defined problems.[3] The focus on solving problems has resulted in reform designs that are "pragmatic and cooperative rather than ideological... directed more at enhancing internal productivity and increasing efficiency than at rolling back the state."[4] Other leading examples of public sector institutional reform can be similarly described. New Zealand made path-breaking changes in the late 1980s and early 1990s largely because economic and financial crises had created problems that could not be solved by preexisting institutions.[5] Sweden's far-reaching reforms over the past two decades began as a response to major economic and governance problems in the early 1990s as well.[6] Fiscal rules emerged directly because of past problems in the budgetary system, for example, and have become embedded largely because political and bureaucratic insiders recognize their importance in stemming future problems.[7]

This chapter argues that problems open doors to better understanding institutional contexts and shaping reforms that are relevant to such contexts. The first section introduces this argument using evidence from health sector reforms in South Asia and Africa. Recent evaluations note that these reforms commonly fail because they do not account for contextual complexities. The evaluations recommend more *ex ante* risk analysis as a solution. A review of forty-four projects suggests that such analysis should not be relied on as a device for better understanding context, however, or for facilitating reform designs that are better fitted to context. It shows, rather, that projects with greater results gained their fit through the combined influence of a "problem focus" and "flexibility."

A second section discusses how these two characteristics facilitate a process of problem-driven learning that ultimately stimulates contextually fitted institutional change. Such processes allow problems to become windows through which opaque contextual realities are made increasingly visible

---

[3] http://www.oecd.org/dataoecd/10/26/2731577.pdf.

[4] Christensen and Laegreid 2003, 13.

[5] G. Scott 2001.

[6] See interview with Sweden's former Prime Minister Göran Persson on the subject, http://www.mckinseyquarterly.com/Reforming_the_public_sector_in_a_crisis_An_interview_with_Swedens_former_prime_minister_2358.

[7] Andrews 2008.

and open to adjustment. Problem-driven processes facilitate questioning of preexisting institutions and the identification of alternative solutions that work, even with difficult-to-see, contextual impediments. These processes are like that one imagines a carpenter goes through in shaping a peg to fit a multifaceted hole, with lots of learning by doing and shaping to size.

A conclusion contrasts this process with the prominent isomorphic approach to institutional reform in development discussed in past chapters. It argues that externally influenced reforms adopting a problem-driven process will likely foster greater institutional change, but the results of such may only be seen over long periods – not in the lifetime of a project-based "reform." Significant change typically happens through accumulated, endogenous responses to multiple problems over long periods. External interventions can instigate and feed such responses, framing issues as problems that force governments in developing countries to look at their situations, explain their own institutional weaknesses, and change these institutions.

PROBLEMS, FLEXIBILITY, AND THE CONTEXTUAL CONSTRAINTS OF HEALTH SECTOR REFORM

Health sector reform has been a staple of development assistance since the 1980s. External support has focused on addressing specific diseases and building health systems. The former type of engagement is commonly called "vertical" (where work is in a narrow disease domain), whereas the latter is "horizontal" (across many diseases). Both embed institutional reforms that change the rules of health care policy development, service delivery, and demand. Interventions commonly change laws, for instance, that determine who can provide medical treatments or how drugs should be procured. Projects also target norms and standards, changing treatment protocols used by medical practitioners and addressing behavioral norms in the general population (affecting areas like sexual behavior and child health). Cultural-cognitive mechanisms are also common focal points, with engagements often attempting to shift the way agents think – providing educational opportunities to professionalize the sector, for instance.

Many countries pursued such reforms in the 1990s and 2000s, aided by entities like the World Bank and World Health Organization and more recently by players like the Global Fund to Fight Aids, Tuberculosis and Malaria. Unfortunately, many of these projects have underperformed. A 2009 World Bank evaluation found, for example, that a third of its health care projects had unsatisfactory ratings, and a number of satisfactory projects were anything but.[8] They delivered hospitals that were never occupied, for instance, and health laws that were not implemented. Few projects could show that institutions had improved or that the poor were benefiting from better health care after projects ended.[9]

The evaluation argues that failing projects were typically hobbled by intractable challenges that emerged in demanding contexts. It posits that these challenges, and their related risks, were "often neglected" in projects,[10] calling reforms designed in such situations "inappropriate."[11] This argument resonates with that made in Chapter 3, which suggests that context is often overlooked in institutional reforms – and that this commonly leads to muted reform results. The argument is further reinforced by recent articles on health sector reform, which use similar institutional language to that employed in this book. Sundeep Sahay and colleagues note that a new institutional logic was at the heart of information management reforms in Tajikistan's health sector. The reform was, however, overwhelmed by a "strongly historically embedded system."[12] The incumbent logic of this system was not considered in the reform or in a similar intervention in Mozambique's health sector, where "the ambitious plans of reformers are made in a formal and top-down manner, conceiving [reform] as a technical process . . . ignoring the informal constraints."[13]

These stories suggest that context is an important influence on the success of health sector reforms. Interventions routinely overlook context, however, and pay in failure. This cannot always be the case, however. Some projects must deal with contextual issues better than others. To test this idea, a sample of forty-four health sector projects was constructed, with one World Bank and one Global Fund intervention chosen in each of twenty-two different countries. The nations and projects were drawn randomly from two regions where the 2009 World Bank evaluation found reforms were most likely to fail – Africa and South Asia.[14] The project list is shown in Table 7.1. Project documents produced by the World Bank and Global Fund at the start and end of all interventions were used as the main reference material.[15]

---

[8] World Bank 2009a, xvi.
[9] Ibid., xvi.
[10] Ibid., xvii.
[11] Ibid., xvii.
[12] Sahay, Sæbø, Molla, and Asalefew 2009, 15.
[13] Piotti, Chilundo, and Sahay 2006, 104.
[14] Countries and projects were selected from full populations using random number selections.
[15] Project completion reports were used to determine the results, based on assessments by the two organizations. Appraisal and proposal documents were referenced to identify ways in which projects were designed and how they responded to contextual pressures. A full list of documents is available from the author.

Table 7.1. *The full sample of 44 World Bank (WB) and Global Fund (GF) projects*

Country	Project
Afghanistan	Health Sector Reconstruction and Development project (WB), Building Afghanistan's Capacity to Address AIDS, TB and Malaria (GF)
Angola	HIV/AIDS, Malaria and TB Control project (WB), Reducing the burden of HIV/AIDS in Angola (GF)
Bangladesh	Expanding HIV/AIDS Prevention in Bangladesh (GF), Health and Population Program Project (WB)
Benin	Population and Health Project (WB), Intensification of the fight against HIV/AIDS (GF)
Bhutan	Scaling up HIV prevention (GF), HIV/AIDS and STI Prevention and Control Project (WB)
Botswana	First Family Health project (WB), Scaling up the Botswana Multi-Sectoral Response to HIV/AIDS (GF)
Burundi	Multisectoral HIV/AIDS control and Orphans project (GF), Strengthening of the Burundian Initiative in the field of prevention and treatment of people living with HIV/AIDS (WB)
Cameroon	Scaling up Treatment and Care of People Living with HIV/AIDS (GF), Multisectoral HIV/AIDS project (WB)
Cape Verde	HIV/AIDS project (WB), Strengthening Cape Verde's response to HIV/AIDS (GF)
Comoros	Fight against malaria (GF), Population and Human Resources Project (WB)
Cote d'Ivoire	Prevention of the spread of HIV/ADS in the context of severe political and military crisis (GF); Integrated Health Services Development (WB)
Ethiopia	Multisectoral HIV project (WB), malaria and other vector borne diseases prevention and control (GF)
Gambia	HIV/AIDS (GF), HIV/AIDS rapid response project (WB)
Guinea Bisssau	Scaling up the response to the HIV/AIDS epidemic (GF), HIV/AIDS Global Mitigation project (WB)
Lesotho	Health Sector Reform (WB), Strengthening Prevention and Control of HIV/AIDS (GF)
Madagascar	Prevention of HIV/AIDS and other STI (Global Fund), Sustainable health system development project (WB)
Malawi	National Response to HIV/AIDS in Malawi (GF), Health Sector Support Project (WB)
Mali	Expansion of the Integrated Prevention and Care Networks for STI/HIV/AIDS in Bamako and the eight Regional Capitals of Mali (GF), Health Sector Development Program (WB)
Nepal	Health Sector Reform Project (WB), HIV/AIDS Prevention among Labor Migrants and Young People (GF)
Pakistan	Enhance HIV/AIDS service impact in targeted communities (GF), HIV/AIDS prevention project (WB)
Sri Lanka	Health Services Project (WB), Scaling up the National Program Activities for the Prevention, Control and Treatment of HIV/AIDS in Sri Lanka (GF)
Tanzania	Second Health Sector Development Project (WB), Scaling up effective district HIV/AIDS response (GF)

Source: Countries and Projects were selected using a random number generator.

This sample includes a number of health sector projects where contextual impediments undermined reform success in the ways described by the 2009 report. The Population and Human Resources Project in Comoros is an example. Sponsored by the World Bank, it ultimately yielded an "unsatisfactory" result, largely because of sociopolitical conflicts in the country and the lack of formal, central systems on which to build. Cote d'Ivoire's Integrated Health Services Development project is another example. Also supported by the World Bank, it intended to modernize and decentralize management mechanisms and systems in the public sector. The project foundered because of growing political strife (which led to civil war) as well as what emerged as the government's resistance to the prescribed change, given substantial prior investment in a different health care model (focused on centralized medical, not decentralized managerial, issues).

Interestingly, one can find projects in the same difficult contexts that yielded better results. An example is the Global Fund's grant for Cote d'Ivoire titled Prevention of the Spread of HIV/AIDS in the Context of Severe Political and Military Crisis.[16] Initiated in the midst of civil war, the intervention was led by an internationally affiliated nongovernmental organization (NGO) and managed to produce significant results. It ramped up condom distribution behind the lines of rebel forces through private sector entities and NGOs, introduced awareness and treatment campaigns in military camps and schools, and trained service delivery agents in community clubs and NGOs on how to use new protocols. Similarly, the Comoros received a Global Fund grant for the Fight Against Malaria that also turned out to be successful.[17] It facilitated expanded access to treatment for this disease, the number-one killer in Comoros. It also registered some important successes in facilitating institutional change: treatment protocols were introduced and reinforced as new regulative and normative mechanisms; behavioral norms needed to ensure a low-risk environment were encouraged; and problematic cultural-cognitive understandings of the disease were addressed through training and communication programs.

The Comoros and Cote d'Ivoire examples show that external interventions are not always constrained by contextual impediments. Projects in the same difficult contexts can yield vastly different results, sometimes proving quite successful and even sparking institutional adjustments. This observation holds across all forty-four interventions, which were rated differently in project completion reports (World Bank) and grant performance reports

---

[16] Global Fund 2007.
[17] Global Fund 2010a.

(Global Fund). Thirteen projects were given average scores on evaluations; considered marginally satisfactory by the World Bank and adequate by the Global Fund.[18] The two organizations rated fourteen projects below this level; as less than adequate. By contrast, seventeen projects were considered more than adequate. Interestingly thirteen countries had a project in the extreme groups; one was less than adequate and one was more than adequate. Comoros and Cote d'Ivoire fell into this set of countries.

Similar variation is evident when one looks at results of just the institutional reform content of the forty-four projects. Portions of each project were not institutional in nature – focused, for instance, on simply providing condoms or medicines. That said, all of the projects introduced or implemented a mix of reforms targeting regulative devices, normative mechanisms, or cultural-cognitive structures. This kind of institutional content can be rated separately from the overall project performance, given that World Bank and Global Fund reports assess individual components and indicators. Based on the disaggregated ratings provided in these documents, it appeared that institutional change dimensions produced adequate results (or were moderately satisfactory) in fourteen projects.[19] These dimensions were given less than adequate ratings in eighteen projects.

Performance was lowest in components that tried to change norms – of behaviors considered socially acceptable given health risks, for instance – but even here some projects saw success. The Global Fund's grant to Expand HIV/AIDS Prevention in Bangladesh is an example.[20] It produced positive results from outreach efforts to high-risk groups like drug users and sex workers. These yielded important changes in what such groups appeared to consider appropriate behavior, reflected in increased use of clean syringes and condoms. This experience contrasts with that of the World Bank's

---

[18] These ratings were considered similar. Both constitute de facto midrange ratings for the World Bank and Global Fund. The adequate B1 rating is the midrange score a grant can receive, with two higher ratings (A1 and A2) and two lower ratings (B2 and C). The World Bank's marginally satisfactory rating also has two higher ratings (satisfactory and highly satisfactory), which are used in practice. It has two lower ratings used in practice (marginally unsatisfactory and unsatisfactory), and an even worse rating (highly unsatisfactory), which is seldom used.

[19] Assessments were done by the author, assisted by two research assistants, who identified project aspects related to regulative, normative, and cultural-cognitive change and then registered their performance, as stated in the Project Completion Reports (World Bank) and Grant Performance Reports (Global Fund). Interventions targeting regulative devices (laws, procedures, protocols, and the like) were more successful than others, with seventeen projects assessed as having more than adequate performance (compared with thirteen considered less than adequate).

[20] Global Fund 2011.

Health and Population project, also in Bangladesh.[21] A "behavioral change" component targeting norms of family planning and maternal health was never implemented in a project that ultimately received an unsatisfactory rating. Contextual constraints are blamed for this failure, including weak capacity, complex bureaucratic politics, and resistance to the ideas embodied in new health and population policies.

One wonders why some projects seemed to manage contextual constraints better than others in places like Bangladesh. The 2009 World Bank evaluation suggests that pre-project analytical work makes the difference. It argues that projects stand a better chance of managing contextual risks when their designs are informed by strong studies of such context. One might point to Benin's World Bank–sponsored Population and Health Project in support of this position.[22] Rated satisfactory and with "substantial" institutional development impact, the project design referenced lessons learned from a prior project, a detailed assessment of the country's previous health strategy, draft documents informing a new strategy, a new demographic and health survey, and a risk analysis. The intervention's completion report indicates that these studies helped to guide the design in a way that facilitated success.[23] By contrast, however, one can cite Pakistan's World Bank–sponsored HIV/AIDS Prevention Project. It was prepared over a period of thirty-three months and included many analytical studies and consultations but ultimately yielded moderately unsatisfactory results. The project completion report notes that some of the *ex ante* work was incomplete or incorrect and that contextual constraints emerged that were not properly considered.[24] Preparatory studies identified strong government support as an antidote to potential political resistance, for instance, but did not count on high political and bureaucratic turnover eroding this support. The project completion report notes that the "neglect of these risks contributed to the main implementation bottlenecks" but also admits that this comment was made "with the benefit of hindsight."[25]

The problem in Pakistan was not a lack of preparatory studies, but an overreliance on studies that did not capture all they needed to. This problem often shows its face only with the benefit of hindsight, however. This means that *ex ante* analyses can underpin a false assumption that context has been effectively considered until hindsight reveals this as untrue. The assumption

[21] World Bank 2005b.
[22] World Bank 2003b.
[23] Ibid.
[24] World Bank 2010b.
[25] Ibid., 5–6.

is heroic given that most studies are typically undertaken by outsiders who cannot know the ins and outs of complex developing country contexts.[26] They bring "global, authoritative, formal knowledge" to the project, which helps it appear legitimate.[27] This knowledge does not, however, ensure that a project effectively considers context – especially given that many contextual factors are not visible to those looking at it from an external vantage point (as discussed in Chapter 3).

Given this discussion, it is interesting to note that a number of more successful projects were not informed by vast amounts of analytical work. Nine of the seventeen projects with better-than-adequate results were designed without producing new risk analyses or political economy studies, for instance. This was one of the findings of a simple assessment of the type of preparatory studies cited in project preparation documents. In this analysis, a project was given one point for each of the following criteria: 1. It built on preexisting work about the health sector; 2. It commissioned new work about the health sector; 3. It built on past work about risks and political economy constraints in the country; 4. It commissioned new work about risks and political-economy constraints in the country. When considering these criteria, the seventeen more-than-adequate projects averaged 2.22 points of 4 and the fourteen less-than-adequate projects averaged 1.93, but these differences were not statistically significant.[28] The implication is that many better-performing interventions did not rely on *ex ante* studies to deal with contextual complexities. One wonders how they did account for this.

A hint of an answer comes when one reads the project completion reports for World Bank interventions in Nepal and Afghanistan. The 2005 Nepal Health Sector Reform project was rated satisfactory, even though its completion report repeatedly notes the lack of *ex ante* political economy risk analysis.[29] The project's progress was impeded by political upheaval and regime transfer, with the country undergoing a civil war and change in government during the intervention. Different governments maintained commitment to the project, however, and its implementation stayed on track at all times. The completion report notes that this was partly because the

---

[26] Anderson and Bammer (2005) find that only 1/81 of analytical work on health comes from developing countries. It is assumed that analytical work underpinning projects in this sample is affected by a similar bias.

[27] Van Kerkhoff 2006, 6.

[28] The *t*-test generates a value of 0.17, which is not statistically significant at even the 10 percent level.

[29] World Bank 2011a.

intervention had a clear focus on solving problems about which broad groups cared deeply – providing basic health services to underserved people.[30] The problem was framed in visible data to which politicians and bureaucrats were sensitive – about outcomes (how many children were dying of measles because they had not been immunized, e.g.) and outputs (how many hospitals were functioning in rural areas, for instance). These problems and indicators were a rigid focal point, and beyond this the project was quite flexible. Its technical content, milestones, and even final goals were adjusted at various points as contextual constraints materialized and changed. This flexibility allowed for the scaling back of overly ambitious components, for instance, and facilitated active responses to emergent constraints – like weakened capacity associated with staff turnover. Dynamic adjustments helped the project stay relevant given contextual realities and ultimately become better fitted to address the problems that motivated its genesis and ensured its continued support.

Afghanistan's World Bank–sponsored Health Sector Reconstruction and Development project offers a similar story. Beginning in 2003, it had a limited lead-up period and was introduced when Afghanistan was still in a state of postwar flux. There was no repository of studies on the health sector and little evidentiary basis for any kind of engagement.[31] Formal analyses were only starting to materialize as sector strategies. This meant that project preparation had to be intertwined with nascent political and technical dialogue about the structure and role of health systems in Afghanistan. Even without the preparatory documents, however, the project addressed fundamental problems that drew broad support, including infant, child, and maternal mortality and the extreme (and visible) lack of service delivery mechanisms in provinces. As with the Nepalese example, it was also flexible in implementation. Project content was allowed to morph as lessons about the contextual constraints emerged (like data and capacity weaknesses).

The project completion report alludes to many such adaptations as crucial to the intervention's success. Built-in monitoring mechanisms indicated that key services were not being utilized in some regions, for instance, because of barriers to access that had not been identified in project design. This led to the project introducing a new category of health facility (subcenters).[32] Further, when NGOs reported low service demands from women because most health providers were men from whom women could not receive

---

[30] World Bank 2011a.
[31] World Bank 2010c.
[32] Ibid., 4–6.

treatment (given local norms), the project employed a previously unforeseen strategy of training female staff in health facilities.[33] This flexibility ensured that the project initiated significant institutional changes – challenging gender-based norms of who can deliver key public sector services, for example.

Given these observations, the problem focus and flexibility of all forty-four projects was assessed. Problem focus was measured by giving one point for positive responses to the following questions[34]: 1. Are locally defined, specific problems mentioned as a frame for the project?; 2. Are baseline indicators of these problems measured in the early stages of the project?; 3. Are activities directly determined as solutions to these problems?; 4. Is progress in solving problems routinely evaluated and considered in adjusting content?

Given these criteria, the average problem focus score for projects in the more successful group was 3.05 (on a scale of 0 to 4), compared with 1.6 for the less-successful group. More than two-thirds of the most problem-focused reforms were examples of vertical health interventions – addressing specific diseases like malaria, HIV/AIDS, and tuberculosis. Some criticize such interventions, arguing that they do not yield sustainable institutional reforms. However, all of these interventions had systemic impacts to the rules of the game that are worth noting. The Global Fund grant for tuberculosis prevention in Bangladesh impacted regulations by introducing new procedures for procuring drugs and strengthening new treatment protocols.[35] The World Bank's HIV/AIDS, Malaria and TB Control project in Angola tackled norms governing sexual relationships and cognitive perspectives on causes of HIV/AIDS.[36] This kind of institutional reform content does not guarantee wholesale institutional transformation in the short run, but it can certainly contribute to it over time. A focus on problems seems to facilitate such change, even in contexts where one might have thought institutional adjustment was highly unlikely.

[33] World Bank 2010c, 8.

[34] At least two references were required to show that criteria were met. For instance, a project received points for having a locally defined problem if there were two pieces of evidence that the project was addressing an issue raised by local players in planning documents, strategies, or political strategies. The subjective nature of the measures is unavoidable, especially given the nature of this work. This subjectivity is not considered a serious concern, however, in that the analysis is not focused on proving a hypothesis but rather frames a broader theoretical argument. The approach should be supported by more rigorous research where measures of problem focus and flexibility are developed according to stringent protocols involving multiple raters and highly specified criteria.

[35] Global Fund 2011.

[36] World Bank 2011b.

Flexibility was analyzed on a four-point scale as well, on which projects received a point for each of the following: 1. Evidence of ongoing assessment of progress and results (not just periodic accountability-based monitoring and evaluation); 2. Evidence of constant feedback on how well the project is addressing key problems, what lessons are being learned, and what issues are being encountered; 3. Evidence that opportunities were created to adjust project content, given lessons from ongoing assessments; 4. Evidence of new ideas actually emerging and being incorporated into project activities during implementation. The average flexibility score for more successful projects was 2.72, compared with 1.06 in the less successful group (again, where 0 is the lowest and 4 is the highest). This reflects the tendency of more successful projects to have ongoing internal evaluations, provide routine feedback, allow adaptation, and show evidence of strategic change in implementation.

These characteristics allowed projects to remain relevant when contextual constraints became apparent or changed. They contributed to a "spirit of 'learning by doing'" in Burundi's Multisectoral HIV/AIDS Control and Orphans project,[37] where antiretroviral treatment activities were added to the project when medicine costs decreased enough to become affordable. The characteristics are also evident in Pakistan's Global Fund grant on HIV/AIDS for targeted communities.[38] Regular progress summaries for this project noted contextual challenges as they emerged. These included early warnings that NGO contractors needed standardized reporting mechanisms to ensure smooth project implementation, and red flags about the limits of programmed activities to address the social stigma associated with HIV. The warnings fed ongoing adjustments to reporting mechanisms, choices of NGO contractors, and methods for advocacy and community mobilization. The adjustments helped ensure this grant's success. By contrast, the World Bank's similarly timed HIV/AIDS Prevention Project failed to identify and respond to such contextual complexities (especially NGO contracting challenges) and was ultimately rated as moderately unsatisfactory.[39]

The differences in average problem focus and flexibility scores for more successful and less successful projects are statistically significant.[40] This indicates that more successful interventions do have a higher problem focus and more built-in flexibility than others. The two scores were highly

---

[37] World Bank 2009b.
[38] Global Fund 2010b.
[39] World Bank 2010b.
[40] The *t*-test statistic for differences in problem orientation is 5.27. This suggests a statistically significant difference at 0.01. The *t*-test statistic for differences in flexibility is 9, which is also statistically significant at 0.01.

correlated (0.82), which suggests that both characteristics combine to facilitate a greater, dynamic responsiveness to context in externally influenced institutional reforms. One might ask, "How?" and "What does this mean for doing institutional reform better?"

HOW PROBLEM-DRIVEN LEARNING FOSTERS CONTEXTUALLY RELEVANT REFORMS

In 1986, Kim Cameron wrote an article that helps answer these questions. He posited that "[i]nstitutional change and improvement are motivated more by knowledge of problems than by knowledge of success."[41] His argument was based on a simple proposition that agents are concerned more with "overcoming obstacles to basic institutional effectiveness" than with looking for ways of improving already-effective institutions.[42] This perspective is reflected throughout the new institutional literature and is discussed via the idea of "disruptions" in Chapter 3. The chapter argued that disruptions can create change opportunities in contexts characterized by complex interactions of multiple incumbent institutional logics.

Not all disruptions or problems generate institutional change, however. This is apparent in the world of development, where corruption, fiscal distress, and even festering poverty often fail to foster adjustments in the rules of the game. "Bad" governments are often observed to fester in the midst of such disruptive conditions. Chapter 3 explained these observations by noting that the degree of institutional change depends on the severity of disruption, how much it tests the legitimacy of preexisting dominant logics, whether viable alternatives exist in the context, and whether agents are in place to struggle for and facilitate a transition. This perspective channels the ideas of authors like Christine Oliver, who suggested in 1992 that problems foster political, social, and functional pressures for institutional change. They only do so, however, where these "performance problems... raise serious questions about the appropriateness or legitimacy" of preexisting institutions and "provide the basis for internal disagreement over which organizational activities need to be abandoned or revised in order to rectify existing organizational problems."[43]

A central idea in this argument is that problems offer a potential window onto the often-opaque institutional context in which change occurs or is thwarted. Hence the idea of problem-driven learning. When problems are

[41] Cameron 1986, 67.
[42] Ibid., 69.
[43] Oliver 1992, 564.

made more apparent, this window grows, allowing a view on the context. This view is further expanded when agents dialogue about the problems and their relationship with incumbent structures. This discussion can stimulate a process of deinstitutionalization, where dominant incumbent institutions are questioned and the "legitimacy of an established or institutionalized organizational practice erodes or discontinues."[44] It can also guide what Roy Greenwood and colleagues call preinstitutionalization, where agents look for solutions within alternative logics already present in the context.[45]

Problem-Driven Learning Reveals Contextual Complexities

Chapter 3 argued that one cannot ignore contextual realities when designing institutional reforms; the potential for change is always contextually determined. It noted as well that these realities are often difficult to see, especially for outsiders but also for insiders who take the most entrenched rules of the game for granted. The question for this chapter, then, is how potential reformers – particularly those operating externally – can get a view on something that appears unviewable and ensure this view spawns thinking about change. It is an important question given that a critical awareness of context tends to preface major institutional change in most models. Roy Greenwood and his co-authors argue, for instance, that the process of nonisomorphic institutional adjustment begins only after agents recognize deficiencies of preexisting structures.[46] In essence, change that goes beyond limited versions of isomorphic mimicry discussed in Chapter 6 requires an awareness of contextual weaknesses. Seo and Creed similarly posit that institutional change demands a "reflective shift in collective consciousness" about the value of extant mechanisms.[47]

Most models of institutional change suggest that this reflection has to be provoked and usually emerges only when forced by a major disturbance to the status quo. External jolts are common examples of such disturbances, including social upheaval, technological disruptions, and economic disasters. Some authors posit that such exogenous shocks or crises are a prerequisite for significant change.[48] As discussed in Chapter 3, however, studies show that endogenous disruptions can also yield the necessary self-consciousness, especially when these manifest in "the constant

---

[44] Oliver 1992, 564.
[45] Greenwood, Suddaby, and Hinings 2002.
[46] Ibid.
[47] Seo and Creed 2002.
[48] Fligstein 1991.

experience of problematic situations."[49] One can think of these disruptions as problems that extant institutional structures cannot solve. They create windows through which agents are forced to examine their contexts, identify necessary changes, and explore alternatives.

The idea of a window is reminiscent of Kingdon's work on policy change.[50] The many applications of his "multiple streams" theory show that problems commonly bring policy and institutional issues onto the change agenda.[51] Faced with problems they cannot ignore, agents across the social and political spectrum become aware of structural weaknesses they usually do not consider. This awareness often becomes the basis for coalition building across networks, where agents at different positions are drawn together to deal with a common concern.[52] These coalitions are crucial to facilitating the reflective shift in collective consciousness of which Seo and Creed speak, given that they connect peripheral and central agents who enjoy different perspectives on incumbent structures (discussed in Chapter 5).[53] As they share their different perspectives, agents become collectively aware of the contradictions, ambiguities, and deficiencies of entrenched structures. A process of change that emphasizes problems thus facilitates learning about context.

Not all problems garner the attention required to lead such learning, however. Valéry Riddle shows, for instance, that health care reformers in Burkina Faso were quite inattentive to the problem of unequal access in the country.[54] He explains various reasons for this, including the lack of widely shared measures of access and inequality. Without such measures, "verbal gymnastics" allowed different stakeholders to hold varying views about the issue, some even believing it had been solved by past initiatives.[55] His observations support Kingdon's argument that "issues" have to be politically and socially constructed to gain attention as "problems." This involves raising the visibility of issues through spectacular "focusing events" like crises, the use of statistical indicators, or manipulation of feedback from previous experiences.

Constructing problems in this way also requires the use of tools like Ishikawa diagrams or the "five-why technique."[56] These are commonly

---

[49] Seo and Creed 2002, 233.
[50] Kingdon 1995.
[51] Barzelay and Gallego 2006; Guldbrandsson and Fossum 2009; Riddle 2009.
[52] Zakocs 2006.
[53] Seo and Creed 2002, 233.
[54] Riddle 2009.
[55] Ibid., 944.
[56] Ishikawa and Loftus 1990; Serrat 2009; Wong 2011.

used to deconstruct problems, identify root causes, and help agents reflect on contextual inadequacies. Ishikawa diagrams require agents to identify the effect of a problem (what the consequence looks like, usually described with data) and its causes (again, with data to show the extent of the cause). The five-why technique pushes agents to identify a problem and then answer "why" it is a problem five times. The rationale is that agents typically focus on issues and need to think beyond these to specify the problem that could motivate processes of reflection. A nurse might say that her problem is a lack of money, for instance, but will get more precise when asked repeatedly why this matters. Imagine the following:

- The problem is a lack of money.
- *Why does it matter?* Because we don't have enough equipment.
- *Why does it matter?* Because we cannot provide proper care.
- *Why does it matter?* Because patients are still sick after we see them.
- *Why does it matter?* Because sick patients die or cannot contribute.
- *Why does it matter?* Because the high death and disability rate is weakening our social and economic strength.

This kind of specification could lead to the use of death and disability rates and social and economic participation levels as indicators of a specified problem that many agents are likely to care about. Such specification helps frame issues as problems and draw attention to these problems as windows for learning. Many theorists argue that such specification and framing are a vital part of the process of institutional change. Snow and Benford argue, for instance, that change agents get to mobilize resources required for change "only when they are able to frame the grievances of aggrieved constituencies, diagnose causes, [and] assign blame."[57]

This discussion helps explain why health sector projects with a problem focus and flexibility tended to have better results than others, regardless of common contextual constraints. The problem focus helped turn issues into shared problems that commanded attention and provided a window onto the institutional landscape. The 2004 Global Fund grant for targeted HIV/AIDS interventions in Pakistan is a good example. It addressed regulative, normative, and cultural-cognitive issues associated with the spread and treatment of HIV/AIDS. These issues had been kept off the national agenda for a long period. Many resisted the idea that they were really problems, given perceptions of low infection rates in the population and

---

[57] Snow and Benford 1992, 150.

entrenched stigmatization of the infected.[58] This began to change in the early 2000s, when data showed that infection rates were probably higher than previously believed and that the risk for more widespread infections was significant.[59] A group of internal agents assembled to devise the Global Fund grant proposal,[60] evincing the common awareness that "it is a time for us to be really alarmed."[61] In looking at the disease, they identified a number of institutional deficiencies that warranted closer interest, using narratives and indicators to explain why these were a problem.

The proposal notes, for instance, that "societal resistance to open discussion of sexuality with young people" increased youth vulnerability to HIV/AIDS.[62] Estimates showed that fewer than 5 percent of senior students in Karachi and Peshawar private schools could correctly identify ways to prevent the transmission of HIV. This problem was linked back to various weaknesses in the institutions governing what students learned, from whom, and how. Regulations did not allow for life-skills teaching in the curriculum, and thus there had been no investment in finding or training teachers to provide it. This observation led back even further to obvious questions about why such education was missing. These questions helped reformers identify cultural norms that made it inappropriate to discuss sexual issues in schools and associated cognitive barriers (whereby people thought that such education could facilitate promiscuity, for instance).

Figure 7.1 builds on Figure 3.1 and illustrates how a problem-driven analysis opened windows on the dominant logics informing education and why teaching about life skills and sexuality was so limited. Looking at the context through a problem window allowed reformers to see "below the waterline" elements of the institutional iceberg dominating lifestyle education.

Other problems provided similar windows on the weaknesses of pre-existing institutions. For instance, new reflection followed the revelation that only 20 percent of NGO blood banks (responsible for a quarter of national supply) screened blood for HIV.[63] This led to the awareness that national laws requiring screening were having limited impact on NGOs, largely because government agencies were not monitoring these entities. In asking why, reformers started to find out about unseen institutionalized behaviors, political relationships, and the like that were undermining service delivery

---

[58] World Bank 2003.
[59] Global Fund 2002.
[60] Ibid.
[61] Qureishi 2011, 1.
[62] Global Fund 2002, 27.
[63] Global Fund 2002, 30.

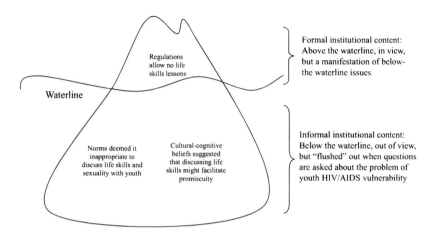

Figure 7.1. Problems allowed reformers to identify contextual challenges in Pakistan.

in the public health domain. These questions also opened up a discussion about the role of government and NGOs in the health sector, which led to a new understanding of trust issues, concerns about NGO capacities, and the like. Data, indicators, and past lessons about this are referenced in the grant proposal, structuring festering issues as problems needing attention.[64] The problem diagnosis reflects a thought process like that facilitated by an Ishikawa cause-effect analysis, as illustrated in Figure 7.2.

Problem-driven learning continued after the Pakistani grant was approved, as was common for flexible projects. Quarterly reviews noted problems in management mechanisms, for example, with NGOs contracted to supply services, and in the form of continuing stigmatization of and institutionalized impediments to serving HIV/AIDS sufferers.[65] The details of these contextual constraints emerged in response to indicators that showed that problems were not being solved or that grant implementation was slowed. These details revealed difficult-to-see norms and ways of thinking that had not been considered in design. The intervention was flexible enough to adjust to emerging lessons about this kind of contextual impediment, reflected in design changes even three years into the four-year engagement. The grant did not achieve all its goals and was ultimately rated only adequate by the Global Fund. This was, however, significantly more successful than the World Bank's similarly timed HIV/AIDS Prevention Project.

The World Bank project's completion report cites as reasons for failure many of the contextual constraints referenced in the Global Fund proposal

[64] Global Fund 2002.
[65] This discussion is based on Global Fund (2010b).

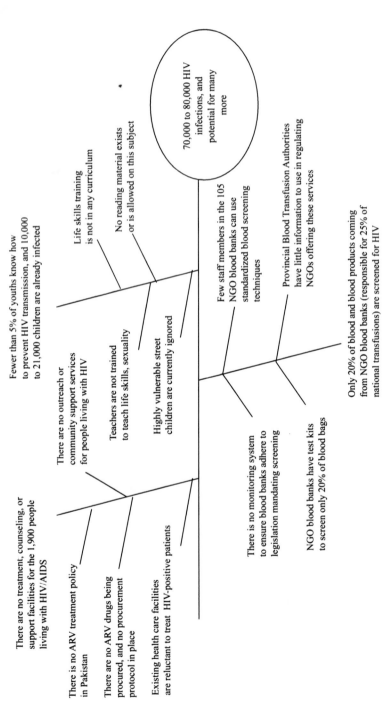

Figure 7.2. How the Pakistani proposal diagnoses its focal problem. *Notes:* Author's representation of textual descriptions in government's proposal to the Global Fund, using the Ishikawa cause-effect diagram for illustrative purposes.[66]

[66] Ishikawa and Loftus 1990; Wong 2011.

and emergent during its implementation.[67] It appears that these issues were not addressed in the project, partly because the project was never constructed to address key problems. The project adopted indicators that were described as controversial and ultimately inaccurate, for example, which is a sure sign that issues were not yet considered shared problems. Furthermore, project preparation documents note that various components were placed on the agenda by external World Bank experts even though government resisted. These World Bank experts believed that "political dynamics" would not have led to their inclusion, which should have been an indicator of a contextual constraint but was rather overlooked.[68] Furthermore, the project lacked the flexibility required to adjust to emerging challenges. The completion report notes that project designers "missed the opportunity to adjust the result framework with the ground realities"[69] that became apparent through implementation, for instance. In acknowledging these realities, the final report provided a rearview mirror onto context. Unfortunately, however, the project did not have an active window facilitating change while it was being implemented.

Problem-Driven Learning Motivates Deinstitutionalization

As noted, the completion report of this World Bank project shows that lessons were ultimately learned about contextual constraints. These were reflected only at the end of the project, however, and did not facilitate responses to the context in the project itself.[70] The lessons in such interventions are thus always about how context thwarts change and reform instead of how reform designs might have led to a change in context itself. An example in the literature relates to a 2005 Asian Development Bank–supported reform of Tajikistan's Health Management Information System (HMIS).[71] Reform designers proposed a modern system that offered decentralized users access to strategic information. This was rejected by bureaucrats attached to a seventy-five-year-old system that external reform designers

---

[67] This discussion is based on World Bank (2010b).
[68] World Bank 2003c, 22.
[69] World Bank 2010b, 19.
[70] The author is not aware of studies on how new projects build on lessons from past projects. In the example of this World Bank project in Pakistan, for instance, the Project Appraisal Document actually notes lessons about governmental opposition to certain components, low trust between government and NGO organizations, and the like. Although cited in the document, they are not appropriately addressed and become the lessons of this project as well.
[71] Sahay et al. 2009.

criticized as inefficient. In retrospect, these designers note that the old system was difficult to challenge because it fostered vastly different logics about how information should be collected and used. These incumbent logics emphasized embedded preferences for paper-based reporting and the use of information for central planning and control. The reform designers argue that their greatest contribution at the project's end was starting a conversation about these incumbent logics, which is a key step in deinstitutionalizing such mechanisms.

Externally influenced institutional reforms with a problem focus and flexibility arguably facilitate these conversations during the reform *and* accommodate action based on them. The Global Fund intervention in Pakistan is an example. Contextual impediments were identified and addressed through the project, given its construction of problems. Provoked by these problems, agents in Pakistan looked critically at their institutional context and ultimately began a process of abandoning or revising faulty incumbents – the basic steps involved in deinstitutionalization.[72] Norms driving stigmatization were not just identified, for instance. They were also tackled through carefully targeted interventions. Similarly, institutionalized trust and access issues between government and NGO entities were not only identified as contextual factors that undermined the impact of blood-screening regulations. The project also allowed for dynamic responses to such impediments, revising the rules that were not working.[73]

The basic idea here is that a problem-driven learning approach brings context into focus as a target of change – not just as a constraint to change. Extant mechanisms are not only identified through a new window onto this context but also challenged through actions that then facilitate more learning, opening space for new institutions. Such deinstitutionalization is like erasing images on an already-full slate before trying to draw something new. It is a vital stage in prominent models of institutional adjustment posited by people like Greenwood and colleagues and Seo and Creed.[74] Solution-driven reforms seldom tackle this stage of institutional change, however. As discussed in Chapters 3 and 4, these reforms seem to assume that preexisting structures will fade away when new and "better" institutions are introduced. When preexisting structures prove obstinate – and dominant – they are commonly blamed for failure of such reforms.

---

[72] Oliver 1992.
[73] Global Fund 2010.
[74] Greenwood, Suddaby, and Hinings 2002; Seo and Creed 2002.

The Afghan Health Reform Project may well have proved an example of this failure. A set of activities aimed to expand service delivery by providing new facilities – including hospitals and clinics. Many of these were not being used by the people most needing services, however, as social norms meant that women could not accept services from the predominantly male medical practitioners. This context-specific constraint was picked up early on through indicators measuring health access for women and children, however, given that deficiencies in such access were major problems the project addressed (and assessed continually to facilitate learning).[75] The project was flexible enough to allow for the addition of new activities aimed at training female practitioners. This was a direct affront to entrenched norms and practices contributing to the prevailing health problems – a key step in deinstitutionalizing dominant but troublesome incumbents. If the reform had simply ignored these incumbents, the problems would not have been solved.

A contrasting example comes from Cote d'Ivoire, where the Integrated Health Services Development project tried, inter alia, to decentralize the health sector and introduce a more managerial approach into it. Unfortunately, new laws and structures introduced through the intervention were abandoned thereafter. The project completion report notes that reforms were "pertinent" but not "achievable" given preexisting cultures in the Ministry of Health, civil service rules, and political structures that supported other approaches to providing health (described as centralized and medicalized).[76] There were no efforts to deinstitutionalize these incumbent institutional mechanisms and no problem focus to motivate deinstitutionalization by internal agents. "Most cadres of the MOH [Ministry of Health] did not share the changes implied . . . and felt rather comfortable with the traditional system of providing health services."[77] The new structures thus had no space in which to fit.

This experience can again be contrasted with a later Global Fund project in the same country titled simply "Prevention of the spread of the HIV/AIDS epidemic in the context of severe political and military crisis." As its name reflects, this intervention had a strong problem focus and ultimately provided the decentralized health care that the prior project had failed to implement. Most of the project's content was aimed at deinstitutionalizing extant normative and cognitive mechanisms that increased vulnerability to HIV/AIDS. It also included work with NGOs focused on creating an

[75] World Bank 2010a.
[76] World Bank 2005c, 7.
[77] Ibid., 24.

appreciation for managerial mechanisms like monitoring systems.[78] Gains in these and other areas were built on in a follow-up grant led by the Ministry of Health, which had gradually accepted the need to deinstitutionalize entrenched mechanisms.[79]

The problem-driven learning approach in this and other examples fosters such deinstitutionalization by establishing a new awareness of deficiencies in extant structures and a sense that these must necessarily and urgently be abandoned or revised. These steps are vital in any institutional change process, providing space for the introduction of new mechanisms – or preinstitutionalization.

Problem-Driven Learning Yields New Solutions

Problems motivate change most effectively when they point to undesirable aspects of the status quo and lend guidance to "feasible remedial action [that] can be meaningfully pursued" to address them.[80] In this respect, "useful" problems unlock what Greenwood and colleagues call deinstitutionalization and preinstitutionalization. Preinstitutionalization was introduced in Chapter 5 as the stage of institutional change where groups begin innovating, "seeking technically viable solutions to locally perceived problems."[81] Two points are important to emphasize here: institutional change solutions must be identified in response to locally perceived problems, and solutions must be viable, given the context.

The idea of solutions emerging through responses to locally perceived problems sounds basic. It is, however, potentially revolutionary for designers of externally influenced institutional reform. Chapters 3 and 4 argued that these reforms are often solution driven (where best practices define what is appropriate). Earlier chapters also posit that these kinds of solutions are often limited, however. Chapter 6 showed, for example, that they are frequently adopted in form without function. One reason is that these kinds of solutions do not provide the motivation internal agents need to absorb political and transitional costs associated with finding and implementing new institutional structures.

The motivation to look for and implement new institutional alternatives is more apparent when agents find solutions through discourse about shared problems. In this light, Guldbrandsson and Fossum's recent study

---

[78] Global Fund 2007.
[79] Ibid.
[80] Chan 2010, 3.
[81] Greenwood, Suddaby, and Hinings 2002, 60.

finds that problems triggered health reform in eight of the nine Swedish municipalities they examined.[82] Tiffany Galvin argues similarly that the rise of market-based logics in the U.S. health care system emerged from the public exploration of "problems of access, efficiency, and costs."[83] New social and political groups emerged around these problems to counter established interests and generate a coordinated process of "finding" new alternative institutions in the sector.

Galvin's study also helps underscore the importance of solutions being viable, given the context. Reflecting on the way problems facilitate deinstitutionalization, she notes that the discourse around health costs and inefficiency challenged the notion of "the doctor knows best."[84] Over time, discussion around such problems also spawned "emerging and alternative logics in the field"[85] that ultimately became the basis for new laws, relational paradigms, and norms. Her commentary resonates with Marc Scheinberg's argument that solutions to U.S. economic problems generally emerge over time from within change contexts and are not dramatic path adjustments, as some would argue. He suggests that elements of alternative institutional orders or logics are ever present, no matter how dominant one logic may be, and "represent resources for endogenous institutional change."[86] This perspective reflects the discussion in Chapter 3 of multiple logics always being present in any setting and emphasizes the importance of building change off these alternatives. Extant alternatives already enjoy a degree of contextual legitimacy and supporting capacity, and so could be politically and technically viable options to at least begin the search for a solution.[87]

Studies find that endogenous institutional change typically builds off elements of such alternatives. Meyer and Hammerschmid find, for instance, that Austrian bureaucrats have begun adopting a managerial logic that has been emerging progressively as an alternative to the established administrative logic.[88] As such, managing for results and other innovations are not novel external transplants; they have become part of the language and practice of government as a legitimate alternative to incumbent logics. Scott and colleagues show, similarly, that San Franciscans pursued preexisting

---

[82] Guldbrandsson and Fossum 2009.
[83] Galvin 2002, 681.
[84] Ibid., 681.
[85] Ibid., 681.
[86] Schneiberg 2007, 50.
[87] Misangyi, Weaver, and Elms 2008.
[88] Meyer and Hammerschmid 2006.

alternative logics when faced with problems of excessive health costs.[89] Logics of the state, corporation, and market offered alternatives to the dominant logic of "doctor knows best" and allowed patients to choose service delivery mechanisms (like health maintenance organizations) that differed from doctor-driven services but already were politically legitimate and technically functional. These established structures gave consumers an exit option to the problems of dominant structures.

Similar findings in areas as different as accounting and higher education publishing show that institutional change often involves the strengthening of an already-apparent alternative logic, which gains prominence because of problems with extant institutions. The already-present alternative is more viable than a completely new set of elements that need to be legitimated and capacitated from scratch. These alternatives are built up over long periods in many cases, however, as Galvin found in looking at institutional change in the U.S. health sector.[90] Change began when problems raised questions about incumbent institutions in the 1960s. Answers to these questions fostered the gradual emergence of new logics over following decades. Rules of the game have changed in this period, typically building off these emerging alternatives.

Experience across the forty-four health projects shows that problems do indeed motivate a search for viable solutions. There is also evidence that problem-driven solutions build off extant alternatives that provide relevant starting points for institutional change. By contrast, many reforms that are not founded on problems propose largely new, externally sourced logics as solutions that often prove unviable. Cote d'Ivoire's two projects showcase these differences. The Integrated Health Services Development project aimed to introduce a public sector logic of decentralized health service provision in accordance with better practice ideals of what a good health system should look like.[91] It failed, however, because the new logics were not supported politically and there was no capacity to operate such a system given prior investments in a more centralized model. By contrast, the grant focused on solving problems of deficient HIV/AIDS services in rebel territories embraced a more successful multisector logic of decentralized health service provision. It was spearheaded by international and local NGOs that had established legitimacy and capacity providing services in these areas. The regulative, normative, and cognitive mechanisms these entities employed in delivering services provided an important foundation

---

[89]   Scott et al. 2000.
[90]   Galvin 2002.
[91]   This discussion is based on the description in World Bank (2005c).

for expanding services.[92] These mechanisms have also been used in follow-up projects that are institutionalizing rules of multisector delivery mechanisms in other disease areas as well.

Benin's World Bank–sponsored Population and Health project is another example of an intervention that found extant alternatives to be more useful starting points for change. The country's high fertility rate was identified as a core problem to be addressed by this initiative. Modern contraceptive methods were proposed as a solution, but regular progress assessments showed that this was not being embraced as needed. Ultimately, established religious and cultural norms undermined this solution in select areas, and modern contraceptive use increased by less than half of the initial goal.[93] Reform designers balanced this "new external" solution with a more established local solution, however, in the form of traditional contraception methods (like birth spacing). These traditional methods were used as points of intervention, especially in areas where resistance to modern approaches was strongest. Elements of these alternative solutions were already in place in Benin and offered viable starting points for a broader discussion about the norms, practices, and cognitive awareness necessary for controlling population growth. Although not international best practice and potentially not as effective, these locally legitimate methods constituted short-term solutions to the problem.[94]

Burundi's Multisectoral HIV/AIDS Control and Orphans project provides a similar example. The project had a strong problem focus and was also very flexible. Designers had assumed that government would lead project implementation. This proved difficult, however, as the public sector lacked many institutional elements required for this role.[95] It was not set up to reach those needing services and lacked basic capacities to do so. By contrast, civil society had already been empowered by law to do this job, was accepted as the appropriate service provider by beneficiaries, and had the necessary capacities. The project gained momentum once reform designers adjusted its implementation modalities, doubling the role of civil society activities to address the problems identified. Using the language of institutionalism, one could say that the logic of civil society service delivery proved an established and viable alternative to the status quo (of no service delivery), whereas a logic of public sector delivery was too new and demanding to be viable.

---

[92] This discussion is based on the description in Global Fund (2007).
[93] This use increased from 3.4 to 7 percent, with the initial target at 11 percent.
[94] This discussion is based on the description in World Bank (2003b).
[95] This discussion is based on the description in World Bank (2009a).

INSTITUTIONAL REFORMS CAN BE IMPROVED THROUGH PROBLEM-DRIVEN LEARNING

These examples contribute to this chapter's basic argument: externally influenced institutional reforms are more successful when they foster problem-driven learning. This happens when interventions exhibit a problem focus and flexibility in design and implementation. A problem focus provokes reflection on contextual constraints that is necessary to instigate change. Flexible mechanisms facilitate dynamic reform responses to the challenges emerging in difficult contexts. A problem focus also points to the weaknesses of preexisting institutions, guiding reformers in how and when to deinstitutionalize them. Flexibility ensures that this guidance is incorporated in reform design and implementation. A problem focus further motivates a search, within the context, for viable alternatives to replace faulty or ineffective institutions. Flexible design and implementation processes allow these emerging alternatives to influence reform content, leading to solutions that fit contextual realities.

Readers may question this argument, positing that institutional change is also facilitated by positive opportunities; when reform provides an innovative way of doing better. Roy Greenwood and colleagues examined a change process that began with this motivation in Canada's accounting profession.[96] They found that the failure to articulate reform in the language of problems fostered indifference to change. When change was articulated in response to a generalized threat faced by the accounting profession, however, it became more accepted and even urgently demanded. These findings echo various examples in the sample of forty-four health projects analyzed in this chapter. Many "better" institutions – laws, procedures, standards of care, and ways of thinking – were met with indifference. They offered opportunities for improvement, but would have been better framed as ways of overcoming problems and failure. A problem focus provides this frame.

Employing a problem focus in reforms is like ensuring that a carpenter keeps his eye on the hole he is trying to fill, noting both opportunities and constraints it poses for peg design as well as the importance of filling the hole as a final objective. It is not good enough to create a poorly fitted peg that does not solve the problem. Project flexibility allows the same carpenter to learn progressively about what sized peg to create and how to fit it, ensuring effective functionality regardless of form. When combined in a reform setting, the two characteristics can accommodate significant institutional

---

[96] Greenwood, Suddaby, and Hinings 2002, 72.

Table 7.2. *How problem-driven learning helps reformers consider and address contextual factors*

Reform approach	Solution-driven isomorphic coercion, mimicry	Problem-driven learning reforms
Change conditions	*Small-hole conditions, conducive to low degree of change*	*Large-hole conditions, conducive to high degree of change*
Severity of disruption	Disruptions moderated by external support (finance and other), decreasing severity and length, undermining the need for reflection	Disruptions constructed as problems (using data, stories, focusing events) provoke reflection on context and need for change
Strength of dominant logic	Incumbent structures not questioned, not made open to deinstitutionalization	Awareness of problems leads to questioning of incumbent structures, opening them to deinstitutionalization (revision or abandonment)
Evidence of alternative logics	No motivation to look for, invest in local alternatives emerging as potential solutions to problems	Problems motivate search for, investment in, local alternatives already emerging as viable solutions to problems
Activity of change agents	Agents at organization's boundary buffer external demands, agree to change as signals; reforms adopted in form but decoupled to minimize influence	Agents are broadly engaged, drawn together by shared problems, looking for local solutions; reforms adopted to effect change, improve functionality

change. Table 7.2 contrasts this approach with the more common solution-driven isomorphism discussed in Chapters 4 and 6.

Reading from top to bottom in Table 7.2, the right-hand column shows basic ways in which problem-driven learning can draw attention to disruption, contribute to the weakening of entrenched institutions, and motivate the search for alternatives. Combined with the way problems draw groups of agents together, these effects all foster what Chapter 3 called large-hole conditions conducive to a high degree of institutional change. Isomorphic approaches, by contrast, foster small-hole conditions. They emphasize solution mimicry instead of problem solving, provide little impetus for reflection on incumbents, and demotivate the search for in-context alternatives. As argued in Chapters 5 and 6, agents engaged in such change are often located in narrow cohorts at the organization's boundary, allowing just enough external influence to ensure the organization looks legitimate without really having to change (as per strategic decoupling). As a result, change is limited to the visible dimensions, and reforms are limited to making organizations look better than they are.

This discussion informs various recommendations on ways to improve institutional reforms in development, particularly related to the way context is considered in the design and implementation of these interventions.

- *Focus reforms on problems, not solutions.* External organizations typically focus reforms on solutions. Reforms should focus rather on solving problems and being flexible about solutions. There are practical implications of this approach. Projects, as the major vehicle for externally influenced reform, should describe the problems being addressed in detail and focus on metrics reflecting a solved problem. Projects should not detail the solutions to these problems or insist on the adoption of visible elements of best practice solutions as measurable objectives.

- *Facilitate the construction of problems from issues.* The difference between an issue and a problem is important. Issues are like problems that society marginalizes because their importance is unclear. Many externally influenced reforms lack traction because they focus on such issues. External agents can increase the influence of the interventions they support by helping to construct problems from these issues. This could involve the use of data and other evidence to show the extent of a problem, constructing a narrative that cannot be ignored. Externally supported interventions should emerge from processes that construct problems in this way, and project documents should routinely tell the story about how severe the problem is, why it matters, and who cares.

- *Facilitate the deconstruction of problems for deep reflection.* Problems are often difficult to specify, having many facets and causes. This detail tends to be ignored by agents trying to fast track the search for solutions. Many external reform projects make this error, forcing project designers to specify solutions in constrained periods before projects even begin. Deconstructing problems is vital, however, because the process of identifying causes and effects facilitates reflection, provokes questions about extant structures, and guides reformers toward appropriate entry points for change. This process takes time and often requires active intervention (which flushes out contextual weaknesses that are not obvious *ex ante*).

- *Provide opportunities for local agents to reflect on problems.* Agents commonly have different views on what is and is not a problem warranting institutional change. One should not assume that agents needed to contribute to reform agree on the problems they face. Rather, external agents should provide opportunities to convene constituencies of potential reformers and discuss problems. The opportunity to reflect on problems in groups of agents who do not regularly engage is crucial to constructing and deconstructing problems and provoking change.

- *Pay attention to deinstitutionalization requirements.* Contextual weaknesses are seldom directly addressed by institutional reforms, even when identified as threats. Projects might note that incumbent political or government structures create political or capacity constraints to doing effective reform, for instance, but rarely facilitate the deinstitutionalization of such structures. These structures frequently get in the way of introducing new mechanisms, however, and need to be addressed as part of reform.

- *Establish flexible pathways to exploring problems and finding solutions.* Externally influenced institutional reforms frequently impose linear change processes on reform contexts. Specific solutions are identified before project activities even begin. This locks reformers into a change path. Flexibility is needed, however, to accommodate the exploration of problems and solutions in complex contexts. This flexibility requires active evaluation of the context, gathering of lessons about constraints and opportunities, and acceptance of dynamic and strategic changes to project design and implementation modalities. This requires decreasing the current *ex ante* specification of projects and moving away from the current approach of having one or two big ex post evaluations designed to report on compliance issues.

This chapter used examples from health sector projects to illustrate the idea that externally influenced reforms can incorporate these kinds of recommendations and foster problem-driven learning about contextual constraints and opportunities. The relative success of projects pursued using this approach speaks to its value. One should note, however, that many of the cases cited as successful here may not have led to significant institutional changes in the project period. Getting 7 percent of Burundi's sexually active population to use condoms may not constitute a deep change for many readers. Such examples are evidence of a growing awareness that change is needed, however, and reflect challenges to incumbent structures and attempts to bolster alternative structures. These are the early steps in institutional change. Realistically, these steps may be the most one should expect to achieve from external reforms working through three-, four-, or

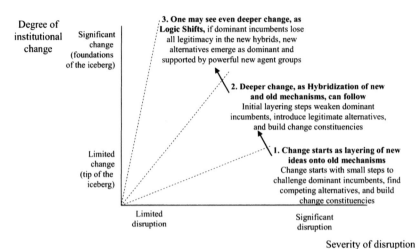

Figure 7.3. How problem-driven learning can foster deep change over time.

five-year projects – especially in difficult contexts that often prove unready for more expansive change.

The hope of many externally influenced reforms is surely that additional steps will build on these kinds of gains, endogenously or with further outside support, and lead over time to expanded possibilities for change. This is like facilitating change in small steps as repeated acts of layered adjustment[97] (shown as step 1 in Figure 7.2, a revised version of Figure 3.2 discussed in Chapter 3). These steps are the feasible starting points in contexts where incumbent institutional mechanisms dominate, alternatives have yet to be identified and capacitated, and there are only narrow groups of agents engaged in change. If these steps are built on, they may lead to greater change opportunities in the form of new hybrids and maybe even complete shifts in logics. These steps are shown as 2 and 3 in the figure.

Figure 7.3 is intended to show that change is iterative and involves creating more contextual opportunity over time – and then acting on such opportunity. This is much like a carpenter working to make a hole larger so that it can fit a larger peg. It is important to note that problem-driven learning is central to this prolonged change process and not just the early steps. As an example, Tulia Faletti's study of health sector reform in Brazil indicates that an accumulation of responses to problems yielded significant change over decades.[98] Reforms transpired and deepened over this time

---

[97] The idea of layering draws from Thelen (2003).
[98] Faletti 2010.

as agents drew attention to emerging problems associated with the weak national health system. These problems were dynamic, changing shape and severity as the country decentralized and service demands grew. The overall reform has involved decades of responses to these disruptions, leading ultimately to far-reaching change in the size, shape, and orientation of Brazil's health sector.

This process typifies endogenous institutional change in many contexts. It is implied in the introductory discussion of Norwegian and Swedish public financial management reforms. A similar process of iterative problem solving characterizes the history of change in the U.S. civil service system, which has involved many incremental interventions provoked by problems.[99] Patronage was considered an important aspect of this system until the problems of low-merit bureaucrats and the assassination of President James A. Garfield led to change in 1882. The assassination was a "focusing act" that drew attention to patronage as a problem, not just an issue. Nearly sixty years later, concerns about the political activity of civil servants also flared into a problem that facilitated the Hatch Act.[100] Perceived problems with civil service activities again emerged in the 1970s, leading to far-reaching reforms at the end of that decade as well.

These examples are intended to provide a contrast with the experience in many developing countries. Governments in these contexts commonly face pressures to introduce a range of externally defined best practice reforms in short periods across health sectors, public financial management domains, civil service regimes, and beyond. Bolivia stands out as an example, where externally influenced reforms decentralized the government, professionalized the civil service, and introduced performance management in the period between 1988 and 2002.[101] The country had been a centralized military dictatorship before this, with entrenched patronage. These systems ultimately proved resistant to much of the proposed reform, and Bolivia was criticized for failing in its commitment to reform.[102] In retrospect, it seems that a better explanation was that many Bolivians did not see their incumbent systems as problems and hence did not choose to support new systems.[103] Repeated efforts to introduce these deep and extensive reforms

---

[99] Andrews 2010.
[100] Public disclosures that Works Progress Administration officials used positions to win votes for Democratic politicians helped Senator Carl Hatch to force through regulations limiting political activities by civil servants.
[101] Montes and Andrews 2005.
[102] Montes and Andrews 2005.
[103] World Bank 2000b.

routinely fail, and they also fail to build on opportunities for change that do in fact exist.

The example is meant to show that externally influenced institutional reforms often assume that change can happen in deep ways, across multiple domains, and over short periods of time on the strength of interventions that introduce externally identified best practices. This assumption does not reflect typical patterns of institutional change, however, or the way in which contextual realities create opportunities for adjustment. Opportunities arise as issues turn into problems in many episodes that often accumulate over long periods, provoking reflection on deficiencies in incumbent structures, deinstitutionalization of these, and a search for new alternatives. This process takes time, is typically incremental, and cannot be downplayed. It is naive to think that reforms demanded and designed from the outside can short-circuit this process and force reforms across governments in short periods.

Externally influenced reforms can, however, play a role in facilitating genuine change processes or contributing at important points when such processes are already under way through interventions with a problem focus and flexibility. Such interventions should be underpinned by patience and humble expectations, however, and a commitment to empower endogenous institutional change mechanisms as the ultimate goal. In a sense, success is about creating adaptive governments that can modernize and improve by identifying and working through problems.

EIGHT

Finding and Fitting Solutions That Work

REFORMS CAN BE RELEVANT

In many respects, China has been *the* development story of the past thirty years. Institutional change has been a key part of this story. Government officials have collaborated with external agents in engagements focused on making institutions work better, not just on producing reforms as signals. In the area of interest rate liberalization, for instance, China's leaders realized the need to liberalize in the 1980s, given financial constraints on business development.[1] It worked with organizations like the International Monetary Fund (IMF) and World Trade Organization on this issue. Instead of liberalizing interest rates over two or three years (like many other countries), however, Chinese officials are still busy with the reforms today. They have used the time to learn about common mistakes, experiment with different options, and fit new solutions into the particular context.[2] The result is a hybrid system that is still in process of development. It is questioned by some but credited by others as a reason why China's financial sector weathered the 2008 financial crisis so well.

The Chinese experience shows that externally influenced institutional reforms can fit the needs and capabilities of a particular country context. This is so even when the contextual realities are complex and make reform difficult, which was certainly the case with financial liberalization in China in the 1980s: the country lacked much of the content it needed to facilitate liberalization (including a market-based banking sector). Content like this is often missing in developing countries, as discussed in Chapter 4. Change from one rule to another demands new regulative, normative, and cultural

[1] Feyzioğlu, Porter, and Takáts 2009.
[2] Andrews 2012a.

cognitive content that is commonly absent in resource-deficient developing countries.[3] The Chinese example shows, however, that it is possible to craft reform pegs that fit holes in such situations using the limited resources at hand and to expand these incrementally over time. Put differently, not all interventions are like those discussed in Chapter 4 – blunted, poorly shaped best-practice implants with overly demanding content that reforms simultaneously fail to provide. This raises a vital question, however: how are relevant solutions found and fitted?

The current chapter addresses this question. It starts by discussing two cases: Rwanda's decentralization reforms after 1994 and the creation of Indonesia's post-2003 Corruption Eradication Commission. Historical narratives of these experiences provide insight into ways developing countries can find and fit institutional reforms that facilitate new functionality and contribute to problem solving. This insight is fleshed out in the second section, which emphasizes that finding and fitting relevant reforms require a process of "purposive muddling" that (i) takes time and is incremental, (ii) requires a localized focus on problems and contextual realities, and (iii) involves broad scanning – externally and internally – and the formation, through bricolage, of hybrids. A conclusion translates these observations into recommendations for improving institutional reforms in development.

REFORMS CAN BE FOUND AND FITTED TO CONTEXT

The first two chapters of this book argue that many institutional reforms do not lead to better governments. Chapters 3 to 6 deconstruct reasons for these results. Chapter 4 posits, for instance, that many reforms fail because they impose specific best-practice solutions into developing country contexts but then do not provide the unseen content required to make such solutions work. Using language employed earlier in this book, these reforms introduce new logics but fail to build normative and cultural-cognitive elements that give them life. As an example, Chapter 4 showed that many reforms introduce laws that require African firms to use international accounting standards, but these reforms do not build local business support around the idea of expanded disclosure. As a result, businesses ignore the new laws, leaving failed reforms and countries with less than effective accounting institutions.

There are other experiences, however, where institutional reforms have had a positive influence on the structure, operation, and impact of governments and markets. This section chronicles two of these: Rwanda's

---

[3] Mair and Marti 2009.

post-1994 decentralization initiatives and Indonesia's efforts to build an anticorruption commission in the period after 2003. Brief narratives are constructed to tell the story in both cases using established approaches that construct historical trajectories from primary and secondary accounts.[4] The narratives build on evidence from documents produced by the governments in question and the development partners that helped facilitate reform, written at various points during these reforms and in end-of-period retrospectives (produced between 2010 and 2011).[5]

Rwanda's Decentralization Reforms

Officials in Rwanda hold that overly centralized government structures were a primary cause of the 1994 genocide. They argue that tight hierarchies allowed for the rapid passage of hate messages from society's top to its bottom and that centralized structures led to weak service delivery and social unrest.[6] Given this, post-1994 efforts to decentralize state structures are justified by the claim that "[l]ocalised democratic institutions and [an] active citizenry ... would have prevented the genocide from happening."[7]

Decentralization is a common reform type. It is often less than successful, however, partly because of its far-reaching political, financial, and administrative requirements. Such requirements had been found wanting in Rwanda prior to 1994, as evidenced by failed attempts to support decentralized activities. These attempts are shown toward the left in Figure 8.1, which provides a time line of decentralization reform in the country.[8] Built on the basis of government and donor accounts, the time line identifies a selection of the most important events and products contributing to this reform. Government initiatives are shown above the line and World Bank activities are below the line (simplifying donor engagements).

What the time line does not show is the success of this reform, which is best described in reflecting about what elected local representatives faced on the ground. In 1999, many representatives had no way of providing

---

[4] Büthe 2002; Faletti and Lynch 2009; Nasra and Dacin 2009.
[5] Source documents are cited in the text; a full listing is available from the author. Documents were first analyzed to identify key events. At least two records were used to corroborate evidence.
[6] The World Bank (1998c, 3) notes that "centralized authority essentially impeded the effective fight against poverty at the community level and led to dramatic socio-political consequences."
[7] Government of Rwanda 2005, 3.
[8] The time line reflects an approach taken in Nasra and Dacin 2009, 595.

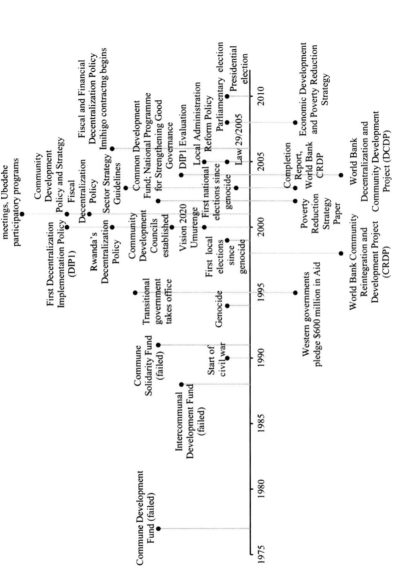

Figure 8.1. A time line of Rwanda's decentralization reforms. *Notes:* This time line illustrates the narrative of Rwanda's reform. Based on sources cited in endnotes.

services to citizens,[9] for instance, but by 2010 they had administrative mechanisms complete with plans, performance contracts, and monitoring mechanisms.[10] Hundreds of community projects had been facilitated through a new matching grant system by this time; more than 80 percent met output and outcome goals, and regular surveys showed that more than 50 percent of citizens actively participated in local government activities.[11] One wonders how solutions were found and fitted to produce these positive results in such a difficult context and (relatively) short period.

An attempt to answer this question must go back to the 1970s, when Rwanda's government failed in an early attempt to craft a development fund that could finance local activity. Two similar initiatives also foundered before the genocide in 1994.[12] Following this tragedy, the transitional government committed to decentralize once again, seeking support from international agencies like the United Nations Development Programme (UNDP), Swedish International Development Cooperation Agency (Sida), USAID, and World Bank. As shown in the time line, the latter initiated a Community Reintegration and Development Project (CRDP) in 1998.[13] This project experimented with block grant funding to twelve communes over three years in support of local activity. To facilitate decision making and implementation processes, the project helped foster the creation of Community Development Councils (CDCs) at local levels, bringing together political and administrative agents in government, nongovernmental organizations (NGOs), and other citizens.[14] It also introduced community development planning, participatory rural appraisal methods, and organizational and financial management mechanisms in these governments. A last component helped national policy makers learn about other decentralization experiences.

The government held its first local elections at the start of this project period (in 1999) and followed with a flurry of initiatives in 2000. These included Rwanda's Decentralization Policy and an associated fifteen-year implementation strategy. This was broken down into three periods, during which activities would be driven by Decentralization Implementation Policies. The first, called DIP 1, ran for three years from 2000 to 2003 and emphasized local-level service delivery initiatives and learning from

---

[9] World Bank 1998c; Government of Rwanda 2000.
[10] Scher 2010; World Bank 2011c.
[11] World Bank 2011c.
[12] World Bank 1998c.
[13] Ibid.
[14] World Bank 1998c; 2003d.

them.[15] The Ministry of Local Administration, Information and Social Affairs (MINALOC) began using a manual developed to implement the World Bank's CRDP during this time, and the CDC concept – introduced to facilitate CRDP activities in the twelve pilot districts – was approved for national rollout by presidential decree.[16] Participatory projects running through CDCs were an integral part of the 2000 Vision 2020 Umurenge, which was a precursor to the 2001 Poverty Reduction Strategy Paper.

Government's decentralization reforms were at the heart of these national strategies. The reforms supported what the United Nations' John-Mary Kazuya calls "decentralizing within the logic of a unitary state."[17] As such, national policies in 2001 and 2002 on fiscal decentralization, community development, and good governance shaped local-level interventions. Building on past experience – including the CRDP's block grant pilot experiments – these policies paved the way for a model whereby subnational government projects would be financed through central grants. Subnational governments would have to prove their capacity to plan and implement, however, and to provide some kind of local, matching contribution to each project.

Old Rwandan traditions were revived to provide avenues through which these contributions could be made, including Umuganda (the tradition of voluntary work in the common interest), Ubudehe (the custom of collective action for community development), and Unusanzu (in which norms stressed supporting the needy).[18] At the same time, government issued guidelines clarifying the modern planning and project management mechanisms required for sectors and localities to access resources.[19] The Community Development Fund was established to service district and Kigali City projects, with 10 percent of national revenues set aside for such activities.

The guidelines that were being developed in 2003 drew from lessons learned in the World Bank's CRDP (based on the project completion report in 2003) and early initiatives by other donors (including the Netherlands and UNDP). Also reflecting these lessons, donors like the European Union and World Bank started new projects. The European Union supported Ubudehe initiatives at the local level, and the World Bank initiated the

---

[15] Government of Rwanda 2000.
[16] World Bank 2003d.
[17] Kazuya, undated, esango.un.org/event/ . . . /Second%20Committee%20Panel-Kauzya.ppt.
[18] Government of Rwanda 2007a.
[19] Ibid.

Decentralization and Community Development Project (DCDP) in 2004.[20] The latter project's explicit focus was on implementing the new planning, implementation, and monitoring mechanisms government had identified as necessary to make decentralization work – especially in districts. It also included mechanisms to educate people about the decentralization reforms that were now taking shape across the country. The importance of such education was obvious in the years between 2005 and 2007, when government introduced a raft of measures to further implement and formalize its reforms. These included a law on the administrative entities of the country, a new Fiscal and Financial Decentralization Policy, and the Rwandan Decentralization Strategic Framework – all drawing on lessons emerging from the 2004 evaluation of the first Decentralization Implementation Programme.

Government now began bolstering its reforms and started engaging more aggressively than before through the Community Development Fund. Districts were required to be a part of the initiative and were supported through external vehicles like the World Bank's DCDP. President Kagame engaged personally with district mayors and, in March 2006, challenged them to adopt the precolonial tradition of Imihigo – whereby leaders would publicly vow to accomplish certain deeds.[21] On Kagame's request, MINALOC assembled a small team to integrate the practice of Imihigo into a comprehensive performance strategy for all mayors. The 2007 Economic Development and Poverty Reduction Strategy (EDPRS) identified Imihigo contracts as the way in which national priorities would be driven through local governments, with all levels of government held accountable to citizens.[22]

Reflecting this vision, Imihigo mechanisms had covered all districts by 2010, combining a "performance-management system, planning tool, multi-layered oversight mechanism, and way of using social and traditional pressure to push mayors to greater levels of achievement."[23] A majority of these districts were implementing their Imihigos through annual action plans when assessed by the World Bank in 2011, and hundreds of projects had been satisfactorily completed through the Imihigo contracts.[24] Even more impressive was the fact that infrastructure projects had maintenance plans in place, financed by the local governments (where maintenance is usually the forgotten part of infrastructure building). Furthermore, every district had executed budgets satisfactorily, and few had qualified 2010

[20] World Bank 2004.
[21] Scher 2010.
[22] Government of Rwanda 2007b.
[23] Scher 2010, 2.
[24] World Bank 2011c.

audit reports. Drawing on such evidence, government officials noted in 2011 that reforms were creating the kind of governance structures so unfortunately absent prior to 1994.[25] They point to surveys by civil society in 2011 as further proof of this. These show that a healthy percentage of citizens are actively involved in their local governments and link decentralization reforms to improved service delivery. More importantly, perhaps, is the fact that citizens and civil society groups are engaged in discussions on how to make things even better in the future. This is evidence that norms and cultural-cognitive mechanisms are supporting the emerging regulative instruments and facilitating a logic of decentralization within the unitary state.

Indonesia's Corruption Eradication Commission

Like Rwanda, Indonesia could reference a myriad of governance problems in the late 1990s. The country was particularly infamous for its high levels of corruption. It was ranked forty-six of fifty-two countries in Transparency International's 1997 Corruption Perceptions Index, scoring 2.72 of 10.[26] It also had a history of failed attempts to deal with this issue, dating back to 1957 operations targeting corruption in the military.[27] This is the first event shown in Figure 8.2, which provides a simplified time line of anticorruption activities.

The time line becomes congested after 2003, when the Corruption Eradication Commission (KPK) was created to investigate and prosecute corruption and monitor state governance. Most commentators did not expect the KPK to be effective, given a legacy of failed reforms in this area and the fact that many anticorruption commissions have not enjoyed success (as argued in the discussion of Malawi in Chapter 3). Skepticism is evident in comments made in 2004 from the Washington-based organization Global Integrity: "The new Anti-Corruption Commission has been installed and sworn in. It is expected to commence work soon, although expectations about its success prospects are low."[28] Global Integrity's 2004 indicators gave Indonesia a perfect 100 for the quality of laws creating the KPK, but

---

[25] This comment reflects press releases about the success of decentralization, as evidenced in recent surveys. See Rwanda: Imihigo On Track-MINALOC, allafrica.com/stories 201110311124.html.

[26] See www.transparency.org.

[27] Jasin 2010; Sunaryadi 2005.

[28] Global Integrity, Indonesia Integrity Indicators 2004, http://back.globalintegrity.org/reports/2004/docs/2004Indonesia.pdf.

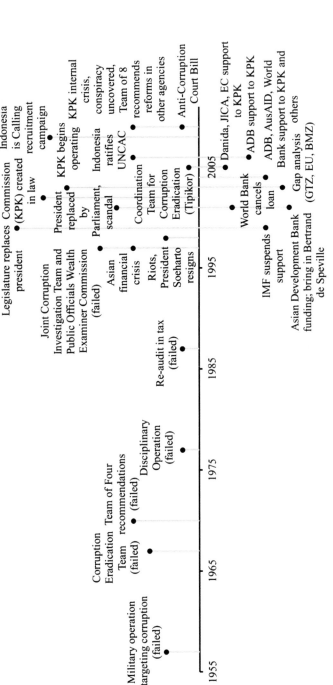

Figure 8.2. A time line of Indonesia's Corruption Eradication Commission reform. *Notes:* This time line illustrates the historical narrative of the KPK reform. Based on various sources.[29]

[29] This historical narrative aims to tell a systematic story of how the KPK emerged. To do this, a selection of publicly available documents on Indonesia's anticorruption struggle was selected. These provide reflections at different points in time between the late 1990s and 2011 and retrospective analyses of reforms from as far back as the late 1950s. They are written by agents internal to this process (KPK commissioners) and external agents in donor organizations and academia. The historical narrative was built on the basis of triangulation of different sources and the creation of linkages between written accounts at different points in time. The sources include Bolongaita (2010), Buehler (2009), Fane (2000), Hamilton-Hart (2001), Indonesian Corruption Eradication Commission (2006), Jasin (2010), Lindsey (1998), McLeod(2000), Sunaryadi (2005, 2007), UNODC (2011), and World Bank(2003e).

only 72 and 25 when reflecting on the agency's effectiveness and accessibility by citizens. The KPK has survived since that time with an impressive record of investigating, prosecuting, and convicting officials. Given such, Global Integrity rated KPK effectiveness at 94 of 100 in 2008 and its accessibility to citizens at 75 of 100 in 2009.[30] As with Rwanda, this experience begs the question: how was this obviously effective reform found and fitted?

The year 2003 is a useful point of reference for answering this question. KPK was created by law in this year after Indonesia survived a difficult period of economic and political turmoil. The 1997/1998 Asian financial crisis revealed many weaknesses in the country and drew attention to its corruption. Domestic riots led to the resignation of longtime president Soeharto shortly after this, and the next five years saw presidents come and go amid a growing number of serious corruption-related scandals.[31] Government took various steps to try and address this, acting under pressure from external agents like the IMF and World Bank.[32] They created the Joint Corruption Investigation Team and Public Officials Wealth Examiner Commission, for instance, but these entities proved incapable of mounting serious investigations and had no authority to prosecute cases.[33] The police and other law enforcement bureaus enjoyed this mandate but were considered ineffective and corrupt themselves.

Key decision makers in government and civil society started thinking about more aggressive strategies as crises deepened and the corruption problem became more apparent – with contaminated presidents replaced by parliament and both the IMF and World Bank halting operations.[34] At this time, the Asian Development Bank (ADB) funded technical assistance for these officials to learn about how other countries had addressed the problem.[35] This generated interest in the example of Hong Kong's Independent Commission Against Corruption (ICAC). The ICAC experience was considered attractive because it was more aggressive than many other anticorruption commissions, enjoyed a comprehensive scope and power, and showed that results could be quickly achieved (in the form of high-level prosecutions). Given this interest, and using ADB resources, the government employed consulting services of Bertrand de Speville, the founding ICAC

---

[30] Global Integrity, Indonesia Integrity Indicators Scorecard 2008, http://report.globalintegrity.org/Indonesia/2008/scorecard; Global Integrity, Indonesia Integrity Indicators Scorecard 2009, http://report.globalintegrity.org/Indonesia/2009/scorecard.
[31] Bolongaita 2010; Fane 2000; Hamilton-Hart 2001.
[32] Buehler 2009; Lindsey 1998; McLeod 2000; World Bank 2003e.
[33] Jasin 2010.
[34] Bolongaita 2010; Sunaryadi 2005.
[35] Bolongaita 2010.

commissioner. Drawing on lessons from their own history of toothless anti-corruption agencies, ICAC's experience, and the input from de Speville, the Indonesian reformers designed a new agency – the KPK – with more power than any that had previously existed.[36] They stipulated that the KPK would only have an impact on corruption if given legal authority to investigate and prosecute cases and kept independent from the executive.[37]

This strong agency was created by law in 2003. It passed through a legislature stunned by the gravity of prolonged crisis and facing another turnover in government – from the Megawati administration to that of incoming President Susilo Bambang Yudhoyono. The latter picked up on the political importance of the anticorruption struggle and offered public support to the KPK. This manifested particularly in 2005, when he created the Coordination Team for Corruption Eradication (Tipikor), where cases could be prosecuted. Support was also forthcoming from external partners, with agents supporting a variety of initiatives that were mostly focused on building the KPK's capacity to function as a legitimate and results-oriented anticorruption agency. Following on this support, the KPK proved instrumental in facilitating Indonesia's 2006 ratification of the United Nations Convention Against Corruption (UNCAC). Its own performance was also noteworthy, with 135 preliminary investigations and 78 full investigations completed by the end of 2007.[38] These had led to fifty-three prosecutions and forty sentences in this period. The agency investigated fifty-three cases in 2008, with forty-three prosecutions and thirty-six sentences achieved in that year alone. Its convictions included members of parliament, senior officials from powerful agencies, governors and mayors, officials from the national police, and prominent businesspeople.

These achievements are best appreciated when contrasted with the limited activities of other anticorruption commissions. Chapter 3 noted that Malawi's commission initiated thousands of investigations but got very few cases to court, for instance, which Emil Bolongaita shows is also the case with the Philippines' Ombudsman.[39] Bolongaita ascribes the KPK's success to a number of factors, including the way it drew on lessons from Hong Kong. He also notes that the agency adopted a number of novel strategies relevant to the Indonesian situation and necessary to make the KPK function as desired. For instance, the KPK has a unique and rigorous hiring and personnel management system designed to ensure its staff can carry

---

[36] Indonesian Corruption Eradication Commission 2006; Jasin 2010.
[37] Jasin 2010, 18.
[38] Data come from Bolongaita (2010) and are supported by Jasin (2010).
[39] Bolongaita 2010.

out the investigations and prosecution mandate. In order to quickly get the most skilled people, the KPK chose to attract staff from the Indonesian National Police and attorney general's office and other executive agencies. Many anticorruption experts advised against this, given fears that these officials were embedded in corrupt systems themselves. The KPK mitigates this risk by outsourcing the hiring process and having potential recruits undergo a battery of tests and background checks. All KPK employees are hired according to performance contracts as well and have to complete daily Balanced Scorecards to show their activities and results.

Other novel ideas have made the KPK an attractive place to work and an effective messenger about anticorruption. In 2008, its "Indonesia is Calling" campaign yielded thousands of applicants to work in the field, and recent initiatives to educate government employees and businesspeople on the problems of corruption have proven successful. The KPK's public support was most visible in 2009, when an internal scandal erupted. High-level employees were charged with corruption themselves, and one was even implicated in a murder. Although some of these charges have led to the individuals facing charges, the scandals also uncovered a conspiracy against the KPK within the government. A presidential commission ultimately found that agencies like the National Police were targeting the KPK and called for reforms in such entities.[40] These calls echoed with similar demands from civil society, which was overwhelmingly supportive of the KPK's role – endorsing its past work and advocating for even more aggressive anticorruption initiatives in the future. The KPK not only continues to build on the past but also faces new challenges in a constantly changing context. A 2009 law has decentralized authority over some kinds of corruption investigations and prosecutions, for instance, which will require the KPK to adjust its structures in order to remain relevant.[41]

HOW REFORMS ARE FOUND AND FITTED THROUGH PURPOSIVE MUDDLING

Although neither the Rwandan nor Indonesian reform is complete, both cases show that externally influenced institutional reforms can be relevant and can achieve anticipated goals, even in short periods and in complex environments where collaboration is needed. The examples are intended to guide an answer to the important question about how reformers in such

---

[40] Bolongaita 2010.
[41] Jasin 2010.

situations choose the content of their interventions. Seo and Creed asked this question in 2002: "How do institutional change agents . . . develop and deploy alternative logics and frames in a way that they can overcome the limits of the present institutional arrangements and effectively mobilize the commitment and resources of other participants for reconstruction?"[42]

This question is moot when countries adopt reforms as signals. As discussed in Chapter 2, reform designers responsible for such interventions simply need to identify the best practice mechanisms that they believe will most strongly signal the intent to change. As Chapters 3 through 6 noted, however, these kinds of reforms frequently do not overcome the constraints of context, deficiencies of local institutional content, or resistance of embedded agents. These reforms are seldom successful in achieving results that the Rwandan and Indonesian examples show can be achieved. With reference to these more successful examples, the current section makes observations about how content is chosen when reforms are not adopted as signals. These emphasize that finding and fitting relevant reforms require purposive muddling, which (i) takes time and is incremental, (ii) requires a localized focus on problems and contextual realities, and (iii) involves broad scanning – externally and internally – and the formation of hybrids through bricolage and experimentation.

Finding and Fitting Takes Time and Is Incremental

Chapter 7 argued that institutional change commonly emerges in response to problems. This was undoubtedly the case in Rwanda and Indonesia. It is interesting to note, however, that both countries took a number of years to "find" reform solutions after problems initially became apparent. Rwanda's problems centered on conflicts that led to the genocide in 1994 – a focal event that made local-level tensions and service delivery problems impossible to ignore. The country's first post-1994 attempt at crafting a formal Decentralization Policy emerged only in 2000, however. Similarly, Indonesia created the KPK in law in 2003 and put it into practice in 2004, which was a number of years after the 1997 Asian financial crisis began revealing the extent of its corruption problems.

Reforms continued to take shape after the initial designs were set in place in both countries as well. Although Rwanda formalized some aspects of its design in 2000, for instance, it left a lot of detail open to further adjustment and introduced a process that would allow the content to emerge. The

---

[42] Seo and Creed 2002, 236.

2000 first-period Implementation Strategy for Decentralization (DIP-1) was adopted in tandem with the Decentralization Policy, for instance, and set in motion a three-stage course of action to define, adopt, and implement its reforms.[43] This process purposefully included many reflection points, including the 2004 DIP-1 evaluation, which were meant to feed into incremental design decisions. Lessons learned from this and other initial steps (including the 1998 World Bank project, completed in 2003) informed reform design choices in 2005 (including a new law and Local Administration Reform Policy). These choices built on prior design decisions and were followed by even more stepwise adjustments that continue today.

One gets the impression of a gradually emerging reform solution in Rwanda. The situation is similar in Indonesia. The 2003 law that created the KPK was not the first iteration of Indonesia's post-1997 attempt to build an anticorruption commission. The Joint Corruption Investigation Team and Public Officials Wealth Examiner Commission were created immediately after the crisis and provided the initial experience on which future reforms could be built. Mochammad Jasin, a KPK Commissioner in 2010, noted that the KPK's post-2003 success "owes much to its comprehensive contemplation" of these early interventions, which helped inform the design of the 2003 law.[44] The full KPK reform continued to emerge beyond the law as well. The agency only developed initial strategies for employing investigators and prosecutors in the window between 2003 and 2004, for instance, and adopted important policies for motivating and overseeing staff activity after this point. Further changes were made in 2008, when the KPK decided to introduce a broad-based Indonesia is Calling employment campaign. Policies guiding engagement with civil society and business have been crafted and adopted at different points in time after this starting date as well, often in response to demands that were not foreseen in 2003.

The Rwandan and Indonesian experiences remind one of theoretical arguments about how policy and institutional solutions often emerge: as a puzzle, over time, given the accumulation of many individual pieces. Modern versions of this perspective are commonly called incrementalism or gradualism, and attributed primarily to Charles Lindblom.[45] In what is also termed "muddling through," the approach holds that groups typically "find" institutional solutions through a series of small, incremental steps. These steps commonly foster positive deviations from extant realities and generate lessons about how these deviations are achieved – what one might

---

[43] Government of Rwanda 2000.
[44] Jasin 2010, 19.
[45] Lindblom 1959; 1979.

call purposive muddling. An example comes from Rwanda, where positive results from selected community funding activities in the late 1990s generated lessons that fed into the design of later intergovernmental grant mechanisms. The KPK also offers examples, even in the way it began investigations while still forging basic standards of operation. The aim in both instances was to start activity, learn from it, and build toward larger interventions.

Small reform steps like the initial Rwandan community funding experiments are relatively cheap and have the prospect of early success or quick wins. The blend of cheapness and demonstrable success characterizes positive deviations and is important in contexts where change faces opposition, which is usually the case with institutional change in development. The small steps also help flush out contextual challenges, including those that emerge in response to the interventions themselves. Facilitating such positive deviations through incremental steps is especially relevant in uncertain and complex contexts where reformers are unsure of what the problems and solutions are and lack confidence in their abilities to make things better. A gradual step-by-step reform that incorporates active opportunities to reflect on experience helps inform new reform solutions and inspire would-be reformers to find and fit these in their contexts. This kind of process typifies cooperative structures studied by authors like Elinor Ostrom, where the combination of "muddling through" and "efforts to learn and the capacity to adapt . . . [have] contribute[d] to the emergence of effective" institutional solutions.[46]

Finding and Fitting Requires a Relevant, Localized Focus

Muddling through does not mean being muddled in the search for reform options. Instead, it implies taking a gradual approach to addressing particular problems, which Chapter 7 noted are key entry points for institutional change. In reflecting on this, Bonnie McCay describes "muddling through" as "a go-slow, incremental approach to problem solving."[47] Given this, one would expect incremental reforms to be focused on solving specific problems and addressing the contextual realities in which these fester. This is not necessarily a formal focal point but reflects what Elinor Ostrom calls a set of "more or less informed expectations about potential outcomes" and factors affecting them.[48] One would also not expect the focal point to be

[46] McCay 2002, 368.
[47] Ibid., 368.
[48] Ostrom 2008, 58.

written in stone, but rather changing dynamically to reflect lessons learned in past stepwise engagements.

This kind of focal point is evident in the Indonesian case, at least after 2001, when reformers began specifying the type of anticorruption reform that would be relevant given contextual challenges. They wanted a vehicle that could address the systemic nature of Indonesia's corruption problem, given the constraints they saw in anticorruption reforms between 1997 and 2001.[49] In these past reforms, new agencies had drawn attention to cases but could never facilitate prosecution and punishment because they lacked jurisdiction and capacity and because they were always beholden to political masters.[50] KPK designers learned from this experience and used lessons to focus their reforms. The focus centered first on the "problem" the KPK would be required to address. Reformers constructed this problem by reflecting on the number of corruption cases past agencies had unearthed but failed to resolve. They built political support for change by drawing attention to these cases, creating an appetite for reform that would have a better record of finalizing cases in the future. This problem focus guided Indonesian reformers in their search for a solution. Over time, it became a focal point for the KPK itself, embodied in indicators the agency adopted as performance goals.

The KPK solution was also informed by an awareness of the local context. Given past experiences, for example, reformers were aware that a new agency would fail to address the focal problem if it did not have independence and authority to investigate and prosecute cases.[51] This fed the choice of a strong Hong Kong–style reform and the rejection of other less aggressive models of anticorruption agencies.[52] After the law creating the KPK was passed as an early reform step, officials found themselves facing new contextual challenges. They recognized deficiencies in the investigative and prosecutorial capacity needed to produce short-term results that would keep political support alive. This led to a policy of hiring from existing agencies like the national police force. As noted, a number of international experts decried this policy as a mistake, given perceptions that these officials were themselves corrupt.[53] The choice made sense, however, given the problem

---

[49] Jasin 2010, 19.
[50] The KPK Commissioners routinely cite these past experiences when describing why the KPK looks the way it does. Amien Sunaryadi (2007) does so in the review of KPK for the United Nations, and Mochammad Jasin (2010) does similarly in a retrospective analysis of the KPK.
[51] Sunaryadi 2005.
[52] Bolongaita 2010.
[53] Ibid.

focus reformers had adopted and the limited resources they had to fight corruption in the country – a contextual reality that constrained the choice of solution. In drawing on an existing pool of talent, KPK reformers were making do with what they had to address the problems at hand.

One sees a focused approach guiding Rwanda's reform search as well. This is evident in a review of the content in one of the first official documents produced by government (the 2000 Implementation Strategy for Decentralization, or DIP-1). The first six pages of this twenty-page document deconstruct the problem warranting reform.[54] The social and political natures of this problem are clear, given references to the 1994 genocide and the need to ramp up service delivery. Eight dimensions of the problem are identified in this section. These eight dimensions give structure to the rest of the document, which sets out a direction for reform and the specific goal of decentralization: empowering local people within what Kazuya calls a logic of the "unitary state."[55] The document also has a six-page section discussing contextual realities titled "Current Capacities, Environmental Opportunities, and Challenges." This shows that government was aware of the constraints it faced and wanted to ensure that reform decisions would be made within these constraints.

The focus on problems and context guided policy choices repeatedly over time in Rwanda. The DIP-1 evaluation in 2004 informed policy documents in 2005 and 2007, for instance. A case in point is the 2007 Strategic Framework, which looks very much like the 2000 Implementation Strategy in that it starts by focusing the discussion on the problem and then on the context, and only then proposes next steps.[56] There are differences between the problem definitions and contextual analyses in 2000 and 2007, however, that reflect dynamic adjustments of the focal point, given experiences with muddling through. In 2007, for instance, the problem is presented up front but in a much shorter section, with more precision than in 2000. It appears that reformers needed less detail about the problem at this point, ostensibly because there was more certainty about it and political buy-in was already high. The contextual analysis, by contrast, is more detailed, given lessons about challenges that emerged while implementing the 2000 strategy. This dynamic focal point kept attention on the problem and contextual realities that shaped which solutions would be possible.

---

[54] Government of Rwanda 2000.
[55] Kazuya, undated, at esango.un.org/event/ . . . /Second%20Committee%20Panel-Kauzya .ppt.
[56] Government of Rwanda 2007a, 6–13.

The idea that incremental institutional reform processes should be informed by some kind of dynamic criteria – or strategic focal point – is not new. As already referenced, authors like Bonnie McCay note that incrementalism is often an appropriate approach to complex problem solving – where the problem guides the route to finding a solution.[57] McCay references Elinor Ostrom's work on the process of resolving water rights in Los Angeles as an example.[58] This work shows that different sets of actors worked together in an incremental process to resolve a common problem, given an awareness of contextual constraints. Richard Rose's work on policy diffusion also points to the importance of such focal points,[59] given that they help ensure the "relevance" of reform choices. In his language, relevant institutions are "politically acceptable and within the resources of government."[60] He argues that "[w]hile relevance is no guarantee of a programme's success, it avoids the certainty of failure due to the promotion of programmes that governments do not want or lack the resources to implement."[61] The argument applies seamlessly when we think about institutional reform in development, incrementalism, and the experiences in Indonesia and Rwanda. Both interventions are proving relevant in their contexts, and in both cases the reason seems to be that solutions are politically accepted and practically possible. The focus on goals has helped build political support in both cases, with stepwise reform gains consolidating such support. Similarly, the awareness of contextual realities has ensured that chosen solutions are possible, given contextual constraints, and stepwise reforms have contributed to building capacity and loosening constraints over time.

A focused approach to muddling through is similar to the interaction of a problem focus and flexibility, discussed in Chapter 7. The examples of successful health projects in that chapter reinforce the idea that interventions have more traction when focused on problems and adopted through a flexible step-by-step strategy. Using Rose's term, these reforms enjoy greater chance of being relevant – politically accepted and practically possible – which enhances the potential for institutional change. Another applied example comes from the literature on change in Enterprise Resource Planning (ERP) systems. These are organization-wide information technology (IT) mechanisms that many readers will know as ORACLE, SAP, and others.

---

[57] McCay 2002.
[58] Ibid.
[59] Rose 2003.
[60] Ibid., 20.
[61] Ibid., 20.

These systems are regularly changed, and often the changes yield limited results where new systems are not fully adopted or used. These experiences have motivated research into why some projects work while others do not. Commonly referenced critical success factors include (i) having a clear understanding of the functional deficiencies the new system should address, (ii) paying attention to contextual factors that impact implementation, and (iii) having a process in place to ensure that systems work as they should.[62] These success factors contribute to ensure that reforms involve locally focused processes of finding and fitting. Studies show that they help to facilitate the production of relevant and functional ERP change solutions.

Finding and Fitting Requires Broad Scanning and the Bricolaged Formation of Hybrids

Beyond being incremental and locally focused, the Indonesian and Rwandan reforms both drew their content broadly from a wide variety of sources. The broad and incremental process of scanning for options is obvious when one looks at reform time lines. Figure 8.2 shows a simplified set of influences on the KPK reform in Indonesia. These include past initiatives that KPK commissioners note influenced their reform designs.[63] Prominent examples are the efforts to create versions of an anticorruption commission in 1967 and 1997. Other internal influences were more contemporaneous, with ideas emerging in the process of ratifying the United Nations Convention on Corruption in 2006 and through opportunities arising from the president's creation of the Coordination Team for Corruption Eradication (Tipikor) in 2005. Reformers also built on preexisting internal sources, drawing on investigative and prosecutorial personnel and processes in entities that had previously done such tasks. Ideas were forthcoming from external sources as well. The Asian Development Bank (ADB), for example, sponsored visits to regional anticorruption commissions and facilitated a consultancy by Bertrand de Speville (the founding commissioner in Hong Kong). Other external agencies, like the World Bank and Danish, German, and Australian governments, provided support and offered ideas on how the KPK should be structured, engage with civil society, and so forth.

Rwanda's decentralization reforms also drew on a variety of sources. Early government and World Bank documents note past efforts to foster decentralized activity through nationally managed funds from which local

---

[62] Holland and Light 1999; Hong and Kim 2002.
[63] Sunaryadi 2005; Jasin 2010.

entities would draw grants (in 1977, 1988, and 1991). Building loosely on this experience, the 1998 World Bank CRDP funded activities in a selection of districts, and it is here that one starts to see the idea of matching grants emerge.[64] Organizations like the World Bank were touting these grants as useful fiscal decentralization tools at the time and were also introducing modern management mechanisms at local levels in many countries (like participatory planning and performance-based financing).[65] Such practices were introduced gradually in Rwanda, and donors paid for government officials to visit other countries and see how mechanisms worked. In some cases, external examples led to ideas being dropped as poorly fitted, given the reform focus discussed earlier. The idea of NGO-led decentralization, for example, was not seriously explored because government wanted to build its own community structures and district administrations.[66] In other cases, ideas were adopted through pilots before being hardwired. Aspects of strategic planning, for instance, were introduced in the 1998 project but adjusted significantly before being formalized in 2003 national planning guidelines.[67]

Many of these external ideas had been internalized to quite some degree by the time Rwanda mainstreamed its decentralization reforms in the period between 2006 and 2010.[68] Laws were in place to allow matching grants, for instance, and the central ministry had developed capacities to manage such grants. Participatory, local-level planning, budgeting, and implementation methods had also been in place in enough local governments to be considered legitimate alternatives to previously hierarchical systems. Those leading reforms had been careful to couch new practices in Rwandan vernacular as well, reviving traditional mechanisms to which local people could relate. By 2008, for example, all mayors were subject to Imihigos (performance contracts) and all districts practiced Ubudehe (participatory project implementation).[69] Some of these locally sourced ideas entered the reform process in 2001, including the tradition of Ubudehe, which reformers "found" in looking for ways to mobilize local communities for project implementation. The idea of Imihigo performance agreements became part of the agenda only in 2006. Reform designers (including the president) were

---

[64] World Bank 1998c.

[65] Bahl 2000.

[66] World Bank 2004.

[67] See documents related to a retreat in late 2005, where lessons were learned about past interventions and fed into reforms, at www.devpartners.gov.rw.

[68] World Bank 2011c.

[69] McConnell 2009; Scher 2010.

looking for ways to hold local governments accountable for using funds and providing services to citizens, and this tradition seemed appropriate to the task.

The decentralization institutions emerging from Rwandan reforms are interesting combinations of these different internal and external ideas. They are not, therefore, a pure-form replica of any one individual idea or institutional model. External ideas have become embedded in regulative and cognitive elements, like the 2005 law on territories and the 2007 strategy on decentralization. Both draw on international thinking about the principle of subsidiarity, for instance, which is central to Rwanda's decentralization effort. Traditional internal ideas also provide for important institutional content. Imihigo performance contracts are used to ensure accountability relationships in the decentralized structures, for example. These kinds of mechanisms have also provided the normative and cognitive foundations of the new participatory structures. Citizens and officials know what is expected of them with regard to traditional concepts like Imihigo and Ubudehe, for example, which has the effect of embedding a new initiative in deep cultural soil.

The same blend of ideas characterizes Indonesia's KPK. The reform design drew external inspiration from Hong Kong's commission, aspects of which are embedded in the 2003 law that created the KPK. Internal ideas were also crucial, however, in providing regulative, normative, and cultural-cognitive content for the new institution. Lessons from prior internal reforms led to the 2003 law giving the KPK authority to prosecute, for instance (which Hong Kong's model does not have). Furthermore, the KPK developed transparent, merit-based hiring mechanisms to draw skilled people from established agencies like the National Police, building on their extant capacity. These Indonesia-specific ideas emerged within the context and were intended to ensure that the agency built on alternative logics of anticorruption that had existed in the country (but were frequently overwhelmed by the dominant logic of corruption). These alternative logics – complete with cognitive and normative mechanisms and formal procedures informing investigations and prosecutions activities – could be introduced fast and already enjoyed some legitimacy and capacity.

Hybrids Instead of Best Practice Solutions

One of the emerging lessons from these experiences is simply that successful institutional adjustments involve the emergence of mixed-form solutions – and not what Elinor Ostrom calls "optimal" institutions (which are embodied in the idea of "right rules," or one-best-way or best practice reforms discussed in Chapters 1 and 4).[70] The bottom line is that incremental reforms focused on addressing problems frequently result in combinations of elements that work together to get the job done given the resources at hand, including extant rules of the game, alternative rules, and supporting capacities. In their 2002 article on institutional change, Dacin, Goodstein, and Scott describe this process and product as bricolage.[71] John Campbell examines change as bricolage as well, explaining this as the process whereby actors recombine available institutional principles and practices in ways that yield change.[72] It has also been described as "making do" with resources and institutions at hand to foster new structures and mechanisms.[73]

Bricolage solutions emerge from available resources and options and not as best practice solutions practiced outside the context and demanding novel and unavailable content. The degree to which bricolage solutions involve a change from extant rules of the game thus depends on the number of options that already exist to choose from and combine in a given context. This raises a second lesson from the two cases, which emphasizes the importance of scanning broadly for reform ideas and developing these ideas over time so that they enter into the context as viable reform options. The lesson is reflected in work that talks about "multiplicity" in institutional fields – or the presence of many institutional referents. This work notes that institutional change is limited in contexts that are closed and do not have many institutional referents – alternatives to dominant incumbents. By contrast, a multiplicity of options enlarges the toolbox from which reformers can draw in crafting new solutions, facilitating deeper change.[74] This lesson is also apparent in Ostrom's work, where she describes the process of finding and fitting institutional solutions as follows: "There must be the generation of new alternatives, [and] selection among new and old combinations of attributes that are successful in a particular environment."[75]

New and old, internal and external ideas can form a menu of alternatives to consider in the change process, but in many senses Ostrom is talking about going beyond this. Scanning processes that facilitate the identification of multiple alternatives must also provide detailed descriptions of their attributes – the laws that make them work, norms that give them credibility,

---

[70] Ostrom 2008.
[71] Dacin, Goodstein, and Scott 2002, 50.
[72] Campbell 2004, 65.
[73] Mair and Marti 2009.
[74] Aldrich and Fiol 1994; Dorado 2005; Douglas 1986; Swidler 1986.
[75] Ostrom 2008, 47.

and cultural-cognitive mechanisms that allow them to function. In this way, scanning must provide a menu of alternatives, with the recipes included. Reformers need this detail to see which ideas match the problems being addressed, which can be introduced with extant ingredients, and what new ingredients need to be cultivated or found – so that they are made to be "at hand" and can feed a bricolage solution.

Carriers, Translators, and Experimentation

This leads to additional lessons about the scanners and scanning processes required to facilitate the "finding and fitting" of relevant institutional reform content. Reform ideas come from agents engaged in the change process who act as "carriers." Organizations like the World Bank have been called carriers of external ideas, responsible for "promulgating new conceptions, standards, and practices."[76] They can only provide for part of the scanning activity necessary in bricolage situations, however. Internal agents must also be engaged to carry past and present ideas into the discussion about potential reform solutions. Without groups of carriers like this, reforms are likely to be narrowly informed, which limits the potential of finding relevant "combinations of attributes" (using Ostrom's term).

Carriers need to do more than just propose alternative ideas, however. They must play the role of a translator as well, deconstructing an idea so that reformers can determine if it fits in its context. In a practical sense, this means explaining where the idea emanated, why it was adopted, how it was adopted, and what its core regulative, normative, and cultural-cognitive content looks like. This is ostensibly what Bertrand de Speville did in Indonesia, explaining the Hong Kong model as more than just a best practice in the region. His consultancy helped KPK reformers to better understand the kind of laws required to authorize a strong anticorruption agency, for instance, and the staffing and process needs of this agency. This translation is similar to a chef explaining how she cooks items on her menu and is a vital part of the finding and fitting process. It breaks interesting reform ideas down into the constituent attributes that are ultimately combined as new hybrid solutions. It also helps inform the process of adapting these attributes to local contexts, which Rose notes is often an overlooked part of best practice transfer: "If a relevant programme of another country is selected for adoption, it must still be contextualized, that is, altered to suit the specifics of one's own national setting."[77]

---

[76] Dacin, Goodstein, and Scott 2002, 50.
[77] Rose 2003, 22.

In many situations, ideas are not translated well through carriers, either because these agents do not know details behind the ideas they are proposing or because they do not have the time or incentive to explain them. Translation can still happen in these cases, however, through the incremental process of trying ideas, experiencing mixed results, and learning from them. In referencing this approach, Elinor Ostrom argues that "[t]he process of choice ... always involves experimentation."[78] This, she notes, is because "[i]t is hard to find the right combination of rules that work in a particular setting" and one has to "try multiple combinations of rules and keep making small adjustments to get the systems working well."[79] Experimentation allows reformers to act on ideas that emerge from the scanning process, to get a better "translation" of what makes them work, and to see how they interact with other institutional elements that either preexist in the reform context or are being introduced through other reforms. It also facilitates bricolage, in that new ideas become part of the landscape of ideas and capacities "at hand" from which new arrangements emerge in resource-constrained settings.[80] Some call this "trying out solutions," whereas others refer to it as continuous testing of new combinations of ideas.[81]

Rwandan officials learned a great deal about introducing grant-based funding to districts from the pilot experiments undertaken in the 1998 World Bank project. This experience informed later reform designs and capacity-building initiatives after 2002.[82] The experimentation did not stop at this point, however. Imihigo performance contracts were introduced in an experimental process after 2006. This allowed reform designers in the Ministry of Local Administration, Information and Social Affairs (MINALOC) to add modern management mechanisms to the traditional performance contracting practice. The experiments ultimately led to the creation of a new hybrid performance management device that is thoroughly "Rwandan." One sees similar experimentation in Indonesia's KPK reform. Although not an official experiment, the failed attempt to create a Joint Corruption Investigation Team yielded important lessons about what would be required to address corruption in Indonesia. The lessons were captured systematically by reformers, as in any meaningful experiment, and informed KPK design.

It is important to note what experimentation did and did not look like in these two examples. First, experimentation is not about performing a

---

[78] Ostrom 2008, 47.
[79] Ibid., 49.
[80] Dorado 2005; Garud and Karnøe 2003; Mair and Marti 2009.
[81] Baker and Nelson 2005, 334.
[82] Government of Rwanda 2007a; World Bank 2004.

scientific experiment in which the context is suspended (as in many randomized trials with potential policy solutions). Rather, it is about trying a real intervention in a real context, allowing on-the-ground realities to shape content in the process. Second, this is not about proving that specific ideas or mechanisms work or do not work. It is rather about allowing a process to emerge through which attributes from various ideas can coalesce into new hybrids. This requires seeing lessons learned about potential combinations as the key emerging result. Third, experimentation requires having mechanisms to capture lessons and use them to inform future activities. It is not, therefore, about allowing a thousand flowers to bloom without focus. The lessons learned through these experimental reform steps helped reformers in Rwanda and Indonesia make sense of reform alternatives, choose attributes from different options that best fitted their contexts, and ultimately create hybrids that addressed the problems on which they were focused.

Institutional Reforms Can Be Improved through Purposive Muddling

It is important to remember that both the Rwandan and Indonesian reforms had significant external influence. They are thus evidence that externally influenced institutional reforms can support endogenous processes of finding and fitting content. As such, the lessons they offer are important for organizations like the IMF, World Bank, and bilateral development agencies in governments of wealthier countries. The lessons have been discussed here through three observations, which emphasize that purposive muddling can lead to relevant institutional reforms that provide functionality necessary to address stubborn problems in complex contexts. The first observation was that purposive muddling takes time and is incremental, emerging as multiple small steps through which reformers learn about what works and why, build their capacities to introduce these new mechanisms, and achieve short-term results to grow political support for greater change. The second observation was that this kind of finding and fitting requires a localized focus on problems and contextual realities, such that reform choices address matters that are politically relevant and viable given capacities and constraints. The third observation was that these reforms emerge through broad scanning, during which external and internal ideas are introduced for discussion, translation, and experimentation. Fitted solutions take shape through a process of bricolage as hybrid blends of different attributes – with some external content and some internal content – rather than as pure-form replicas of any one idea.

These lessons indicate that the process of institutional reform matters as much as the final product – or potentially even more. The finding and fitting process yields new and viable institutional forms by gradually building capacity to implement and political support to legitimize the final product. It is a starkly different approach from that characterizing many institutional reforms in development, which emphasize products over process and impose demanding external best practice solutions on resource-poor contexts. As discussed in Chapter 4, this kind of reform overspecifies the content of reform in an *ex ante* manner by focusing on reproducing the content of external models. Much of this content is not found in the local context, however. This is particularly problematic because, as Chapter 4 argues, external reforms seldom address unseen informal institutional content needs. Norms and cultural-cognitive mechanisms required to facilitate new laws and procedures are often not provided by reforms. The result is an incomplete reform that does not yield improved functionality or contribute to solving problems.

This is illustrated in the left-hand column of Table 8.1, which is a revised version of Table 4.4. It is contrasted with a purposive muddling approach described in this chapter, where problems and contextual realities guide selection. This alternative approach involves the incremental selection of attributes from a broad set of options, such that the final hybrid has regulative, normative, and cultural-cognitive elements that may look strange and poorly connected but ultimately combine into functional new rules of the game.

The process of finding and fitting institutional reform through purposive muddling is similar to the iterative route carpenters might follow when crafting pegs for difficult-to-fill holes. They may look at different types of pegs for inspiration, considering some square oak pegs, round pine pegs, small pegs, rough pegs, smooth pegs, and so forth. Ultimately, their selection would draw on attributes of many examples, building on the tools and material at hand – perhaps leading to a hybrid round, rough oak peg that fits the hole needing filling. This kind of hybrid is evident now in Rwanda and Indonesia, where decentralization and anticorruption reforms have yielded new institutions that incorporate some aspects of external best practice with other aspects of internal tradition. Neither of the two examples is a pure form of any preexisting best practice, and neither emerged by pursuing best practice. Rather, as has been shown, they came about as a result of incremental, iterative processes supported by external partners.

Experience in these cases yields recommendations for ways to improve the process and product of institutional reforms in development. These

Table 8.1. *Contrasting best practice and purposive muddling approaches*

Key content area	Results of a best practice reform approach	Results of a purposive muddling reform approach
Problems	Problems not considered in design; at best, issues are addressed but not fleshed out to reveal complexities	Problems are focal point of design, content selection; problems are progressively identified and constructed
Contextual complexities	Contextual issues not considered in choosing content, or are loosely referenced	Contextual issues are focal point of design. Incremental reforms flush issues out, allow for adjustments and learning
Regulative mechanisms	Best practice reforms focus on visible elements only	Purposive muddling allows regulative, normative and cultural cognitive elements to emerge incrementally, focused on problems and context, though broad scanning activities helping reformers identify institutional attributes that work in their contexts
Normative mechanisms	Best practice reforms seldom provide for these less visible elements	
Cultural-cognitive mechanisms		

recommendations focus particularly on ensuring that the content of reforms is relevant to context – that is, politically accepted and practically possible.

- *Focus on small next steps, not final solutions.* Best practice reforms often introduce long-term solutions – like international accounting standards – in short time periods, promising final products from four- to six-year projects. The idea behind incrementalism is different. Reforms should start with small first steps that lead to learning and additional next steps, which cumulatively provide a path to long-term change. Externally supported short-term projects should focus on the short-term actions that facilitate this kind of gradual change and emphasize as results the degree to which governments "find" new ideas and build new capacities and political appetite for bigger next steps.
- *Capture lessons and cultivate stories of positive deviation.* Reforms commonly fail because of deficiencies in political will, capacity, and

internal confidence in the possibility of change. None of these factors is enhanced by best practice interventions that impose impossible
demands on resource-deficient contexts. These interventions disem-
power local agents who ultimately need to build the political support,
ability, and self-belief required for change. A stepwise reform process
can have the opposite effect, especially when it is composed of manage-
able next steps that demonstrate what is possible given extant resources.
External agents could support such steps by capturing lessons from
these activities and cultivating stories about the way these yield positive deviations from the status quo – generating quick wins, growing
capacity, and political support, and pointing toward more comprehensive solutions.

- *Always build on past steps.* Donor agencies are frequently criticized
for introducing reforms that bear no semblance to what governments
have done in the past or even to what other donors are doing concur-
rently. This is particularly the case when external agents introduce best
practices that have no legacy in the reform context. By contrast, incremental reforms should always build on what is there already, especially
in developing country contexts where all next steps are likely to be
constrained by resource deficiencies. Change comes through the accumulation of small steps, which cannot happen if reforms are always
centered on de novo ideas.

- *Identify, and pay attention to, "relevancy criteria."* Many reforms fail
because they are not politically accepted or practically possible. Richard
Rose calls such interventions "irrelevant."[83] Reformers can counter the
risk of choosing such reforms by using locally defined relevancy criteria
when specifying the content of interventions. A first criterion involves
focusing on problems to gain political acceptance. A second criterion
relates to considering preexisting institutional realities in the reform
context, which influence the practical possibility of reform.

- *Foster multiplicity.* Change is often most needed and limited in contexts where institutional options are constrained. Faulty rules of the
game may prevail for long periods in these situations simply because
agents lack alternatives. By contrast, change is facilitated by the presence of many alternatives – what has been described as institutional
multiplicity. Externally influenced reforms can foster multiplicity by
introducing new external ideas and provoking internal searches for

---

[83] Rose 2003.

alternatives hidden in forgotten traditions or marginalized groups. This is not the same as representing one-best-way models and narrow sets of external ideas, however. It requires providing and facilitating the search for broad sets of ideas, with details about where they emerged, when, under what conditions, and with what prerequisites. The goal should be to construct a host of menu items with the attached recipes, encouraging and informing choice.

- *Facilitate learning and bricolage.* Many reforms specify solutions *ex ante*, often based on externally sourced best practices. As discussed in Chapter 4, these practices are often not fully supported in resource-deficient contexts. Evidence suggests that relevant institutions emerge in such contexts through processes of bricolage, where agents construct hybrids from the attributes of available institutional alternatives; given resources at hand. This is a core part of the muddling through process and involves creating opportunities, often through experimentation, for action-based interventions – with organized evaluation, learning, and feedback mechanisms. Those facilitating such approach should be open to locally relevant but potentially strange-looking hybrids emerging from such process.

These recommendations combine to facilitate purposive muddling in reform processes. This purposive muddling can be introduced in externally influenced reform processes, as shown in the cases of Rwanda and Indonesia. The spirit of purposive muddling is also evident in many of China's institutional reforms. As discussed in the introduction, for instance, the country's financial sector reforms reflect a hybrid of government and market mechanisms that has emerged gradually from stepwise reforms over decades and is still taking shape today.[84] The long process allowed China to develop political support for its reform and to establish market structures and informational and other abilities to ensure liberalization without crisis. China's public financial management reforms have arguably emerged along a similar trajectory, slowly and purposefully addressing specific problems – one step at a time.[85] One can contrast this approach with the quick and often problematic public financial management and liberalization attempts of other developing countries, which have frequently gone hand in hand with crisis and financial sector failure.[86]

---

[84] Feyzioğlu, Porter, and Takáts 2009, 16.
[85] Lou and Wang 2008.
[86] Noy 2004.

There is active discussion about whether one can generalize from China's reform approach to other countries.[87] The Chinese experience with reforms like financial liberalization differs with regard to both process and final product when compared with what one typically sees in developing countries. Key aspects of state control have been retained, even with liberalized interest rates. Banks have professionalized and globalized before being privatized, for instance, through an incremental process of identifying and introducing reforms that are relevant to the context. This kind of hybrid is apparently functional but defies description in terms of any one best practice model. This is the case for China's government and economic structures generally, which reflect a model of "authoritarian capitalism"[88] for some and an example of standard neoliberal ideas for others.[89] Opting out of relating China's hybrid system to any given model, Joshua Cooper Ramo suggests that the "Beijing Consensus" is about the process of finding and fitting new institutions.[90] He notes that this process is based on innovation and experimentation and the need for contextualized, politically sustainable solutions and self-determination.

It is important to note that external agencies have not always supported the processes and products in this hybrid system. Such agencies have not turned their backs on China, however, partly because the country's geopolitical position makes it less dependent than others – and thus less pressured to pursue isomorphic change. Singapore is another country that decided not to routinely mimic external best practices. After a number of years of failed efforts to create economic institutions in the 1960s, the country adopted a bricolaged system of strong global capitalism (led by multinational enterprises) and strong government. This hybrid went against the grain in various respects. Multinational companies were frowned on by many development voices, for instance, portrayed as mechanisms of

---

[87] The question emerged after a 2008 presentation on China's public financial management reforms at the IMF. A blog entry on the exchange noted that the key question was "Could the Chinese experience provide lessons for other developing countries?" In response to this question, "[p]anel members expressed the view that while of course China and every other country is unique in its needs and its reform path, there is ample scope in institutional reforms for learning from each other's experience. Public sector reforms were seen as successful due to the Chinese willingness to experiment with new models – in public financial management this has often taken place at the provincial level – and to accept that which works well." See full entry at http://blog-pfm.imf.org/pfmblog/2008/02/new-challenges.html.

[88] Halper 2010.

[89] Yao 2010.

[90] Ramo 2004.

"neocolonialist exploitation."[91] Similarly, developed countries were moving away from strong central government structures after the 1970s, making Singapore's pursuit of government-owned entities like airlines unfashionable. Singapore adopted its hybrid despite opposition, however, because it provided an appropriate fit for their needs at the time. According to Lee Kuan Yew, "We had a real-life problem to solve and could not afford to be conscribed by any theory or dogma."[92]

Many countries aspire to be the new Singapore, one of the world's great (and few) examples of economic development in the past fifty years. This is demonstrated by the fact that tourists can buy T-shirts that herald Rwanda as "The New Singapore" at Kigali's airport. The model of institutional reform Singapore provides is very much about process, whereby solutions were found and fitted to the problems of the day. This process of purposive muddling is vital to effective institutional reform. It can be facilitated and supported by outside parties, but the active engagement of internal agents like Lee Kuan Yew is arguably even more important. These agents demand a functional orientation in change agendas and build leadership structures that make this happen. These leadership structures are discussed in the next chapter.

---

[91] Lee 2000, 59.
[92] Ibid., 59.

NINE

Broad Engagement, Broader (and Deeper) Change

CONVENING AND CONNECTING FOR CHANGE

As noted in the Chapter 8, many developing countries aspire to be a new Singapore, characterized by robust economic growth and stable, successful market and government institutions. Observers commonly argue that Singapore's development story was all about its president's heroic leadership. Although Lee Kuan Yew was certainly one of the great national leaders of the twentieth century, his autobiography casts doubt on this idea of individualistic heroism. In it, Lee likens governments to orchestras and reflects on the multiple functions played by multiple agents in producing orchestral sounds.[1] He calls himself a conductor but names many others who, metaphorically, led the tubas, oboes, and clarinets. These are not just "bit players," in his estimation. They are leaders of their sections in the orchestras, armed with the knowledge and skill to do something that the conductor cannot. They included local people in the president's core team and those working a few arms' lengths away from this team, as well as external advisors, supporters, and influencers.[2] The deep social, economic, and institutional change that helped Singapore move from third world to first was a product of broad-based engagement and leadership across all of these agents.

Chapter 5 discussed the need for broad engagement at two levels to facilitate institutional reform. The first involved establishing groups of agents to stimulate change – institutional entrepreneurs, for want of a better name. The second related to the idea of engaging with distributed agents who have to implement change. The chapter argued that dominant approaches

---

[1] Lee 2000.
[2] Like Albert Winsemius, a Dutch economist who worked for the United Nations Development Programme (UNDP) and became a longtime advisor to the government–working closely with the president and with the president's various policy teams.

to doing development focus narrowly on champions, not even acknowledging the importance of broad engagement among the first group of entrepreneurs. The chapter provided evidence that distributed players are all but forgotten as potential agents of change but are treated rather as targets. This often results in change that either lacks entrepreneurial energy or fails to diffuse and become institutionalized by the distributed agents. The reforms are like pegs fashioned by a single carpenter who does not have access to all of the materials, methods, or tools required and cannot see the holes he is meant to fill. No matter how good he is, this carpenter is unlikely to complete the job on his own.

This chapter presents a different vision of agency in institutional reform. It builds on the ideas introduced in Chapter 5 and Lee Kwan Yew's perspective of leadership involving an orchestra with multiple leaders in multiple sections. It argues that these multiple leaders provide a variety of functions needed to facilitate institutional change – including ideas, financing, inspiration, implementation capacities, and formal authority. Different combinations of these functions are required at different points in the change process, calling for different sets of broadly engaged agents at all times. These agents and their functions only lead to change when combined, which points to the importance of mobilization and the agents who mobilize others. These are identified as motivators, conveners, and connectors, and are considered pivotal role players in any change process.

The first section of the chapter presents a study on leadership in twelve interventions that seem to be delivering better functionality in complex settings. Section 2 discusses evidence from this study, which supports the view that multiple leaders provide multiple functions to facilitate institutional change. It also reinforces the argument that mobilizers – especially conveners and connectors – are vital role players. These mobilizers allow for broader engagement of institutional entrepreneurs and also facilitate dynamic interaction between these entrepreneurs and distributed agents – who then become active agents of change instead of passive targets. The evidence from section 1 also helps inform a discussion about potential roles external agents play in supporting institutional change in development. This role is smaller than that played by internal agents, centered on some key functions that external agents may be uniquely located to provide.

A conclusion draws on the evidence and discussion to identify three key lessons for purveyors of externally influenced institutional reforms in development: (i) Instead of focusing on lone champions, reformers should establish broad-based engagements; (ii) instead of emphasizing agents who provide authority and ideas, reforms should cultivate mobilizers – motivators, conveners, and connectors; and (iii) external agents themselves should be aware of the limited roles they can play in facilitating institutional change and play these roles as effectively as possible.

INSTITUTIONAL CHANGE COMES WITH HELP

Agents are required to make successful institutional change happen. This is a common assumption and the gist of the argument in Chapter 5. It raises many questions, however: Who needs to provide such agency, when, and how? In 2008, a multidonor group called the Global Leadership Initiative commissioned work to ask these questions.[3] The research approach was simple. It started by selecting reforms in which institutional change seemed to be progressing successfully in spite of contextual difficulties. These are listed in Table 9.1. They included efforts to build cadres of deputy ministers in Afghanistan; to craft development plans for Afghanistan and the Central African Republic; to stimulate service delivery in Burundi, Rwanda, Kenya, and Sierra Leone; to establish legislative and policy-making structures in Kenya and Uganda; and to create local anticorruption mechanisms in Kosovo. All of these reforms involved small interventions that were showing success in the face of more limited larger reforms, which made them particularly interesting. Why would a program equipping Afghan deputy ministers produce positive results while broader civil service reforms were generally failing? How did a group of local governments in Kosovo develop anticorruption mechanisms while national attempts to do so had stalled?

To better understand the change experienced in these initiatives, participants and close observers of the reforms were identified and interviewed,[4] using a structured and common protocol in all cases.[5] The protocol built on examples in prior work on leadership and change across the literature, and a variety of controls were adopted to ensure the validity of interview data.[6] Questions asked particularly about (i) who led reforms at two points

---

[3] Andrews, McConnell, and Wescott 2008.

[4] Selective identification and snowballing approaches were used together given complementary strengths and weaknesses of each. The former ensures access to actors considered key from an external perspective. It can lead to limited access for those who were not externally visible. Snowballing allows access to this latter group of agents.

[5] See Andrews, McConnell, and Wescott 2008.

[6] Interviews are commonly used to gather information about organizational and institutional change. Research employing this method usually focuses on interviews with small groups of agents who were engaged in the change process. Although interview numbers are low in such studies, the interviews themselves are structured, lengthy, and "thick" with qualitative detail. See Greenwood, Suddaby, and Hinings (2002), Hennessey (1998), and Rimmer et al. (1996).

Table 9.1. *Basic details about each case and intervention*

Country/Period/ Intervention title	Contextual complexity	Intended goal of the intervention
Afghanistan (06–08) Civil Service Leadership	The new government was being built after 30 years of conflict and lacked top and middle layers of civil servants	Develop cadre of top- and middle-level leaders/managers in the Afghan government
Afghanistan (2002) Towards a National Plan	Postwar government lacked vision around which to organize	Establish National Development Framework and planning process
Burundi (07–09) Rapid service delivery	Government emerging from war lacked structure, struggled to provide services	Improve service delivery, confidence, accountability
Central African Republic (04–05) Post-conflict planning	Government emerging from conflict but limited consensus about role, legitimacy	Build political consensus around plan, deliver services
Kenya (04–09) Rapid results and performance management	Adjustment at the end of Moi administration, pressure for service delivery	Improve service delivery in key areas, mainstream results-based management
Kenya (00–09) Legislative reform	Parliament had been weakened during Moi administration	Strengthen parliament
Kosovo (04–06) Municipal anticorruption	Concerns about corruption in new municipalities	Develop municipal inspectorates
Rwanda (07–09) Imihigo performance contracting	Government lacked mechanisms for ensuring local service delivery	Develop accountable and effective local governments
Rwanda (07–09) Rapid service delivery	Government lacked mechanisms to deliver services	Promote rapid service delivery
Sierra Leone (07) Empowering women in government	Women were underrepresented in the postwar government	Introduce more women to political leadership
Sierra Leone (04–09) Decentralized service delivery	Government lacked mechanisms to deliver services	Promote rapid service delivery
Uganda (06–07) Preparing for government transition	Uganda lacked multiparty policy-making processes	Develop multiparty policy and process, assist transition to nonpartisan work

Source: Derived from Andrews, McConnell, and Wescott, 2010.

in time – at its start and years afterward during implementation – and (ii) why these agents were considered leaders.[7] Data from 148 interviews told a consistent story of multiagent leadership in both periods.

Agency at the Start of Reform

When asked who led at the start of reform, the 148 respondents pointed to 103 agents across the twelve reforms. The median number of "leaders" identified per reform was seven. Organizations like donor entities and ministries were nearly twice as likely to be identified as leaders than individuals, and there were surprisingly few references to national leaders or "bosses." With regard to Afghanistan's 2006 to 2008 civil service leadership program, for example, there were no references to President Karzai, and only three people identified the vice president responsible for administration as the leader. Eight respondents pointed to the Civil Service Commission when identifying the leader, six to the United Nations Development Programme (UNDP), two to the World Bank, and a further four to technical specialists in these organizations.

Similarly, interviewees noted that efforts to strengthen Kenya's legislature were led at the start by a number of organizational entities. These included the U.S. Agency for International Development (USAID) and its contractors, civil society groups, and parliament as a whole. Interviewees also identified people who provided early leadership, mentioning parliamentarians by name and using terms they were given when change transpired (e.g., the "Young Turks"). Other individuals were also identified, however, who were not in prominent positions. These more "mundane" characters included three women who held secretarial and administrative positions in USAID, its primary contractor in Nairobi, and a nongovernmental organization (NGO). One of these agents was identified more often than others, apparently recognized as the glue that held all of the others together.

Interviewees were asked why they identified these agents as leading reforms at the start. All responses were fully transcribed, summarized, and then classified according to emerging themes.[8] This yielded a variety of "reasons" why interviewees identified their leaders:

---

[7] Interviews were conducted in eleven cases. A participant observation method was adopted in Burundi, given that government did not authorize interviews. Four interviewers were involved in the eleven other cases, and interview data were captured in writing and through voice recording.

[8] A full explanation of the classification process is available on request from the author. Three people were involved in the coding process.

- Some identified leaders as those who provided formal authority at the start of the change process or inspired and motivated change. Authorizers were the people or organizations "commissioned," "mandated," or "appointed" to pursue reform. Motivators were the individuals credited with "spearheading," "driving," and "working at the front" of the change. Together, such descriptions accounted for about a third of all the leaders identified.
- About 15 percent identified leaders as those who recognized the problems needing change or supplied ideas for solutions. A third of these were those whom Chapter 5 called distributed agents, responsible for implementation. For example, a Kenyan was identified as a leader because he "could articulate the problem" with weak service delivery better than others. Additional examples come from Kosovo and Afghanistan, where agents were considered leaders because they "could understand the problem" and "knew the problem better than others."
- Agents were also named as leaders because they provided financial resources needed to initiate change. An agent was recognized as doing this in eight of the cases. An international organization was credited for "providing funding" to facilitate activities in the Central African Republic, for instance. Another was a "critical provider of funds" in the early days of Kenya's legislative reform.
- About 10 percent of the named leaders were recognized for empowering other agents to engage in reform at its start through practical support. A government official in Afghanistan was identified as a leader because he "protected others from political attack," for instance, whereas another "got the front-end approvals to allow change." Other agents provided training that empowered agents proposing reform.
- About 17 percent of the leaders were credited with assisting engagements between small groups of agents directly involved in designing reforms. These were classified as "conveners," given the way they facilitated meetings. A person involved in Kenya's legislative reform, for instance, "helped people engage, then took a back seat." An individual in Kosovo "built teams," and a civil society agent in Sierra Leone "got everyone to come to meetings" and "facilitated discussions between key players."
- A further 10 percent of the leaders were classified as "connectors" because they reached out beyond core groups and teams, facilitating indirect engagements with more distributed agents. Examples include government officials in Rwanda and Uganda who "ensured the rest of government was on board" and "communicated with the rest of

Table 9.2. *Why agents were identified as "leaders," and the roles played by external agents*

Role	Proportion of all responses at start of reform (%)	Proportion of all responses related to external agents at the start of reform (%)	Proportion of responses during reform implementation (%)	Proportion of all responses related to external agents during reform implementation (%)
They had formal authority to lead reform	16	0	19	0
They motivated and inspired reform	19	4	14	3
They constructed and/or communicated problems	4	2	7	0
They came up with the ideas for reform	9	3.5	2	0
They are implementation leaders	6	0	17	0
They provided financial resources	9	9	3	3
They empowered other agents	9	1	12	2
They convened key groups	17	5	11	1
They connected to distributed groups	10	1.5	14	3
Total	99	26	99	12

Source: Author's analysis of interview data. Two other researchers also participated in the coding, to ensure objectivity.

the public service." An international consultant in Afghanistan was both a convener and connector, "reaching out to the most important stakeholders who reached out to others."

Interviewees identified conveners or connectors in every case. About a quarter of these "relational leaders" were external agents – typically employed by donor agencies. In total, external agents made up about a quarter of all those identified as leaders at the start of reform. This is shown in Table 9.2, which breaks down the roles played by all of the leaders and those from external agencies at this early reform stage. Data point to the fact that external agents were most commonly called leaders because they provided funding for interventions. Their roles were interspersed across other functions as well, but they had no contribution in two key areas: providing formal authority and "leading" as a reform implementer. These roles were purely internal to the governments or communities undergoing change.

Agency in Reform Implementation

In all cases, interviewees agreed that reforms had enjoyed success but were still in the process of implementation. They identified 146 agents when asked who the reform leaders were in the current state of implementation. This is 43 more than were cited as leading at the start of reforms. Sixty percent of the implementation leaders were organizations, which is about the same proportion identified as playing key roles at the start of reform. Interestingly, there were many more local organizations named as leading implementation than had been previously mentioned. The corollary of this is evident in the last column of Table 9.2, which shows that external agents from donor organizations made up a smaller proportion of those considered leaders at this stage (comprising 12 percent, compared with 26 percent at reform initiation).

When asked why they identified such agents as implementation leaders, interviewees once again reflected predominantly on what the agents did to facilitate change. Table 9.2 shows that a larger proportion of leaders provided formal authority in this stage than at the start (19 percent compared with 16 percent). This expanded group reflected the greater formalization of most reforms. Agents had been "appointed" to lead the emerging change in a variety of cases and "elected" in others, with one respondent noting that the "reform has now been centralized and he has been made responsible." Four additional leadership functions were more prominent in the implementation stage:

- The proportion of those identified as leaders because they were at the forefront of implementation efforts increased from 6 percent to 17 percent. These included three Afghans who had "shown commitment to do the reforms" slated in the national plan, were "the most successful implementers," and "had the greatest capacity to do the work." Kenyan agents were recognized similarly because they "knew best how to implement the reform" and "have been at it longest, showing best results and teaching others."
- The share of those seen as empowering other groups to participate rose from 9 percent to 12 percent. Two agents in Rwanda's decentralization reforms were recognized for "supporting the people and

giving them advice" and "building confidence across the community." A senior Kenyan official was acknowledged for "helping junior officials to partake in decisions" affecting results-oriented reform.

- The contribution of agents noted for helping identify problems rose from 4 percent to 7 percent of the total. These included a person in Kosovo who "listened to the problems emerging through the process" and an organization in Sierra Leone that was "close to the ground and can understand the situation well." It is interesting that problem identification was still a leadership function in implementation, suggesting purposive muddling (discussed in Chapter 8).
- The slice of those connecting to distributed groups grew from 10 percent to 14 percent. Those fitting this description in Rwanda and Uganda "coordinated across the whole of government" and "engaged with multiple players" to "spread reform to many people and provide the connections."

The proportion of agents helping convene smaller groups of key players was still notable but had declined from 17 percent to 11 percent. The full set of relational leaders (conveners and connectors) made up about the same share as at the start but was now dominated by those forging connections with distributed agents. As with core-group conveners, the group providing inspiration and motivation declined in share but was also still important. Other leadership roles that had been prominent at the start were much more marginal, including those informing change ideas and providing financial support (the share of both dropping from 9 percent to about 3 percent). External agents had been predominantly engaged in leading these areas at the start of the reforms and still did so during implementation (at least with funding) but now played a smaller part overall.

BROAD ENGAGEMENT, THROUGH MOBILIZATION, FACILITATES BROAD CHANGE

The evidence from these twelve interventions suggests that institutional change requires leadership contributions from multiple agents during initiation and even more during implementation. The idea that institutional change requires broad engagement is not new. The idea that such change requires *broad leadership* engagement is, however, more novel – especially in the development arena. Chapter 1 argued that interventions in this domain typically emphasize narrow, top-down leadership by champions or dominant organizations. Other agents are considered targets of change, not necessarily active in designing, tweaking, and shaping reform engagements.

Chapter 5 provided an example of this in the discussion of Mozambique's public financial management (PFM) reforms. In this example, reform leadership emanated from agents inside or associated with the Ministry of Finance. Other affected ministries, provincial agents, district officers, and the like were simply expected to implement what those champions produced. As the chapter discusses, these distributed agents have not implemented all they were told to, partly because they appear to have different perspectives on the value of proposed (and imposed) changes.

There are similar examples of planning and financial management reforms in the research cases described in this chapter. Although still incomplete, these interventions seem to be yielding smaller and slower but more accepted improvements to the processes of allocating and managing public finances in complex contexts like Afghanistan, the Central African Republic, and Uganda. In all of these cases, leadership has involved multiple agents in multiple organizations spanning government and including external supporters. Other cases analyzed here reflect a variety of common institutional reforms that seem to be facilitating changes to the de facto rules of government in challenging contexts. Broad leadership is evident in all of these cases, with agents playing various roles to facilitate change. A subset of scholars has been arguing for a while that change comes through this kind of broad engagement. This section reflects on such work and how it helps explain evidence emerging in Table 9.2. It discusses the need for broad leadership and mobilization in institutional reform and then comments on roles external agents play in facilitating change.

Change Requires Multiple Agents Providing Multiple Functions

As noted in Chapter 5, any discussion of leadership or institutional entrepreneurship must start by acknowledging the paradox of embeddedness. This asks how agents embedded in institutionalized contexts can simultaneously find and introduce changes to these contexts. It offers a particular challenge to those who believe that change is driven by narrowly defined individual champions, commonly the most powerful ministers or managers in a government setting. Think, perhaps of the centrally located agent A in the shaded circle in Figure 9.1. The circle is meant to represent a defined social network or field – perhaps the civil service of Afghanistan – in which agent A is the elite, powerful de facto leader. Think of the president or vice president in charge of managing public administration (if the formal role also equates with informal power and authority, which is not always the case).

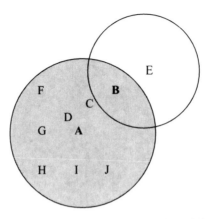

Figure 9.1. Agents in different positions in social networks and the challenge of change.

As discussed in Chapter 5, these centrally located agents (or elites) are commonly considered the most embedded in their contexts. They are empowered by preexisting rules of the game and are the greatest beneficiaries of such – having the most power, biggest office, and largest paycheck. Because of this, they are not expected to perceive the need for change, have access to change ideas, or risk their interests in pressing for change. By contrast, agents at the periphery of the network (like agent B) are more weakly embedded in extant rules. Consider, for instance, a new bureaucrat fresh from doing an extended internship in the New York offices of the United Nations. These agents benefit less from preexisting rules and are thus more open to criticizing prevailing institutions and entertaining change. They often also coexist in other networks; perhaps comprising United Nations colleagues met while in New York, represented in the clear circle. They get to see different rules of the game in and through these other network engagements, potentially fueling ideas for change in their primary social sphere (in this case, the Afghan civil service system). They lack the power to even experiment with these changes, however, given their peripheral location.

Based on such thinking, it should be apparent that change is possible only if at least two agents at very different positions in social, political, and economic networks combine, bringing together the ideas about change and the power to authorize change. At its most simple, this could involve a direct link between a central leader and a frontline agent. This kind of direct link is not always possible, however, especially in hierarchical settings where those with power are often separated from others. Third parties are needed to facilitate links in such situations, which are typical to development. Think of agent C in Figure 9.1, perhaps a civil service colleague in Afghanistan who formerly worked in the United Nations, has a higher rank, and enjoys the ear of those in power.

Although simple, this example and discussion has already identified the need for at least three different, and differently located, agents to facilitate institutional change. It is easy to think of more. Although agent A may have power, for instance, she probably needs to augment it to facilitate change. There is thus a need for other central, elite agents like D to give political support or influence in areas beyond agent A's authority. The vice president in charge of civil service may have authority to change a law, for instance, but needs the support of a minister of finance to pay for the activity of new entities created by the law. Furthermore, the externally sourced ideas agent B has for change need to be detailed and explained, warranting engagement by other external actors – like E in the clear circle, maybe a current United Nations official who knows a lot about proposed reform modalities. Additionally, if distributed agents like F, G, H, I, and J are expected to accept and implement change, they too need to be engaged in some way. As argued in Chapter 5, these agents are often expected to simply "implement by edict" but often implement and facilitate diffusion only when they have been involved in reflecting on the need for change and finding and fitting solutions.

This line of observation resonates with theories on "functional leadership."[9] These posit that leadership is about the actions that agents take, or functions they perform, especially in facilitating change. Different scholars cluster leadership functions differently, but common approaches emphasize three sets: (i) substantive contributions to tasks (like providing ideas about new institutions), (ii) procedural contributions that aid groups in addressing tasks (authorizing mechanisms to allow experimentation, for instance), and (iii) maintenance contributions that improve relationships between agents (like team mechanisms that encourage discussion). Theorists argue that multiple agents provide these different functions, in teams across organizations and other social groupings, at all levels of social hierarchy. An applied example comes from a study of leadership in change within Australian firms.[10] This was often motivated and catalyzed by a chief executive officer but transpired only after "a more complex and pluralistic process involving different stakeholders."[11] Middle managers developed and operationalized plans; external consultants provided knowledge; and union

---

[9] Hackman and Walton 1986; Zaccaro et al. 2001.
[10] Rimmer et al. 1996.
[11] Ibid., 43.

Table 9.3. *Different functions and the likely network location of respective agents*

Function set	Roles, drawn from Table 9.2	Characteristics and likely network location
Substantive contributions	i. Construct, communicate problems	i. See weaknesses in incumbents, ***periphery***
	ii. Come up with ideas for reform	ii. Access to alternative ideas, ***periphery***
	iii. Provide implementation view	iii. Experienced, ***probably periphery***
Procedural contributions	iv. Provide formal authority	iv. In power, ***center***
	v. Motivate and inspire reform	v. Respected, visible, ***varied***
	vi. Empower other agents	vi. Able to support, ***varied***
	vii. Provide financial support	vii. Access to finances, ***center or external***
Maintenance contributions	viii. Conveners of small groups	viii. Trusted, thick connections, ***varied***
	ix. Connectors to distributed agents	ix. Trusted, broad connections, ***varied***

leaders "open[ed] the doors to workforce involvement and the development of trust."[12]

Functional theorists tend to examine roles agents play in forming and managing teams. This is a narrower focus than the current study, in which leadership through teams was only one modality of engagement. The idea that multiple agents provided different functions is, however, consistent with evidence from these cases. The three function sets mentioned earlier are also useful in organizing evidence of the different roles agents play. This is shown in Table 9.3, which also identifies the likely network location of these actors.

The table organizes all nine roles discussed in Table 9.2 into one of the three function sets. It also shows some basic characteristics that seem associated with the various roles and their implications for the likely network location of different agents. Substantive contributions come from those who frame problems, suggest solutions, and provide an implementation view (ensuring new ideas are viable). Given their ability to see problems and access new ideas, these individuals are likely to be located at the periphery or edge of a network or field. By contrast, procedural contributions are

[12] Rimmer et al. 1996, 43.

made by those in positions to provide formal authority, motivation, and money. These are likely to be powerful agents in their own right, located at the center of the network. Maintenance contributions relate to convening and connecting roles that could ostensibly be played by agents in various positions.

Readers are likely to have different perspectives on some of the details in Table 9.3, especially about the likely location of different role players. The salient messages in this table should not be affected by such differences, however:

- Change comes about when multiple functionalities are provided;
- Different functions imply different roles;
- Different roles are likely to be played by different agents at different positions in the network or field slated for change.

These messages combine to underscore the importance of engaging broad groups of agents to facilitate change. It should be emphasized that these include distributed agents who are involved in implementing change. These actors played an important role at the start of a number of the reforms referenced in Table 9.2, providing input about problems and ideas for change. They played one of the more important roles in all cases during implementation, helping keep the focus on problems, experimenting with new ideas, and constantly reworking reform content. These substantive contributions ensured that reforms were grounded in reality, viable, and relevant. Such contributions were made possible by broad-based engagement mechanisms that are vital to effective institutional reform.

The Importance of Mobilizing Functions from Agents

The multiple functions in Table 9.3 reflect what Silvia Dorado calls "resources" that agents provide and which are "integral to change."[13] In noting the importance of such resources, Dorado asks how they can be obtained to facilitate change. She argues that one rarely finds top-down champion-style leaders solving this question effectively. These are the leaders commonly identified in externally influenced institutional reforms, as discussed in Chapters 1 and 5. As Chapter 5 argued, these agents' abilities to force change by edict are routinely weaker than many may assume. Given similar observations, Dorado calls attention to an alternative and more

---

[13] Dorado 2005, 390.

common type of leadership: "More frequently, the diffusion and legitima-tion of new institutional arrangements requires the mobilization of support and acceptance from multiple actors."[14]

Dorado identifies three approaches to mobilization: leveraging, accumu-lating, and convening. Leveraging involves politically skilled agents defining a project and then gaining internal support for and external acceptance of it. There are key agents in this model who initiate change and inspire others to support and participate in the change. Their success is reflected in how effec-tively they engage the functions and resources of a broad set of additional agents, often as motivators and facilitators. Accumulating does not have a key role player but involves a long and probabilistic process whereby new designs emerge and are implemented and diffused through the haphazard interaction of multiple agents. Convening entails the creation of interor-ganizational arrangements that bring different agents, their resources, and functional strengths together to "jumpstart a process of change."[15] This is not focused on specific projects and solutions but on complex problems that defy definition and solution by any individual agent. The key player brings agents together, acting as "the catalytic agent(s) bridging unaware, unsure or skeptical actors to explore the possibilities of cooperation."[16] The key convening player needs to enjoy credibility across many parties, familiarity with the problem being addressed, and a social position that allows many balanced, unbiased engagements.[17]

Dorado posits different conditions under which these three mobilization approaches emerge. Leveraging requires that agents capable of influencing change from a central position can also access alternative ideas to pursue and package these as viable solutions. This requires either a low degree of institutionalization and embeddedness (with what Chapter 3 called weak dominance and the presence of multiple competing alternatives) or con-nections between these influential agents and additional idea providers and translators (as shown in Figure 9.1 and related in Dorado's own exam-ple of change in Bolivia).[18] Accumulation again tends to require a degree of openness, typically occurring in social contexts that allow dynamic and con-structive engagements within and across networks. Convening, by contrast, takes place in contexts beset by complex problems where opportunities for engagement and solutions are not obvious and need to be explored through

[14] Dorado 2005, 390.
[15] Ibid., 391.
[16] Kalegaonkar and Brown 2000, 9.
[17] Ibid.
[18] Dorado 2001.

an interactive process. This process reflects what Chapter 8 described as bricolage, where the active engagement of multiple agents facilitates an expanded set of institutional alternatives (called "referents" by Dorado) to stimulate the emergence of new hybrids.

It is likely that one will find all three approaches arising as relevant in different instances of institutional reform in development. It is also likely, however, that institutional reform in development will be achieved through convening more often than leveraging, which will be more common than accumulation. This is a hypothesis based on discussion in early chapters and on the view that many developing country contexts are characterized by dominant preexisting institutions, deficient sets of viable alternatives, and significantly more complex problems than obvious opportunities or solutions. This hypothesis is supported by evidence in Table 9.2, which shows that the most important leadership function across all twelve reform cases is related to convening and connecting.

Convening agents brought smaller groups of key agents together with direct ties to initiate and guide reform. They did this mostly by hosting formal and informal meetings and gatherings and establishing diverse teams.[19] Connecting agents created indirect ties between other actors to facilitate broad interaction, ensuring that ideas were shared between core groups devising reforms and distributed agents experimenting with new proposals. These connectors were particularly important in implementation, where the role of distributed agents was also greater. It appears that these distributed agents connected to central decision makers through third parties, probably because direct ties were not possible given extant organizational and social structures. Local communities in Rwanda needed third-party coaches to connect to national-level policy makers, for instance, so that both sets of agents could learn about which service delivery experiments were working and why.

These convening and connecting agents accounted for more than 25 percent of named leaders both at the start of reform and in its implementation. Together, these were the only functions identified in both periods and in all cases. There was also a key role for those motivating and inspiring reform, however, especially in early periods. This indicates some leveraging in the mobilization process, although the coexistence of these agents with conveners and connectors suggests that motivation was an insufficient mobilizer. Conveners and connectors were still required, particularly in the implementation period, where the role of motivators was smaller

---

[19] Andrews, McConnell, and Wescott 2008.

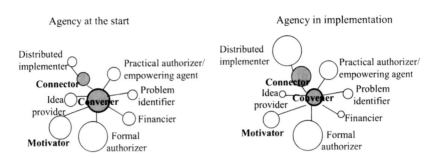

Figure 9.2. Agency functions at the start of reform and during implementation. *Notes:* Circle sizes reflect the frequency that a leader was named as providing a certain function. Based on the author's analysis of data across all twelve cases identified in Tables 9.1 and 9.2.

and the role of connectors grew. This speaks potentially to the importance of third-party ties between agents at the center of fields and networks and those at the periphery. Direct ties between such agents are not common and certainly are not conducive to equal engagement. Peripheral implementers may view centrally located motivators as powerful authoritarians trying to control them – as subordinates – which could foster resistance to change.

Figure 9.2 shows the relative size of these and other functional roles played by leaders across all twelve cases at the start of reform and in implementation. The figure illustrates conveners and connectors as those bringing agents together – as this is what they were explicitly recognized for. Motivators are seen as having an additional function that needed to be mobilized to facilitate change by conveners and connectors.

It is impossible to say whether these figures capture the full story of who mobilized which agents to engage in the twelve reforms. It is likely that mobilization involved a blend of convening, connecting, and motivating in most examples. The salient observation is that these roles were relatively more important than others. Cumulatively, those playing the three mobilizing roles account for 46 percent of the leaders identified at the start of reforms and 39 percent of the leaders identified in implementation. The additional six functions – including provision of formal authority to change, identification of problems and ideas, and experimental implementation with proposed reforms – engaged smaller sets of leaders. These additional functions, it appears, were only bought together because of the mobilization of the conveners, connectors, and motivators. Mobilizing is thus an essential leadership function in any and all institutional reform.

The Role of External Agents in Change Processes

This book focuses partly on externally influenced institutional reform in development. It is pertinent, therefore, to ask what role external agents played in the twelve interventions analyzed – and what relevance this might have for other reforms. The question poses some methodological challenges, especially in defining who an external agent is. Chapters 3 and 5 posited that all actors typically occupy multiple fields, domains, and networks, so that none can be easily identified as an internal or external agent in any one context. Figure 9.1 shows that agents B and E inhabit the gray and clear circles, for instance, potentially being internal to both. Acknowledging this, but seeking simplicity, the current work builds on an approach that identifies external agents as those working in development organizations like the United Nations, World Bank, or IMF. These are the external influencers of reform, with internal agents being government and other actors in the developing countries themselves.

Some clear observations emerge from the twelve cases given this simplified approach. First, external agents are commonly identified as playing important leadership roles in cases where reforms are producing real results, albeit incrementally. They were seen as leaders in all twelve cases. Second, these agents are not the main role players, comprising a minority share of the overall leadership solution in all cases. Altogether, there were 44 references to such agents from about 250 – suggesting that outsiders provide only 20 percent of the functional leadership required for change. Third, the role of external agents is largest when reforms start and diminishes thereafter. External actors accounted for 26 percent of the leaders identified at the start of reform, compared with 12 percent in implementation. Fourth, external agents dominate one role only – the provision of financing in early reform periods. Fifth, external agents collaborate with internal agents to provide a range of other functions, including contributing to reform content and mobilizing agents, but internal actors are the main role players in all of these areas.

The gist of these observations is that external agents do have a role to play in influencing institutional reform, but when reforms are successful this role is often quite marginal. External agents do not provide the primary leadership in defining problems or ideas, as purveyors of best practice reforms might advocate. They are also not the source of authority for change, or the ones who bring implementation know-how to ensure reforms are viable. By contrast, external agents have roles to play in filling missing functions – particularly initial financing. However, it is important to note that providing one functional contribution does not mean having broad influence. For instance, external organizations providing money to the twelve reform initiatives did not commonly tie the money to specific ideas through coercive intervention. Financing supported local ideas in most cases, rather than supporting the introduction of new external ideas.

It is also important that the external agents engaged in these reforms were not wholly outsiders to the reform contexts. In most cases, external agents called leaders were stationed in the country as representatives of bilateral or multilateral agencies. They were known and trusted by local people and seemed to be part of the close working groups that initiated reforms – sometimes even acting as conveners. The research did not go into more depth about their dispositions or backgrounds. It would appear, however, that effective external engagement in institutional reform requires having at least one foot in the grounded reality of the context in which change is being pursued.

REFORM THROUGH BROADLY MOBILIZED AGENTS

This chapter's basic message is that institutional reform, whether externally influenced or not, requires the engagement of a broad set of agents. Individual champions are not enough, and even small groups of centrally located actors are insufficient. Multiple functions are needed to foster an awareness of the need for change, introduce new ideas to drive reform, motivate and authorize adjustment, and more. These functions typically come from different agents at different positions in reform networks. Given this, reforms are likely to emerge and diffuse successfully only where diverse sets of players are mobilized, including elites, peripheral agents, and distributed implementers. This set of players is like the orchestra Lee Kuan Yew argued was behind Singapore's development success. There may have been a central conductor in this orchestra, but the music was a product of many functional contributions by multiple players.

This message stands in contrast to the common approach taken in many institutional reforms in developing countries, described in Chapter 5. This approach advocates reform through narrow champions working with external ideas, demanding that distributed agents implement change by edict. Champions are supermuscular agents in this approach, expected to play multiple roles and fulfill multiple functions. They are like carpenters who source wood, tools, and designs for new pegs, shape the hole into which the pegs are meant to fit, and do the woodwork as well. Distributed agents are simply targets of change, passive responders to top-down commands.

They get to put the peg in place, whether it fits a hole or not. Commonly, champions do not finish the pegs and/or implementers fail to force a fit.

A broad-based approach proposes building communities of agents to engage in making and shaping reform pegs – ultimately ensuring a better fit of these to the holes that need filling. The approach emerges from evidence in twelve reform experiences discussed in this chapter and from theories about network location, functional leadership, and mobilization. The evidence and discussion yields various recommendations about ways to improve externally influenced institutional reform in development:

- *Establish multifunction reform communities, not champions.* Instead of focusing on lone champions, reformers should establish broad-based communities of agents. These are needed to provide the multiple functions required to facilitate change, contributing substance, facilitating procedure, and fostering and maintaining relationships.
- *Cultivate and support mobilizers.* Mobilizers are likely to be more important than the champions commonly considered drivers of change. Motivators, conveners, and connectors facilitate engagements by complex and diverse sets of agents that foster change. They need to be cultivated and supported.
- *External agents should be humble.* External agents should be aware of the limited roles they can play in facilitating institutional change and play these roles as effectively as possible. They have the unique role of providing seed financing for change but should not see this as a reason to dominate other functions.

The last of these recommendations supports the argument that ownership matters in development. The emphasis on ownership has been common in the development community's thinking about institutional reform. A 2000 World Bank strategy document speaks, for instance, about the importance of government being in the driving seat of change.[20] The 2005 Paris Declaration reflected a consensus agreement, by development organizations and developing country governments, that ownership matters. The ownership concept is difficult to deconstruct, however, and lacks sufficient substance to have practical relevance in many cases, where interventions after the Paris Declaration do not look that different from those that came before. Ownership at the start of an intervention means having the minister of finance sign off on proposals. Ownership at the end of an intervention is assessed

---

[20] World Bank 2000a.

by reviewing whether the minister is still supportive of reform. There is seldom any thinking behind what this support looks like when it is sufficient to foster deep change, where it comes from in such instances, or why it is ever forthcoming from deeply embedded political operatives.

This chapter's discussion hopefully addresses such a lack of substance, identifying basic characteristics that seem to equate with real ownership and reforms that foster change – albeit change that is slow and incremental. In so doing, it adds to a growing literature on the topic and a discussion started by David Booth on whether external entities can help build ownership in countries.[21] Given the evidence presented here, it seems that country ownership requires having a group of differently located agents engaged in reform initiation and implementation – not just a powerful minister. Furthermore, ownership implies having members of this group provide different and specific functional contributions, defining the content of change and facilitating the change process. External agents can provide some of these contributions but will be the minority role player providing discrete functions – not defining the content and process as a whole. Internal agents should dominate some roles, however, providing formal authorization for reform and taking responsibility for implementation. Ownership also implies local engagement in key facets of defining problems and finding solutions through a process of mobilization that engages multiple parties rather than one agent who acts as the interface with international actors.

These characteristics are real and demanding. They suggest that ownership requires external actors to pull back and internal agents to push forward in the change process. This may require switching roles in the process and practice of institutional reform in development, which implies changes in the rules of this game. Booth notes that such a change has not been forthcoming in many interventions following the 2005 Paris Declaration – where development organizations committed to pursue necessary adjustments and facilitate country ownership.[22] The next chapter asks whether such change is becoming more likely in the development community over time.

---

[21] Booth 2011.
[22] Ibid.

TEN

Reforming Rules of the Development Game Itself

IS CHANGE POSSIBLE IN THE DEVELOPMENT GAME?

A 2008 evaluation discussed in Chapter 1 asked whether governments improved after World Bank public sector reform projects. Findings were mixed and not altogether convincing.[1] Country Policy and Institutional Assessment (CPIA) scores for governance improved after these projects in about 70 percent of countries but stayed the same or dropped in 30 percent. Public financial management (PFM) scores improved in 62 percent of countries after such reforms but stagnated or fell in nearly 40 percent. Corruption, transparency, and accountability scores improved for 53 percent of the nations with public sector reforms, remaining static or declining in 47 percent. Civil service reforms led to improved quality of public administration scores in 42 percent of countries borrowing for such interventions. Scores were constant or worse in 58 percent of the borrowing nations. Even where progress was observed, most countries registered scores in all these areas that were below levels the CPIA handbook suggests are required to facilitate functional improvements in government – where reforms have "noticeable positive effect on the overall performance of the public sector."[2]

Similarly mixed results have emerged in recent evaluations emanating from international development capitals like Oslo,[3] Washington,[4] London,[5] and Manila.[6] In addition to providing real data to show that externally influenced institutional reforms frequently have limited effects, these studies cite common reasons for this problem. They reference the way many reforms

---

[1] World Bank 2008, 46.
[2] World Bank 2011d, 73.
[3] Norad 2011.
[4] World Bank 2009a.
[5] DFID 2011.
[6] ADB 2009.

ignore context, for instance, promote demanding best practices, and fail to establish broad country-level ownership. *Such narrative resonates with that of this book and supports the argument that institutional reforms in development need to go beyond producing square pegs for round holes.*

The first section of this chapter summarizes such message. It starts by revisiting evidence that many governments do not improve after years of institutional reforms. This is because reforms often follow dominant processes whereby context is largely ignored, poorly fitted best practices are mimetically reproduced, and narrow sets of high-level agents are relied on to champion reform. These interventions commonly yield reforms as signals, where the form of government changes but functionality does not; what you see is not what you get. The section then points out that other reforms show a different way of doing reform, summarized into a new approach called problem-driven iterative adaptation (PDIA). This combines ideas from Chapters 7 through 9, all of which already have some theoretical backing and a practical place in the discussion of development. PDIA proposes that externally influenced institutional reforms should focus on solving problems through a process Chapter 8 described as purposive muddling, incorporating action-based learning by broad sets of agents.

A second section acknowledges that this new approach would itself require institutional change – to the way the international development community pursues institutional reforms in developing countries. It asks whether the current context is likely to facilitate such change. Using a theoretical framework introduced in Chapter 3, this discussion examines the degree of disruption in development's institutional reform field and whether dominant entrenched institutions are weakening, alternatives are available, and influential constituencies exist to advocate for change. In looking at all four factors, one can identify reasons to expect significant change but also see reasons why change will be limited. The skeptical perspective emerges partly from observing the limited change evident in development after prior evaluations of reform results and in the Paris and Accra agreements of 2005 and 2008.

This discussion leads to a concluding section that outlines key steps needed to tip the scale in favor of significant change. These steps focus particularly on changes needed to extant rules of the development game. The current book and PDIA-type reforms it proposes are unlikely to influence behavior if lending rules continue to reward reforms as signals, for instance, or if project preparation processes incentivize a focus on best practice solutions, or if norms make it appropriate to exclude distributed agents from the process of designing interventions. These rules still dominate development and need to be adjusted and deinstitutionalized while new alternative rules – supporting PDIA-type mechanisms – are more aggressively introduced. Such changes will require cognitive shifts in developing countries and development organizations. This is because changes in rules require changes in the way key players think – in this case, about what constitutes success in institutional reform, how quickly it can progress, and who the main role players are.

A SUMMARY OF THIS BOOK'S ARGUMENT

The early chapters of this book tell a particular story about institutional reforms in development. This kind of reform has emerged from nowhere to dominate development dialogue and practice in the last thirty years. Such reforms manifest in similar-looking interventions implemented across highly dissimilar countries. These interventions are, however, producing varying results. Analysis in Chapters 1 and 2 shows that countries often fail to register higher scores on the development community's measures of government effectiveness after decades of expensive reforms sponsored by such community. The disappointing results of these reforms are not easily explained. Countries with poor results have not had systematically lower reform numbers or more unsatisfactory projects, and it does not seem that reforms always have more positive effects over time. Chapter 2 notes that this puzzling evidence points to countries adopting reforms as signals – to garner short-term support from the international community. The problem is that these reforms make governments look better for a few years but do not make governments function better in the long run.

The first column in Table 10.1 summarizes arguments about why these reforms look this way, as discussed in Chapters 3 to 6. These arguments suggest that reforms as signals tend to have similar characteristics that lead to their (often) limited influence. For instance, they typically overlook contextual realities that determine how much change is possible, emphasize best practice interventions beyond the reach of developing countries, and focus on narrow groups of champions that can seldom facilitate implementation and diffusion. Such reforms often produce new laws, systems, and processes that make governments look better. These visible demonstrations of short-term success are commonly supported by narrow groups of concentrated government actors who interface with external development organizations. New laws commonly go unimplemented, however, and new processes are not owned, used or diffused by broadly distributed sets of implementing agents. This means that governments do not get "better" in a

Table 10.1. *Summarizing the book thus far, and introducing PDIA*

Issue	Reforms as Signals	Problem-Driven Iterative Adaptation (PDIA)
Context	*Chapter 3.* Context ignored, or only visible context considered; context seen ex post as constraints	*Chapter 7.* Contextual complexities are revealed and addressed through problem-driven learning
Content	*Chapter 4.* Isomorphic mimicry, where only some (visible) elements of externally defined best practice are mimetically reproduced	*Chapter 8.* Content is found and fitted through purposive muddling involving active, ongoing, and experiential learning and feedback
Agents	*Chapter 5.* Narrow sets of high-level agents are relied on to champion reform; implementation by distributed agents is assumed to happen "by edict"	*Chapter 9.* Broad sets of agents are mobilized into communities of change by conveners, connectors, and motivators, fostering emergence and diffusion of local solutions
Results	*Chapter 6.* Frequent decoupling, where some elements of reform are adopted as signals, but what you see is not what you get and new forms do not improve functionality	*Chapters 7, 8, and 9.* Slow, incremental process whereby localized hybrids emerge to provide functionality needed to solve pressing local problems; new forms may not look impressive, but they function

functional sense after reforms. Although interventions produce results sufficient enough to trigger short-term financial support and even follow-up projects and reforms, what you see is not what you get, and many governments are not ultimately becoming more functional and effective at leading and facilitating development.

The last column in Table 10.1 offers a simplified view on ideas the final chapters offered about doing reform differently to facilitate better (more functional) government. These chapters drew on examples of reforms that seem to be having such impacts, effecting real change in governments and going beyond square pegs in round holes, or reforms as signals. Such reforms have three key dimensions: (i) They facilitate problem-driven learning; (ii) they involve stepwise interventions that allow processes of purposive muddling and action-based learning, which helps change agents see what works, why, and what next steps they should take; and (iii) they engage broad sets of (mostly local) agents providing different functional contributions that ensure reforms are viable and relevant.

When combined, these dimensions yield a potentially new approach to doing reform – PDIA.[7] This approach emphasizes the importance of problems as entry points for change and the reality of iterative process as the means by which change typically transpires. Both of these emphases should already be clear from prior chapters. The idea of adaptation is, however, new, vitally important, and distinctive. Whereas many externally influenced institutional reforms focus on introducing specific rules, PDIA is about building adaptive capacities in developing countries to change as their environments demand such change. These adaptive capacities are more present in some countries than in others, just as in biological species. Biological species that can adapt to environmental changes enjoy more evolutionary success than others. The argument here is similar: countries and governments that can adapt to challenges – without constant external support – are likely to develop more than others. The goal of external support should thus be fostering adaptive capacity through incremental interventions, not just succeeding (on the face of it) in the incremental interventions themselves.

As such, PDIA constitutes a different approach to doing institutional reform in development. Instead of ignoring context in favor of a solutions focus, it emphasizes problems as the entry point to understanding context and the needs and opportunities for change. Instead of fostering demanding and poorly fitted best practices as reform content, it emphasizes facilitating processes of finding and fitting locally relevant solutions to locally felt problems. Instead of assuming that reform ownership comes through narrow sets of champions, it emphasizes building broad groups of agents to diagnose, define, implement, and diffuse change ideas and practices in developing country governments.

While noting the differences between PDIA and common practice, it must be recognized that the fundamental ideas presented here are not novel in the development community; they all have foundations in extant work. For instance, Chapters 7 through 9 used arguments from institutional and organizational theory to argue for a problem-driven, iterative reform approach that engages multiple agents. The chapters also drew on real reform examples to illustrate these dimensions in action from countries as difficult to work in as Pakistan, Rwanda, Indonesia, and Afghanistan. The examples show that externally influenced reforms already offer examples of PDIA-type interventions, albeit often at the margins of larger, more traditional project activities.

---

[7] The term emerges in Andrews, Pritchett, and Woolcock (2012).

Furthermore, the central concepts presented here feature in other work. Brian Levy, Verena Fritz, and Kai Kaiser have long been promoting a problem-driven approach to doing governance work in the World Bank.[8] Levy also emphasizes the need for external organizations to seriously consider context when proposing and designing reforms.[9] Nancy Birdsall and her colleagues at the Center for Global Development have been advocating the use of dynamic processes of finding and fitting reforms for years as well. The idea of "Cash on Delivery Aid" links payments to a specific outcome (solving a problem, for instance) and allows a dynamic, flexible process of finding the solution.[10] Such a flexible, iterative process of finding hybrids is front and center in Nadim Matta's work on Rapid Results interventions as well.[11] This work also touts the message that broad-based agency is required for reform to work, which is reinforced in recent studies by Adrian Leftwich and the Developmental Leadership Program.[12]

HOW MUCH CHANGE SHOULD ONE EXPECT IN THE DEVELOPMENT COMMUNITY?

Many other authors have proposed similar ideas and called for change in the way development organizations seek to influence institutional change in developing countries. The list is long and includes luminaries like Dani Rodrik, Ha-Joon Chang, Bill Easterly, Peter Evans, Merilee Grindle, Lant Pritchett, and Michael Woolcock.[13] These authors' contributions have been augmented by recent publications acknowledging the need for change by development organizations themselves. The 2008 World Bank evaluation referenced in the introduction to this chapter is an example.[14]

It is both humbling and heartening to reflect on this past and current work. One is reminded that very few ideas are new ideas. One is also encouraged that other voices are saying similar things, suggesting a groundswell in favor of new approaches to international development and especially development work involving governance and government capacity building. In observing this groundswell, however, it is important to remember that change in the development community requires adjustments in

---

[8] Fritz, Kaiser, and Levy 2009.
[9] Levy 2010.
[10] CGD 2010.
[11] Matta and Morgan 2011.
[12] Leftwich and Wheeler 2011.
[13] Chang 2003; Easterly 2001; Evans 2004; Grindle 2004; Pritchett and Woolcock 2004.
[14] Rodrik 2007; World Bank 2008.

institutions – rules of the game – which this book argues are stubborn and difficult to change. Acknowledging this, the current section asks how much change one should expect in the development community given the kind of diagnosis provided in this book.

The section employs theory from earlier chapters to address this question, assessing the space for change given four contextual factors introduced in Chapters 3 and 7: (i) the degree of disruption to the institutional reform field; (ii) the strength of dominant incumbents; (iii) the presence and viability of alternatives; and (iv) the activity of potential change agents. In looking at all four factors, one can not only identify reasons to expect significant change but also see reasons to expect more limited change.

Disruption in the Institutional Reform Field

Chapter 3 posited that far-reaching institutional change often happens after disruptions test the legitimacy of incumbents. Chapter 7 noted that such disruptions typically manifest after focal events like crises or when data are used to draw attention to festering problems. These events and data-constructed problems provide new views onto incumbent structures, fostering skeptical reflection that can lead to change.

There are reasons to argue that disruption is currently high in development's institutional reform field. One could point to the 2008 World Bank Independent Evaluation Group Report as a recent trigger of such disruption. As already introduced, this report analyzed the impact World Bank–sponsored reforms had on various aspects of government quality in the 2000s. Although such evaluations were not novel, the 2008 report used data to communicate its results – and the problem – in a new way. Using measures from the World Bank Country Policy and Institutional Assessment (CPIA) indicators, this evaluation showed that many countries failed to improve aspects of government quality even after externally influenced reforms. The proportion of countries seeing post-reform declines or stagnation ranged from 27 percent for measures of "governance"[15] to 58 percent for "quality of public administration."[16]

These data draw attention to the problem of public sector reform failure in development in a way and to a degree that prior qualitative critiques could not. They show in basic numbers that up to 60 percent of countries with public sector reforms in place did not improve scores on indicators

---

[15] World Bank 2008, 38.
[16] World Bank 2008, 46.

of public administration quality. Similar studies also show mixed and disappointing results in a range of other institutional reform areas, including privatization,[17] deregulation,[18] PFM,[19] health system modernization,[20] and financial liberalization.[21] Although data used in these studies are always open to challenge, they all suggest that whereas some countries' governments and markets improve after external reforms, many do not. The current book illustrates this as well. It finds that a majority of countries do not see improved scores on World Governance Indicators (WGIs) or Quality of Governance (QoG) measures after decades of public sector institutional reforms.

Even these data-based stories of failure are not guaranteed to yield change-inducing disruption, however, partly because the analyses are open to fairly easy attack by those resisting change. The 2008 World Bank evaluation notes this clearly, acknowledging that institutional reforms are not easily assessed using empirics.[22] All of the variables employed in these analyses are vulnerable to critique, for instance, given the lack of widely shared measures of external and internal reform activity or of government effectiveness. Given this, one should expect what Valéry Riddle calls "verbal gymnastics," where different stakeholders find reasons to question the evidence and even defend current performance.[23] One would hope that the scope for such gymnastics is decreased through the fact that multiple measures across multiple studies allude to the same problem of poor reform results – even controlling for contextual factors often used to excuse poor performance. The picture is similar whether one looks at CPIA, WGI, QoG, or gross domestic product (GDP) data. *Many institutional reforms do not seem to make governments function better.*

Other verbal gymnastics could arise, however, to dampen the disruptive influence of such data, focused on expectations of reforms and other potential measures of success. For example, the data discussed may not cause disruption for those who consider a 30 percent to 50 percent success rate good for externally influenced institutional reforms. This compares favorably with success rates in the venture capital industry and small business development, for instance, where some might argue that interventions are

---

[17] Boubakri, Cosset, and Guedhami 2009.
[18] Busenitz, Gomez, and Spencer 2000.
[19] Andrews 2011a; de Renzio, Andrews, and Mills 2010.
[20] World Bank 2009a.
[21] Karikari 2010; Obstfeld 2009.
[22] World Bank 2008, 35–36.
[23] Riddle 2009, 944.

similarly risky and uncertain.[24] If this is the expectation for institutional reform in development, it allows organizations and agents involved to use the excuse presented in Chapter 1, of a carpenter successful at producing a glut of pegs that do not fit the many holes needing filling. Such a carpenter may get away with saying, "It would be great if all the pegs fit into all the holes, but give me some credit for what I have done. Look at all the nice pegs I have created, and remember that some of the holes were filled by the pegs. I am sure more pegs will fit more holes in time."

This message seems to be working in the development arena, given evidence of unabated growth in the rollout of institutional reforms. As discussed in Chapter 1, organizations like the World Bank have seen a steadily increasing portfolio of these projects since the 1970s. Project numbers rose from 469 in the 1980s (20 percent of all loans)[25] to 1,700 in the 1990s (62 percent) to 3,235 in the 2000s (65 percent). Reform influence has grown in monetary terms as well, tracking the increased average dollar value of World Bank investment loans (from $80 million before 1999 to $94 million between 2003 and 2008).[26] Total lending volumes for public sector management reforms alone increased from an average annual inflation-adjusted total of $1.8 billion during the 1990s to $2.7 billion in the 2000s.[27] Demand was not dampened after 2008, even with the World Bank evaluation's finding of weak reform results. More than 70 percent of new projects since this time have incorporated some aspect of institutional reform, with an average loan size of $172 million.[28] Nearly $3.6 billion was committed to public sector reform in 2010 alone.[29]

Such evidence suggests that demand for institutional reforms has grown substantially in the last decade and continues to grow despite studies showing limited and mixed results. This increased demand – and expansion in loan numbers and amounts – is not a trivial measure of success for many development organizations, especially those with words like "bank" and

---

[24] Laine and Torstila (2005) find that venture capital success rates are about 30 percent.

[25] These figures reflect analysis in Chapter 1.

[26] These statistics were calculated by the author on the basis of projects in the World Bank projects database as of February 2012. There were 11,869 investment projects in the database at this time.

[27] World Bank 2012, 2.

[28] As discussed in Chapter 1, PAL&J sector spending has been part of 46% of all World Bank projects. This shows a rise in recent years, given that these projects made up 39 percent of the projects started when Moloney (2009) did her study. More than 70 percent of projects approved since Moloney's study had PAL&J content. The $172 million figure is an average of investment project size in the post-2008 period, as calculated from information in the World Bank database.

[29] World Bank 2012, 1.

"fund" in their titles.[30] It may, in fact, be the dominant measure of success for these organizations and for many developing country governments that accede to reforms as signals to ensure continued financial support. These organizations and countries are likely to take data showing limited reform impact with a pinch of salt, given the obviously positive demand and growth in this "industry." They are especially likely to take this position, given that internal measures of reform quality are overwhelmingly positive. For example, project evaluations typically show that more than three-quarters of funded projects are completed satisfactorily, which lets development organizations report that they are responding to growing demand with generally satisfactory supply.[31] What these satisfactory evaluations tend to mean, however, is simply that projects disbursed anticipated funds against anticipated sets of activities, producing anticipated inputs. The problem is that these inputs, activities, and fund flows frequently fail to yield better government and market structures. This failure is only a disruptive problem, however, if better government is the end goal.

Dominant and Alternative Mechanisms in the Institutional Reform Field

There is thus a mixed story on whether and to what extent development's institutional reform community is currently facing change-inducing disruption. The story is similar with regard to the presence and strength of extant rules of the game and potential alternatives to them. In some respects, preexisting rules seem weakened, given a swathe of studies criticizing common approaches to doing reform. As discussed, a number of sources criticize the way dominant processes lead reformers to ignore context, foster best practices, and introduce reforms with limited country ownership. These weaknesses have even been identified in recent studies emerging from multilateral and bilateral organizations. The 2008 World Bank public sector evaluation is one example, as are the 2009 World Bank assessment of health sector reforms,[32] the 2008 Accra Agenda for Action,[33] and the 1998 and 2006 Asian Development Bank reviews of governance projects.[34]

---

[30] A short list yields the International Monetary Fund, World Bank, Inter-American Development Bank, Asian Development Bank, African Development Bank, and European Bank for Reconstruction and Development.

[31] World Bank 2008.

[32] World Bank 2009a.

[33] Accra Agenda for Action, http://siteresources.worldbank.org/ACCRAEXT/Resources/4700790-1217425866038/AAA-4-SEPTEMBER-FINAL-16h00.pdf.

[34] Asian Development Bank 2006.

These documents call for change to various dimensions of the traditional approach to doing reform, as shown in Table 10.1. They also recommend alternatives similar to those reflected in the four dimensions of PDIA, also illustrated in Table 10.1. For instance, a variety of authors have proposed ways of better considering context in reform design and of pursuing incremental change through projects. These alternative approaches have also been adopted in the development arena already, as shown in the positive examples of health care reforms in Chapter 7, the narrative on decentralization in Rwanda in Chapter 8, and the twelve cases of reform through broader ownership in Chapter 9. For example, Rwanda's decentralization initiative was supported initially through a 1998 World Bank project using the novel and flexible Learning and Innovation Loan (LIL) instrument. This allowed the reform to emerge in a stepwise fashion, emphasizing learning as a key goal instead of mimetic best practice reproduction.

This kind of mechanism has not emerged as a strong alternative to dominant rules of project preparation and execution, however, but rather occupies a marginalized position in the field. This is evident when one considers that LILs have been used in fewer than 2 percent of World Bank investment projects since the instrument was introduced in 1998.[35] More than two-thirds of all these innovative and flexible projects were initiated before 2001 as well, meaning that only forty-five LIL projects were initiated in the last ten years of more than four thousand projects (comprising fewer than 1 percent of the investment loans in this period). More than 90 percent of the projects in this period used the traditional Specific Investment Loan (SIL) and Technical Assistance Loan (TAL) instruments.

It is hard to know exactly why preexisting instruments continue to dominate, but one reason may relate to their relative value. The average LIL carried a value of about $5 million (which is, in fact, a limit) compared with more than $150 million for other investment projects. This is a significant difference, especially in organizations like regional and multilateral development banks, where units and individuals are assessed according to the amount of money they move and internal budgets are tied to the size of loan portfolios. These banking-style rules are arguably the dominant rules of the game in places like the World Bank and create incentives to pursue larger, simpler projects. The 2006 Asian Development Bank review on governance

---

[35] The data here are drawn from the World Bank project database in an exercise by the author in January 2012. A total of 151 LILs had been initiated since 1998 of about 5,900 projects (5,126 investment loans and 779 development policy loans). The average LIL was valued at about $5 million, whereas the average investment loan in this period was about $150 million and the average development policy loan was about $175 million.

projects refers to a similar incentive in noting that staff are rewarded based on the size and number of loans they process.[36]

Preexisting rules of the game continue to dominate in other ways as well. Decades-old processes of selecting, preparing, and implementing projects still prevail in many organizations.[37] The 2006 Asian Development Bank review refers to this as the "culture of project approvals."[38] Processes embedding such culture typically require detailed planning and programming before reforms are approved or initiated and provide limited room for adjustment once projects become active. Budgets associated with these projects tend to mirror this emphasis, providing more resources for preparing interventions than for engaging in implementation stages. These processes were designed in the 1970s and 1980s, primarily for infrastructure projects in which technical solutions could be locked in and the quality of a project depended largely on how carefully it was prepared. These processes are not appropriate for institutional reforms, however, especially when one accepts that these involve more than changing technical regulative mechanisms. Preprogramming and forced linearity make it difficult to unearth context-specific normative and cultural-cognitive realities or facilitate the iterative processes of finding and fitting contextually relevant ways of improving such. These processes are particularly problematic in settings where contextual factors are opaque, intractable problems are common, resources are limited, and the isomorphic incentive to pursue reforms as signals is intense. In such situations, dominant project preparation and implementation requirements are likely to yield overambitious reform designs and routine failure in reform implementation.

The pressure to preprogram reform content embeds a solutions-based approach to reform design, undermining the alternative idea of problem-driven change. Projects are unlikely to gain approval if they help construct problems and propose the first steps toward finding solutions to such, or build incrementally on past steps and past lessons. Rather, extant processes force project designers to specify what the solutions are – even if they do not detail the problems needing resolution. This foster a best practice orientation in reform designs as well, given that these offer the most legitimate form of solution available. Projects are more likely to be approved if they promise

---

[36] Asian Development Bank 2006, 34, 47.
[37] For examples, see project cycles of the Inter-American Development Bank and World Bank, http://www.iadb.org/en/projects/preparation,1270.html and http://web.worldbank.org/WBSITE/EXTERNAL/PROJECTS/PROCUREMENT/0,,contentMDK:20109658~pagePK:84269~piPK:60001558~theSitePK:84266,00.html.
[38] Asian Development Bank 2006, 47.

interventions that have a best practice stamp of approval, for instance. A 2012 World Bank public sector strategy document identifies the promise of such legitimacy as a reason for the "continuing attraction of best practices" in public sector institutional reform agendas.[39] It notes that best practice still dominates reform agendas despite a 2000 World Bank strategy that declared the need for "best fit" reforms.

The discussion on best practice in this 2012 strategy amounts to an admission that such practices still dominate reform engagements, despite past promises to pursue best fit. The strategy could go further in explaining why best practices are still so dominant, however. This could include identifying ways in which the development community has actually reinforced a predisposition toward best practice solutions since 2000. The construction and use of indicators stands out as an obvious example of the way this has been done. CPIAs, WGIs, *Doing Business* indicators, and Public Expenditure and Financial Accountability (PEFA) indicators are among many that gained great prominence in the 2000s. As discussed in Chapter 1, donors use these indicators to assess the quality of developing country governments, determine lending decisions, and identify reform content. It is also common to find ministers of finance in developing countries choosing PFM reforms to improve scores on PEFA indicators. Ministers of industry also spend time and money on interventions aimed at improving their country's *Doing Business* ranking.

In specifying good practices and making such specifications the basis of a large part of reform dialogue, the development community has used indicators (implicitly or explicitly) to buttress preexisting cognitive and normative institutional scripts favoring a best practice orientation. Consider some of the messages one could take from the mere fact that the World Bank and other donor organizations define a set of indicators called the "critical dimensions of good international practice"[40]: "We know the problems, and these are the solutions"; "It does not matter the context, these 'good practices' will fit"; "If you want legitimacy, this is the way to go"; and "If you want our support, here is what you should do."

The technical nature of these indicators and the project preparation processes underpinning institutional reforms also undermine the goal of building deep and broad country ownership around and through reforms.

---

[39] World Bank 2012, 15.
[40] The wording here draws from formal descriptions of the PEFA indicators, but equivalent language is commonly used to introduce and describe other prominent indicators, giving them an immediate legitimacy.

Kate Kenny identifies the development community's imposition of technical processes and prepackaged solutions as one of the ways it defines "the other," for instance, excluding local people from key decisions.[41] Lorrae van Kerkhoff observes similarly that solutions emerging from development organizations – and embodied in indicators – are routinely identified by Westerners.[42] Their complexity institutionalizes a metaphoric wall prohibiting access of non-Westernized agents to the development process. This results in a continued overreliance on a few developing country interlocutors in the reform process who can "talk Western." These are often associated with the champions discussed in Chapter 5, at least to outsiders who assume their endless influence and stamina. Sarah Lucas references the institutionalized dependence on such in bemoaning the way officials from the United States' Millennium Challenge Corporation (MCC) undermined efforts to build broad ownership in Mozambique.[43] She writes, "Top public sector managers that have the confidence of the donor community are often pulled in many directions [but] human resource constraints are real, and . . . in the process of fostering 'ownership' . . . the MCC may exacerbate constraints that all poor countries struggle with daily."

Agents of Change in the Institutional Reform Field

As already argued, many voices have criticized the development community and those responsible for designing and introducing institutional reforms in developing countries. These voices are predominantly academic and sometimes seem more focused on generating public debate than on fostering new ideas.[44] These debates have, however, bought the problems of institutional reform and aid into the mainstream of development thinking – and beyond – and opened avenues for new ideas to emerge. This book shows how these ideas can be combined into a potentially new approach – PDIA – to inform change across the field.

There are agents beyond these academics who are advocating for change, however. The last decade has seen actors from the more powerful organizations and capitals of development engaging in regular discussions about

[41] Kenny 2008.
[42] Van Kerkhoff 2006.
[43] Mozambique: Field Report, http://www.cgdev.org/section/initiatives/_active/assistance/mcamonitor/fieldreports/mozambiquefield.
[44] The 2009 debate between Dambisa Moya, Bill Easterly, and Jeffrey Sachs is a good example. It attracted significant attention outside the conventional realms of development theory and practice and is summarized at http://www.huffingtonpost.com/kristi-york-wooten/the-sachs-moyo-easterly-a_b_210473.html.

their own failures. They have convened to pursue such reflections four times since 2002, in the High Level Fora on Aid Effectiveness. Meetings in Rome (2002), Paris (2005), Accra (2008), and Busan (2011) have seen active debate about what aid effectiveness means and how it can be achieved. Such gatherings were instigated because of the "need to understand why aid was not producing the development results everyone wanted to see" and have led to a set of principles intended to guide the activities of development organizations and developing countries.[45]

There is active debate on the degree to which these meetings have facilitated more effective development engagements. Many agree that they have led to new agreements and dialogue, but real action is still lacking. For instance, an evaluation preceding the 2011 Busan meeting shows that only one of the thirteen reform targets identified in Paris in 2005 was met in the subsequent six years.[46] "The Evaluation also found that Accra has attracted little political attention and action on implementation." The biggest problem, it seems, is that agreements in these meetings are voluntary and nonbinding. This means that some agents are present to advocate for change but others are not present or are not present sufficiently to commit to these changes. Those present include agents identifying the need for change, agents producing ideas on which change might be based, and even agents convening ever-increasing groups to promote change. Those absent are the agents who authorize change within development organizations and in developing countries and the implementers of projects in which change ultimately needs to be reflected. Without these agents, it is unlikely that change can move beyond discussions and into real action.

CONCLUSION: TIPPING THE SCALE IN FAVOR OF CHANGE

This book has examined the effectiveness of institutional reforms in development. It argues that these reforms regularly fail to achieve the goals of better governments and markets in developing countries. Indeed, many countries have worse government effectiveness scores, as measured by external organizations like the World Bank, after decades of reforms influenced by the same external organizations. The book posits that this failure is largely

---

[45] This quote is taken from the Organization for Economic Coordination and Development's description of the high-level fora, http://www.oecd.org/document/63/0,3746,en_2649_3236398_46310975_1_1_1_1,00.html.

[46] These are comments from the civil society group AID Watch, based on official evaluations of past actions, http://www.ukan.org.uk/fileadmin/user_upload/09_AW_paper_on_1st_BOD_FINAL.pdf.

attributed to the way institutional reforms are designed and implemented. They are often pursued as signals introduced with insufficient attention to contextual complexities – as poorly fitted best practices by overly narrow groups of agents. The result is a glut of square peg reforms in round-hole governments – laws that are not implemented and systems that are not used in governments that still lack basic functionality years (and billions of dollars) after the laws and systems have been adopted.

The book proposes a new approach, PDIA, to doing institutional reform in developing countries, intended to foster more effective results. PDIA calls for interventions that address context-specific problems through stepwise processes of purposive muddling by broad groups of mostly local agents. This approach builds on ideas various commentators have previously raised as ways of improving institutional reform. Many of the ideas have even been "adopted" by development organizations to improve their interventions. Evidence shows that these ideas are not easily implemented, however, given the challenge of reforming rules of the game in the development field itself.

This chapter examined four factors expected to affect how much change the institutional reform field is likely to accept in coming years. It suggests that there are reasons to expect significant change given disruptive problems, acknowledged weaknesses in extant structures, the presence of viable alternatives, and growing calls for reform. It also notes that change could be limited, however. The disruptive problems could be ignored; "weak" incumbents have proven resistant to change before; viable alternatives may be marginalized (as in the past); and there are missing change agents to authorize and implement change. These perspectives are summarized in Table 10.2. They stand as equally weighty sides of a scale. The final column shows ideas about how the scale might be tilted to facilitate significant change.

The first step needed to facilitate significant change involves changing the money rules in development. It is important to ensure that these reforms are not allowed to continue as signals that simply facilitate financial flows. It is a problem that project numbers and values continue to grow while evidence of project effectiveness is being questioned, and it is highly likely that many projects approved today will fail tomorrow. To counter this, institutional reforms need to be judged according to the way in which they foster more effective and functional government, and financial support offered in relation to these reforms should be tied to such results. This means asking simple questions of reforms: Are new problems being identified and constructed, using data, to provoke action? Are stepwise reforms being introduced to address problems, or are they building on prior steps? Is there

Table 10.2. *Facilitating significant change in the development field*

Factor influencing change	What suggests change may be significant	What suggests change may be limited	Facilitating significant change
Severity of disruption	"The field is disrupted!" Data shows reforms often do not lead to better governments	"What disruption?" Demand is high, growing, money is moving, most projects are satisfactory	Change money rules to reward better functionality, not form-based mimicry
Strength of dominant logic	"The past approach has been weakened." Many criticize the same tendencies: to ignore context, push best practice, focus on narrow champions	"The past approach gives a strong foundation." Recent activities reinforce preexisting approaches, embedding best practices, for instance, as the basis for interventions	Force reflection on preexisting structures (Create hurdles for retaining entrenched institutions) Deinstitutionalize extant institutions where they get in the way
Evidence of alternative logics	"Alternatives exist and are viable replacements." New approaches, like PDIA, are practically viable, more appropriate	"Alternatives are in place already, but at the margin." Many elements of new approaches, like flexible loans, are hardly used	Incentivize the use of new approaches: reward problem construction, stepwise reform, creation of reform communities
Activity of change agents	"Agents exist at the periphery, identifying problems, new ideas." The problems are clear, and agents have ideas to inform change	"Agents at the center support preexisting institutions." Those needed to authorize and implement change have shown a limited appetite for reform	Strengthen alternative authorizers; Introduce and empower new players

evidence of short-term lessons about what works and why? Are reform communities being developed, combining agents providing the functions necessary to achieve change?

The idea is to reward developing country governments for gradually becoming more functional and adaptive. Cash on Delivery Aid[47] is a useful

---

[47] CGD 2010.

starting point here, as long as the "delivery" focus is problem driven and donors are willing to reward small-step achievements and the learning associated with them. Mechanisms like Cash on Delivery Aid will only be effectively implemented when the development community changes its thinking about what constitutes success in institutional reform, however. A functional, adaptive orientation is unlikely to emerge while success is measured through project numbers or promises to adopt new best practice forms (like laws and processes).

A second step needed to tilt the scale in favor of significant change involves challenging dominant institutional incumbents (those rules of the game that pre-exist). These include the processes that institutionalize an ignorance of context, tendency to adopt best practice, and reliance on champions. Because these rules of the game are likely embedded in extant processes, it is important to create high hurdles for agents resisting change. Project leaders should be required to defend solution-based interventions introducing best practices, for instance, and all manifestations of good, better, or best practice should be subjected to stringent tests. The 2008 World Bank evaluation raises useful ideas in this respect, calling for guidance on where "Chilean or Nordic" solutions will and will not work, and "what pace of progress" one should expect from such reforms, "given the initial conditions in a country."[48] Beyond setting up these hurdles to the use of best practices, development organizations should take steps to deinstitutionalize processes and systems that constrain flexibility. Common project preparation processes have been identified as one such rule, as has the tendency of development organizations to link budgets to the value of projects. It is extremely difficult to imagine change toward a PDIA-type approach in the presence of processes that incentivize actors to focus on large, preprogrammed, solution-based projects or that impose a false linearity on the design and implementation of reforms.

Just as entrenched rules of the game must be deinstitutionalized, it is also important to take steps that institutionalize new alternatives. This requires creating new rules that require and incentivize the use of PDIA-type processes. Governments and agents in development organizations should be rewarded for constructing new problems, fostering purposive muddling, facilitating learning, and convening reform groups. Project preparation and implementation processes could be explicitly designed to facilitate this, and resources could be made available in appropriate ways. Development organizations might consider creating institutional reform trust funds in

[48] World Bank 2008, 68, 71.

different regions, for instance, managed by boards of directors drawn from affected countries and disbursing resources to support problem-driven reform requests. More flexible, problem-driven funding streams could be provided to allow problem identification and stepwise implementation and assistance in the form of PDIA mechanisms like rapid results management. Problem identification and analysis tools could be mainstreamed throughout the development field as well, provided whenever a country asks for assistance in tackling institutional reforms.

Finally, reforms to the processes of development will require more support by agents empowered to authorize change. It seems as though actors involved in authorizing and negotiating development interventions are satisfied with the status quo. If a new approach is to take root, more skeptical agents will be required to lead interventions, with a greater appetite for incremental change and problem-driven interventions and bricolaged solutions that may look strange but work. It is likely that some of these agents will need to hail from developing countries themselves, but even here it is important to choose those who have not mastered the art of isomorphic mimicry and reforms as signals. One of the more interesting developments at Busan's 2011 development forum involved the role of new donors like China and India. These entities are moving from their initial focus on infrastructure and commodities investments in developing countries to focus on issues of governance and institutional reform.[49] One imagines that these new players, if empowered, might bring a new message and approach to institutional reform in development. They may even provide the authority and implementation energy needed to facilitate change toward a more flexible approach to such reform.

These steps are required to ensure that more reforms go beyond being square pegs in round holes and facilitate the emergence of more functional governments in more developing countries. There is a danger that even these steps will not yield this shift, however, if they themselves become reforms as signals. Each step will likely make a difference only if it is a product of new thinking in the development community – about the goals of institutional reform and the importance of contextual factors, problems, and broad local engagement in the change process. *As proposed earlier and argued in Chapter 3, changes in thinking foster changes in rules. It is hoped that this book provokes both.*

---

[49] Andrews 2012a.

References

African Development Bank. (2012). *Governance Strategic Directions and Action Plan 2008–2012*. Tunis: African Development Bank.

Ahrens, J. (2001). Governance, Conditionality and Transformation in Post-Socialist Countries. In H. Hoen (Ed.). *Good Governance in Central and Eastern Europe*. Cheltenham: Edward Elgar, 54–90.

Aldrich, H. E., and Fiol, M. (1994). Fools Rush In? The Institutional Context of Industry Creation. *Academy of Management Review* 19(4), 645–670.

Alesina, A. F., and Perotti, R. (1999). Budget Deficits and Budget Institutions. In J. M. Poterba and J. von Hagen (Eds.). *Fiscal Institutions and Fiscal Performance*. Chicago: University of Chicago Press, 13–36.

Anders, G. (2002). Like Chameleons. Civil Servants and Corruption in Malawi. *Bulletin de l'APAD*, 23–24, 2–19.

Anderson, C., and Bammer, G. (2005). Measuring the Global Research Environment: Information Science Challenges for the 21st Century. Proceedings of the American Society for Information Science and Technology, Charlotte, NC: Digital Library of Information Science and Technology.

Andrews, M. (2006). Beyond Best Practice and Basics First in Adopting Performance Budgeting Reform. *Public Administration and Development* 26(2), 147–161.

Andrews, M. (2008). The Good Governance Agenda. Beyond Indicators Without Theory. *Oxford Development Studies* 36(4), 379–407.

Andrews, M. (2010). Good Government Means Different Things in Different Countries. *Governance* 23(1), 7–35.

Andrews, M. (2011a). Which Organizational Attributes Are Amenable to External Reform? An Empirical Study of African Public Financial Management. *International Public Management Journal* 14(2), 131–156.

Andrews, M. (2011b). Examining World Bank Project Documents. Paper prepared for the Public Sector Group, World Bank. Washington, DC: World Bank.

Andrews, M. (2012a). Developing Countries Will Follow Post-crisis OECD Reforms but Not Passively This Time. *Governance* 25(1), 103–127.

Andrews, M. (2012b). The Logical Limits of Best Practice Administrative Reform in Developing Countries. *Public Administration and Development* 32(2), 137–197.

Andrews, M. (2012c). World Bank Public Sector Reforms: 75% Similar, 50% Effective. Paper presented at 2012 Conference of the International Research Society on Public Management. Rome, April 11, 2012.

Andrews, M., McConnell, J., and Wescott, A. (2010). *Development as Leadership Led Change*. Washington, DC: World Bank.

Andrews, M., Pritchett, L., and Woolcock, M. (2012). Escaping Capability Traps through Problem Driven Iterative Adaptation (PDIA). *Center for International Development Working Paper 239*. Cambridge, MA: Center for International Development.

Andrews, M., and Turkewitz, J. (2005). Introduction to Symposium on Budgeting and Financial Reform Implementation. *International Journal of Public Administration* 28(3–4), 203–211.

Asian Development Bank. (2006). *Review of the Implementation of ADB's Governance and Anticorruption Policies*. Manila: ADB.

Asian Development Bank. (2009). *ADB Support for Public Sector Reforms in the Pacific: Enhance Results through Ownership, Capacity, and Continuity*. Manila: ADB.

Asian Development Bank. (2011). *2011 Development Effectiveness Review*. Manila: ADB.

Ashworth, R., Boyne, G., and Delbridge, R. (2007). Escape from the Iron Cage? Organizational Change and Isomorphic Pressures in the Public Sector. *Journal of Public Administration, Research and Theory* 19, 165–187.

Bacharach, S., and Mundell, B. (1993). Organizational Politics in School: Micro, Macro, and Logics of Action. *Educational Administration Quarterly* 29(9), 423–452.

Bahl, R. (2000). *Intergovernmental Transfers in Developing and Transition Countries: Principles and Practice*. Washington, DC: World Bank.

Baker, T., and Nelson, R. E. (2005). Creating Something from Nothing: Resource Construction through Entrepreneurial Bricolage. *Administrative Science Quarterly* 50, 329–366.

Bagdadli, S., and Paolini, C. (2005). The Institutional Change of Italian Public Museums Between Legitimacy and Efficiency: Do Museum Directors Have a Role? Mimeo .neumann.hec.ca/aimac2005/PDF_Text/BagdaliS_PaolinoC.pdf.

Barnett, W., and Carroll, G. (1995). Modeling Internal Organizational Change. *Annual Review of Sociology* 21, 217–236.

Bartunek, J. M., and Moch, M. K. (1987). First-Order, Second-Order, and Third-Order Change and Organization Development Interventions: A Cognitive Approach. *Journal of Applied Behavioral Science* 23(4), 483–500.

Battilana, J., Leca, B., and Boxenbaum, E. (2009). Agency and Institutions: A review of Institutional Entrepreneurship. *Academy of Management Annals* 3, 65–107.

Barzelay, M., and Gallego, R. (2006). From "New Institutionalism" to "Institutional Processualism": Advancing Knowledge about Public Management Policy Change. *Governance* 19(4), 531–557.

Becker, G. S. (2002). Deficit Spending Got Argentina into This Mess. *Business Week* (February 11), 26.

Benton, A. (2009). What Makes Strong Federalism Seem Weak? Fiscal Resources and Presidential-Provincial Relations in Argentina. *Publius: The Journal of Federalism* 39(4), 651–676.

Blustein, P. (2006). *And the Money Kept Rolling In: The World Bank, Wall Street, the IMF, and the Bankrupting of Argentina*. New York: Perseus.

Bolongaita, E. (2010). An Exception to the Rule? Why Indonesia's Anti-Corruption Commission Succeeds Where Others Don't – A Comparison with the Philippines' Ombudsman. *U4 Issue*, August 2010, No. 4. Norway: U4 Anti-Corruption Resource Center, Chr. Michelsen Institute.

Bonvecchi, A. (2010). The Political Economy of Fiscal Reform in Latin America: The Case of Argentina. *Inter-American Development Bank Working Paper No. IDB-WP-175.* Washington, DC: IADB.

Booth, D. (2011). Aid Effectiveness: Bringing Country Ownership (and Politics) Back In. *Overseas Development Institute Working Paper 336.* London: ODI.

Boubakri, N., Cosset, J. C., and Guedhami, O. (2009). From State to Private Ownership: Issues from Strategic Industries. *Journal of Banking and Finance* 33(2), 367–379.

Bourdieu, P. (1977) Cultural Reproduction and Social Reproduction. In J. Karabel and A. H. Halsey (Eds.). *Power and Ideology in Education.* New York: Oxford University Press, 487–511.

Braun, M. (2006). *The Political Economy of Debt in Argentina, or Why History Repeats Itself.* Washington, DC: World Bank.

Braun, M., and Gadano, N. (2007). What Are Fiscal Rules For? A Critical Analysis of the Argentine Experience. *Cepal Review* 91 (April). Argentina: Centre for the Implementation of Public Policies Promoting Equity and Growth.

Bräutigam, D., and Knack, S. (2004). Foreign Aid, Institutions, and Governance in Sub-Saharan Africa, *Economic Development and Cultural Change* 52(2), 255–286.

Bruton, G. D., and Ahlstrom, D. (2003). An Institutional View of China's Venture Capital Industry – Explaining the Differences between China and the West. *Journal of Business Venturing* 18, 233–259.

Buehler, M. (2009). Of Gecko's and Crocodiles: Evaluating Indonesia's Corruption Eradication Efforts. Presentation at CSIS/USINDO, Washington, DC, November 23, 2009.

Busenitz, L. W., Gomez, C., and Spencer, J. W. 2000. Country Institutional Profiles: Unlocking Entrepreneurial Phenomena. *Academy of Management Journal* 43(5), 994–1003.

Büthe, T. (2002). Taking Temporality Seriously: Modeling History and the Use of Narratives as Evidence. *American Political Science Review* 96(3), 481–493.

Cabral, L., and Fernandes, F. (2003). *Experiência com o Cenário Fiscal de Médio Prazo em Moçambique e Opções para o seu Desenvolvimento Futuro,* FoPOS project, National Directorate of Planning and Budget, Ministry of Planning and Finance, July. Maputo: Government of Mozambique.

Cameron, K. S. (1986). Effectiveness as Paradox: Consensus and Conflict in Conceptions of Organizational Effectiveness. *Management Science* 32, 539–553.

Campbell, J. L. (2004). *Institutional Change and Globalization.* Princeton, NJ: Princeton University Press.

Cavanagh, J., and Gustafsson, A. (2009). *SISTAFE at the Crossroads.* Report of 7th Mission. Maputo: SISTAFE Quality Assurance Group.

Center for Global Development. (2010). *Cash on Delivery: A New Approach to AID.* Washington, DC: Center for Global Development.

Chan, N. (2010). Narrative Change and Its Microfoundations: Problem Management, Strategic Manipulation, and Information Processing. Paper presented at the Workshop in Political Theory and Policy Analysis, Indiana University-Bloomington, April 3, 2010.

Chang, H. J. (1998). Korea: The Misunderstood Crisis. *World Development* 26(8), 1555–1561.

Chang, H. J. (2003). Kicking Away the Ladder: Infant Industry Promotion in Historical Perspective 1. *Oxford Development Studies* 31(1), 21–32.

Cheibub, J. A., Gandhi, J., and Vreeland, J. R. (2010). Democracy and Dictatorship Revisited. *Public Choice* 143(1–2), 67–101.

Chirambo, R. (2009). Corruption, Tribalism and Democracy: Coded Messages in Wambali Mkandawire's Popular Songs in Malawi. *Critical Arts: A Journal of North-South Cultural Studies* 23(1), 42–63.

Chisinga, B. (2003). Lack of Alternative Leadership in Democratic Malawi: Some Reflections Ahead of the 2004 General Elections. *Nordic Journal of African Studies* 12(1), 1–22.

Christensen, T., and Lægreid, P. (2003). Administrative Reform Policy: The Challenge of Turning Symbols into Practice. *Public Organization Review* 3(1), 3–27.

Cooper, D. J., and Robson, K. (2006). Accounting, Professions and Regulation: Locating the Sites of Professionalization. *Accounting, Organizations and Society* 31, 415–444.

Covaleski, M., and Dirsmith, M. (1988). An Institutional Perspective on the Rise, Social Transformation, and Fall of a University Budget Category. *Administrative Science Quarterly* 33, 562–587.

Cullen, T. (1994). *Malawi: A Turning Point.* Edinburgh: The Pentland Press.

Czarniawska-Jorges, B., and Jacobsson, B. (1989). Budget in a Cold Climate. *Accounting, Organizations and Society* 12 (1–2), 29–39.

Dacin, M. T., Goodstein, J., and Scott, W. R. (2002). Institutional Theory and Institutional Change: Introduction to the Special Research Forum. *Academy of Management Journal* 45(1), 45–57.

Dambrin, C., Lambert, C., and Sponem, S. (2007). Control and Change – Analysing the Process of Institutionalization. *Management Accounting Research* 18, 172–208.

Denzau, A. T., and North, D. C. (1994). Shared Mental Models: Ideologies and Institutions. *Kyklos* 47(1), 3–31.

de Renzio, P. (2008). Taking Stock: What Do PEFA Assessments Tell Us about PFM Systems Across Countries? *Overseas Development Institute Working Paper* 302. http://www.odi.org.uk/resources/download/3333.pdf.

de Renzio, P. (2011). Can Donors "Buy" Better Governance? The Political Economy of Budget Reforms in Mozambique. *IESE Working Paper no. 9/2011.* Instituto de Estudos Sociais e Economicos (IESE). Maputo: IESE.

de Renzio, P., Andrews, M., and Mills, Z. (2010). Evaluation of Donor Support to Public Financial Management (PFM) Reform in Developing Countries: Analytical Study of Quantitative Cross-Country Evidence. Study of Public Financial Management reform for African Development Bank. http://www.afdb.org/fileadmin/uploads/afdb/Documents/Evaluation-Reports/EvaluationDonorSupportPFMReformDevelopingCountries.pdf.

de Renzio, P., and Dorotinsky, W. (2007). *Tracking Progress in the Quality of PFM Systems in HIPCs.* Washington, DC: The PEFA Secretariat.

de Renzio, P., and Hanlon, J. (2009). Mozambique. Contested Sovereignty? The Dilemmas of Aid Dependence. In L. Whitfield (Ed.). *The Politics of Aid: African Strategies for Dealing with Donors.* Oxford: Oxford University Press, 246–270.

Department for International Development. (2010). *DFID in 2009–2010.* London: DFID.

Department for International Development. (2011). *Governance Portfolio Review Summary.* London: DFID.

Di Maggio, P. J. (1988). Interest and Agency in Institutional Theory. In L. Zucker (Ed.). *Institutional Patterns and Organizations.* Cambridge, MA: Ballinger, 3–22.

Di Maggio, P. J., and Powell, W. W. (1983). The Iron Cage Revisited: Institutional Isomorphism and Collective Rationality in Organizational Fields. *American Sociological Review* 48, 147–160.

Dixon, G. (2005). Thailand's Quest for Results Focused Budgeting. *International Journal of Public Administration* 28(3–4), 355–370.

Djankov, S., La Porta, R., Lopez-de-Silanes, F., and Shleifer, A. (2002). The Regulation of Entry. *Quarterly Journal of Economics* 117, 1–37.

Doig, A., Watt, D., and Williams, R. (2005). Measuring "Success" in Five African Anti-Corruption Commissions. *U4 Issue,* March 2005. Norway: U4 Anti-Corruption Resource Center, Chr. Michelsen Institute.

Dorado, S. (2001). Social Entrepreneurship: The Process of Creation of Microfinance Organizations in Bolivia. PhD Thesis, Faculty of Management, McGill University. Montreal: McGill University.

Dorado, S. (2005). Institutional Entrepreneurship, Partaking, and Convening. *Organization Studies* 26(3), 385–414.

Douglas, M. (1986). *How Institutions Think.* Syracuse, NY: Syracuse University Press.

Dull, M. (2006). Why PART? The Institutional Politics of Presidential Budget Reform. *Journal of Public Administration, Research and Theory* 16, 187–215.

Easterly, W. (2001). *The Elusive Quest for Growth: Economists' Adventures and Misadventures in the Tropics.* Cambridge, MA: MIT Press.

Easterly, W. (2002). *The Cartel of Good Intentions: The Problem of Bureaucracy in Foreign Aid.* Washington, DC: Center for Global Development.

Evans, P. (2004). Development as Institutional Change: The Pitfalls of Monocropping and the Potentials of Deliberation. *Studies in Comparative International Development* 38(4), 30–52.

Ezzamel, M., Hyndman, N., Johnsen, Å., Lapsley, I., and Pallot, J. (2007). Experiencing Institutionalization: The Development of New Budgets in the UK Devolved Bodies. *Accounting, Auditing and Accountability Journal* 20(1), 11–40.

Fafchamps, M. (1996). The Enforcement of Commercial Contracts in Ghana. *World Development* 24(3), 427–448.

Faletti, T. (2010). *Decentralization and Sub-national Politics in Latin America.* Cambridge: Cambridge University Press.

Faletti, T., and Lynch, J. (2009). Context and Causal Mechanisms in Political Analysis. *Comparative Political Studies* 42(9), 1143–1166.

Fane, G. (2000). Survey of Recent Developments. *Bulletin of Indonesian Economic Studies* 36(1), 13–44.

Feyzioğlu, T., Porter, N., and Takáts, E. (2009). Interest Rate Liberalization in China. *IMF Working Paper 09/171.* Washington, DC: IMF.

Fillol, T. (1961). *Social Factors in Economic Development: The Argentine Case.* Cambridge: MIT Press.

Fligstein N. (1991). The Structural Transformation of American Industry: An Institutional Account of the Causes of Diversification in the Largest Firms. In P. di Maggio (Ed.). *The New Institutionalism in Organizational Analysis.* Chicago: University of Chicago Press, 311–336.

Fogarty, T. J., and Dirsmith, M. W. (2001). Organizational Socialization as Instrument and Symbol: An Extended Institutional Theory Perspective. *Human Resource Development Quarterly* 12(3), 247–266.

Fozzard, A. (2002). How, When and Why Does Poverty Get Budget Priority: Poverty Reduction Strategy and Public Expenditure in Mozambique. *Overseas Development Institute Working Paper 167.* London: Overseas Development Institute.

Frandale, E., and Paauwe, J. (2007). Uncovering Competitive and Institutional Drivers of HRM Practices in Multinational Companies. *Human Resource Management Journal* 17(4), 355–375.

Friedland, R., and Alford, R. R. (1991). Bringing Society Back In: Symbols, Practices, and Institutional Contradictions. In W. W. Powell and P. DiMaggio (Eds.). *The New Institutionalism in Organizational Analysis.* Chicago: University of Chicago Press, 232–266.

Fritz, V., Kaiser, K., and Levy, B. (2009). *Problem Driven Governance and Political Economy Analysis.* Washington, DC: World Bank.

Frumkin, P., and Galaskiewicz, J. (2004). Institutional Isomorphism and Public Sector Organizations. *Journal of Public Administration Research and Theory* 14, 283–307.

Galvin, T. (2002). Examining Institutional Change: Evidence from the Founding Dynamics of U.S. *Health Care Interest Associations. The Academy of Management Journal* 45(4), 673–696.

Garud, R. and Karnøe, P. (2003). Bricolage Versus Breakthrough: Distributed and Embedded Agency in Technology Entrepreneurship. *Research Policy* 32, 277–300.

Gibson, E. L. (1997). The Populist Road to Market Reform: Policy and Electoral Coalitions in Mexico and Argentina. *World Politics* 49, 339–70.

Gibson, E. L., and Calvo, E. (2000). Federalism and Low-Maintenance Constituencies: Territorial Dimensions of Economic Reform in Argentina. *Studies in Comparative International Development* 35(3), 32–55.

Giddens, A. (1984). *The Constitution of Society.* Berkeley: University of California Press.

Global Fund. (2002). Pakistan: To Enhance the Health Impact of Public and Private Health Services amongst Target Communities at Risk and Vulnerable to HIV, Pulmonary Tuberculosis and Malaria Infection. Original proposal, July 2002. Geneva: Global Fund.

Global Fund. (2007). Cote d'Ivoire: Prevention of the Spread of the HIV/AIDS Epidemic in the Context of Severe Political and Military Crisis. Grant Performance Report. External Print Version, December 19, 2007. Geneva: Global Fund.

Global Fund. (2010a). Comoros: The Fight Against Malaria at the Community Level in the Union of the Comoros. Grant Performance Report. External Print Version, April 13, 2010. Geneva: Global Fund.

Global Fund. (2010b). Pakistan: To Enhance the Health Impact of Public and Private Health Services amongst Target Communities at Risk and Vulnerable to HIV, Pulmonary Tuberculosis and Malaria Infection. Grant Performance Report. External Print Version, November 29, 2010. Geneva: Global Fund.

Global Fund. (2011). Bangladesh: Expanding HIV/AIDS Prevention in Bangladesh. Grant Performance Report. External Print Version, October 24, 2011. Geneva: Global Fund.

Goldsmith, A. A. (2010). No Country Left Behind? Performance Standards and Accountability in US Foreign Assistance. *Development Policy Review* 28(1), 7–26.

Government of Rwanda. (2000). *Rwanda Decentralization Implementation Program, 2000–2003*. Kigali: Ministry of Local Government, Good Governance, Community Development and Social Affairs.

Government of Rwanda. (2005). *Evaluation of Support to 5 Year Decentralization Implementation Program, 2000–2003*. Kigali: Ministry of Local Government, Good Governance, Community Development and Social Affairs.

Government of Rwanda. (2007a). *Rwanda Decentralization Strategic Framework*. Kigali: Ministry of Local Government, Good Governance, Community Development and Social Affairs.

Government of Rwanda. (2007b). *Economic Development and Poverty Reduction Strategy, 2008–2012*. Kigali: Government of Rwanda.

Government of Rwanda. (2008). *Rwanda Decentralization Implementation Program, 2008–2012*. Kigali: Ministry of Local Government, Good Governance, Community Development and Social Affairs.

Granovetter, M. (1985). Economic Action and Social Structure: The Problem of Embeddedness. *American Journal of Sociology* 91, 481–510.

Gray, S. J. (1988). Towards a Theory of Cultural Influences on the Development of Accounting Systems Internationally. *Abacus* 24(1), 1–15.

Greene, W. H. (1993). *Econometric Analysis*. Englewood Cliffs, NJ: Prentice Hall.

Greenwood, R., and Hinnings, C. R. (1993). Understanding Strategic Change: The Contribution of Archetypes. *Academy of Management Journal* 36(5), 1052–1081.

Greenwood, R., and Hinnings, C. R. (1996). Understanding Radical Organisational Change: Bringing Together the Old and New Institutionalism. *Academy of Management Review* 21, 1022–1054.

Greenwood, R., and Suddaby, R. (2006). Institutional Entrepreneurship in Mature Fields: The Big Five Accounting Firms. *Academy of Management Journal* 49, 27–48.

Greenwood, R., Suddaby, R., and Hinings, C. R. (2002). Theorising Change: The Role of Professional Associations in the Transformation of Institutional Fields. *Academy of Management Journal* 45(1), 58–80.

Greenwood, R., Diaz, A. M., Li, S. X., and Lorente, J. C. (2010). The Multiplicity of Institutional Logics and the Heterogeneity of Organizational Responses. *Organization Science* 21(2), 521–539.

Grindle, M. (2004). Good Enough Governance: Poverty Reduction and Reform in Developing Countries. *Governance: An International Journal of Policy, Administration and Institutions* 17, 525–548.

Guillen, M. (2003). *The Limits of Convergence: Globalization and Organizational Change in Argentina, South Korea, and Spain*. Princeton, NJ: Princeton University Press.

Guldbrandsson, K., and Fossum, B. (2009). An Exploration of the Theoretical Concepts Policy Windows and Policy Entrepreneurs at the Swedish Public Health Arena. *Health Promotion International* 24(4), 434–444.

Hackman, J. R. and Walton, R. E. (1986). Leading Groups in Organizations. In Goodman, P. S. (Ed.). *Designing Effective Work Groups*. San Francisco, CA: Jossey-Bass, 72–119.

Halliday, T. C., and Carruthers, B. G. (2007). Foiling the Hegemons: Limits to the Globalisation of Corporate Insolvency Regimes in Indonesia, Korea and China. In C. Antons and V. Gessner (Eds.). *Law and Globalization in Asia since the Crisis*. Oxford: Hart Publishing, 255–301.

Halper, S. (2010). *The Beijing Consensus: How China's Authoritarian Model Will Dominate the Twenty-First Century*. New York: Basic Books.

Hamilton-Hart, N. (2001). Anti-Corruption Strategies in Indonesia. *Bulletin of Indonesian Economic Studies* 37(1), 65–82.

Hanlon, J. (2004a). Renewed Land Debate and the "Cargo Cult" in Mozambique. *Journal of Southern African Studies* 30(3), 603–626.

Hanlon, J. (2004b). Do Donors Promote Corruption? The case of Mozambique. *Third World Quarterly* 25(4), 747–763.

Hannan, M. T., and Freeman, J. (1984). Structural Inertia and Organizational Change. *American Sociological Review* 49, 149–164.

Harvard Kennedy School. (2007). *Same Bed Different Dreams: The China-Singapore Industrial Park. Case 1859.0*. Cambridge, MA: Harvard University.

Haveman, H. A., and Rao, H. (1997). Structuring a Theory of Moral Sentiments: Institutional and Organizational Coevolution in the Early Thrift Industry. *American Journal of Sociology* 102, 1606–1651.

Heifetz, R., Linsky, M., and Grashow, A. (2009). *The Practice of Adaptive Leadership*. Cambridge, MA: Harvard Business Press.

Heilbrunn, J. R. (2004). *Anticorruption Commissions: Panacea or Real Medicine to Fight Corruption?* Washington, DC: World Bank.

Helmke, G., and Levitsky, S. (2004). Informal Institutions and Comparative Politics: A Research Agenda. *Perspectives on Politics* 2(4), 725–740.

Hennessey, J. T. (1998). "Reinventing" Government: Does Leadership Make a Difference? *Public Administration Review* 58, 322–332.

Hirsch, P., and Lounsbury, M. (1997). Ending the Family Quarrel: Towards a Reconciliation of "Old" and "New" Institutionalism. *American Behavioral Scientist* 40(4), 406–418.

Hodges, T., and Tibana, R. (2004). The Political Economy of the Budget Process in Mozambique. Oxford: Oxford Policy Management. http://www.gsdrc.org/go/display&type=Document&id=1619.

Holland, C. P., and Light, B. (1999). A Critical Success Factors Model for ERP Implementation. *IEEE Software* (May/June), 30–35.

Hong, K. K., and Kim, Y. G. (2002). The Critical Success Factors for ERP Implementation: An Organizational Fit Perspective. *Information and Management* 40, 25–40.

International Monetary Fund. (2003). *IMF Completes Review Under Benin's PRGF Arrangement and Approves US$3.7 Million Disbursement*. Press Release No. 03/156, September 11, 2003.

Indonesian Corruption Eradication Commission. (2006). *Identification between Laws/Regulations of the Republic of Indonesia and the United Nations Convention Against Corruption.* Jakarta, Indonesia: Corruption Eradication Commission.

Ingraham, P., Moynihan, D., and Andrews, M. (2008). Formal and Informal Institutions in Public Administration. In B. G. Peters and D. Savoie (Eds.). *Institutional Theory in Political Science.* Manchester: Manchester University Press.

Inter-American Development Bank. (2003). *Modernization of the State.* Washington, DC: Inter-American Development Bank.

Ishikawa, K., and Loftus, J. H. (1990). *Introduction to Quality Control.* Tokyo: 3A Corporation.

Jackall, R. (1988). *Moral Mazes: The World of Corporate Managers.* New York: Oxford University Press.

Jasin, M. (2010). The Indonesian Corruption Eradication Commission. *Article 2 of the International Covenant on Civil and Political Rights* 9(1), 18–27.

Jin, H. K., Kim, N., and Srivastava, R. K. (1998). Market Orientation and Organizational Performance: Is Innovation a Missing Link? *Journal of Marketing* 62, 30–45.

Jones, C., Hesterly, W. S., and Borgatti, S. P. (1997). A General Theory of Network Governance: Exchange Conditions and Social Mechanisms. *Academy of Management Review* 22(4), 911–945.

Judge, T. A., Thoresen, C. J., Pucik, V., and Welbourne, T. M. (1999). Managerial Coping with Organizational Change: A Dispositional Perspective. *Journal of Applied Psychology* 84(1), 107–122.

Kalegaonkar, A., and Brown, D. L. (2000). Intersectoral Cooperation. Lessons for Practice. *IDR Reports* 16/2. www.jsi.com/idr/IDRepoorts.com.

Kamanga, I. (2008). *Combating Corruption: Challenges in the Malawi Legal System.* UNAFE Material Series No. 76. http://www.unafei.or.jp/english/pages/RMS/No76.htm.

Kanter, R. M. (1983). *The Change Masters.* New York: Simon & Schuster.

Karikari, J. A. (2010). *Governance, Financial Liberalization, and Financial Development in Sub-Saharan Africa.* African Economic Conference, November 2010. http://papers.ssrn.com/sol3/papers.cfm?abstract_id=1733322.

Kaufmann, D., Kraay, A., and Zoido-Lobaton, P. (1999). *Governance Matters.* World Bank Policy Research Working Paper 2196. Washington, DC: World Bank.

Kaufmann, D., Kraay, A., and Mastruzzi, M. (2007). *Governance Matters VI: Aggregate and Individual Governance Indicators 1996–2006.* World Bank Policy Research Working Paper, No. 4280. Washington, DC.

Kenny, K. (2008). Arrive Bearing Gifts. In S. Dar and B. Cooke (Eds.). *The New Development Management: Critiquing the Dual Modernization.* London: Zed Books.

Killick, T., Castel-Branco, C. N. (2005). *Perfect Partners? The Performance of Programme Aid Partners in Mozambique, 2004.* A report to the Programme Aid Partners and Government of Mozambique. Maputo: PAP Secretariat.

Kirkpatrick, I., and Ackroyd, S. (2003). Transforming the Professional Archetype? The New Managerialism in UK Social Services. *Public Management Review* 5, 511–531.

Kingdon, J. W. (1995). *Agendas, Alternatives, and Public Policies.* 2nd edition New York: Harper Collins.

Kmenta, J. (1986). *Elements of Econometrics.* 2nd edition. New York: Macmillan.

Knight, J. (1997). Social Institutions and Human Cognition: Thinking about Old Questions in New Ways. *Journal of Institutional and Theoretical Economics* 153(4), 693–699.

Kolstad, I., Fritz, V., and O'Neil, T. (2008) *Corruption, Anti-corruption Efforts and Aid: Do Donors. Have the Right Approach?* London: Overseas Development Institute.

Kopits, G. (2001). Fiscal Rules: Useful Policy Framework or Unnecessary Ornament? *IMF Working Paper, No. 01/145*, Washington, DC: International Monetary Fund, October.

Kopits, G., and Symansky, S. (1998). Fiscal Policy Rules, *IMF Occasional Paper, No. 162*, Washington, DC: International Monetary Fund.

Kornai, J. (1979). Resource-Constrained Versus Demand-Constrained Systems. *Econometrica* 47(4), 801–819.

Kornai, J. (1980). *Economics of Shortage*. Amsterdam: North-Holland.

Kornai, J. (1986). The Soft Budget Constraint. *Kyklos* 39(1), 3–30.

Kostova, T. (1997). Country Institutional Profiles: Concept and Measurement. *Academy of Management*, Best Paper Proceedings, 180–189.

Krueger, A. O. (2004a). Meant Well, Tried Little, Failed Much. Roundtable lecture at the Economic Honors Society Meeting, New York University, March 23, 2004.

Krueger, A. O. (2004b). Argentina: Remaining Economic Challenges. Lecture to the American Enterprise Institute. Washington, DC, March 31, 2004.

Kurtz, M. J., and Schrank, A. (2007). Growth and Governance: Models, Measures and Mechanisms. *Journal of Politics* 69(2), 538–554.

Laine, M., and Torstila, S. (2005). The Exit Rates of Liquidated Venture Capital Funds. *Journal of Entrepreneurial Finance and Business Venturing* 10, 53–73.

Lee, K. Y. (2000). *From Third World to First: The Singapore Story*. New York: Harper.

Lee, S. Y., and Whitford, A. B. (2009). Government Effectiveness in Comparative Perspective. *Journal of Comparative Policy Analysis: Research and Practice* 11(2), 249–281.

Leftwich, A., and Wheeler, C. (2011). Politics, Leadership and Coalitions in Development: A Research and Policy Workshop Report. Developmental Leadership Program. www.dlprog.org.

Levitsky, S., and Murillo, M. V. (2008). Argentina: From Kirchner to Kirchner. *Journal of Democracy* 19(2), 16–30.

Levy, B. (2004). Governance and Economic Development in Africa: Meeting the Challenge of Capacity Building. In B. Levy and S. J. Kpundeh (Eds.). *Building State Capacity in Africa: New Approaches, Emerging Lessons*. Washington, DC: World Bank, 1–42.

Levy, B. (2010). Development Trajectories: An Evolutionary Approach to Integrating Governance and Growth. *Economic Premise 15*. Washington, DC: World Bank.

Lewin, K. (1947). Frontiers in Group Dynamics. *Human Relations* 1(1), 5–41.

Lienert, I. (2007). Indonesia's Push for Treasury Transparency. *IMF Survey Magazine: Countries and Regions.* December 10, 2007. www.imf.org/external/pubs/ft/survey/so/2007/CAR1210A.htm.

Lindblom, C. (1959). The Science of "Muddling Through." *Public Administration Review* 19, 79–88.

Lindblom, C. (1979). Still Muddling, Not Yet Through. *Public Administration Review* 39, 517–526.

Lindsey, T. (1998). The IMF and Insolvency Law Reform in Indonesia. *Bulletin of Indonesian Economic Studies* 34(3), 119–124.

Lindsey, T., and Taylor, V. (2000). Rethinking Indonesian Insolvency Reform: Contexts and Frameworks. In T. Lindsey (Ed.). *Indonesia: Bankruptcy, Law Reform and the Commercial Court.* Sydney: Desert Pea Press, 2–14.

Linnan, D. (2000). Bankruptcy Policy and reform: Reconciling Efficiency and Economic Nationalism. In T. Lindsey (Ed). *Indonesia: Bankruptcy, Law Reform and the Commercial Court.* Sydney: Desert Pea Press, 94–109.

Lister, S., Baryabanoha, W., Steffensen, J., and Williamson, T. (2006). Evaluation of General Budget Support – Uganda Country Report. Birmingham: International Development Department, School of Public Policy, University of Birmingham.

Loft, A. (2007). Governing Accounting Beyond the State (?): The WTO and the Construction of a "World without Walls" for Accounting Services. Copenhagen Business School Working Paper. Copenhagen: Copenhagen Business School.

Lou, J., and Wang, S. (2008). *Public Finance in China: Reform and Growth for a Harmonious Society.* Washington, DC: World Bank.

Maguire, S., Hardy, C., and Lawrence, T. B. (2004). Institutional Entrepreneurship in Emerging Fields: HIV/AIDS Treatment Advocacy in Canada. *Academy of Management Journal* 47, 657–679.

Mair, I., and Marti, I. (2009). Entrepreneurship in and around Institutional Voids: A Case Study from Bangladesh. *Journal of Business Venturing* 24(5), 419–435.

Malagueño, R., Albrecht, C., Ainge, C., and Stephens, N. (2010). Accounting and Corruption: a Cross-Country Analysis. *Journal of Money Laundering Control* 13(4), 372–393.

Martinez Peria, M. S., and Schmukler, S. (2001). Do Depositors Punish Banks for "Bad" Behavior? Market Discipline, Deposit Insurance, and Banking Crises. *Journal of Finance* 56, 1029–1051.

Matta, N., and Morgan, P. (2011). Local Empowerment through Rapid Results. *Stanford Social Innovation Review* (Summer), 51–55.

McCay, B. J. (2002). Emergence of Institutions for the Commons: Contexts, Situations, and Events. In E. Ostrom (Ed.). *The Drama of the Commons.* Washington, DC: National Research Council, 361–399.

McConnell, J. (2009). Institution (Un)Building: Decentralizing Government and the Case of Rwanda. Paper presented at the European University Institute Conference on the European Report on Development, Accra, Ghana, May 21–23, 2009.

McCourt, W., and Ramgutty-Wong, A. (2003). Limits to Strategic HRM: The Case of the Mauritian Civil Service. *International Journal of Human Resource Management* 14(4), 600–618.

McLeod, R. H. (2000). Soeharto's Indonesia: A Better Class of Corruption. *Agenda* 7(2), 99–112.

Meyer, R. E., and Hammerschmid, G. (2006). Changing Institutional Logics and Executive Identities: A Managerial Challenge to Public Administration in Austria. *American Behavioral Scientist* 49(7), 1000–1014.

Meyer, J., and Rowan, B. (1977). Institutional Organizations: Formal Structure as Myth and Ceremony. *American Journal of Sociology* 83, 340–363.

Miles, C., and Snow, R. (1978). *Organizational Strategy, Structure and Process.* New York: McGraw Hill.

Mintzberg, H. (2010). Developing Leaders? Developing Countries. *Oxford Leadership Journal* 11(2). http://www.oxfordleadership.com/journal/vol1_issue2/mintzberg.pdf.

Misangyi, V. F., Weaver, G. R., and Elms, H. (2008). Ending Corruption: The Interplay among Institutional Logics, Resources, and Institutional Entrepreneurs. *Academy of Management Review* 33(3), 750–770.

Moloney, K. (2009). Public Administration and Governance: A Sector-Level Analysis of World Bank Aid. *International Review of Administrative Sciences* 75(4), 609–627.

Montes C. (2003). Results-Based Public Management in Bolivia. *Overseas Development Institute Working Paper 202.* Overseas Development Institute: London.

Montes C., and Andrews, M. (2005). Implementing Reforms in Bolivia: Too Much to Handle. *International Journal of Public Administration* 28(3–4), 273–290.

Moto, F. (2001). Language and Societal Attitudes: A Study of Malawi's "New Language." *Nordic Journal of African Studies* 10(3), 320–343.

Mussa, M. (2002). *Argentina and the Fund: From Triumph to Tragedy.* Washington, DC: Institute for International Economics.

Nasra, R., and Dacin, T. (2009). Institutional Arrangements and International Entrepreneurship: The State as Institutional Entrepreneur. *Entrepreneurship Theory and Practice* (May), 585–609.

NORAD. (2010). Annual Review of DFID/RNS's Malawi Anticorruption Bureau Support Programme. Norway: NORAD. http://www.norad.no/en/tools-and-publications/publications/publication?key=207030.

NORAD. (2011). From More Effective Aid to More Effective Institutions: Strengthening State Institutions for Sustainable Development. Room Document for Meeting 5 October 2011. Oslo: NORAD.

North, D. (1989). Institutions and Economic Growth: An Historical Introduction. *World Development* 17(9), 1319–1332.

North, D. (1990). *Institutions, Institutional Change and Economic Performance.* Cambridge: Cambridge University Press.

Noy, I. (2004). Financial Liberalization, Prudential Supervision, and the Onset of Banking Crises. *Emerging Markets Review* 5(3), 341–359.

Nutt, P. (1986). Tactics of Implementation. *Academy of Management Journal* 29(2), 230–261.

Obtsfeld, M. (2009). International Finance and Growth in Developing Countries: What Have We Learned? *IMF Staff Papers* 56, 63–111.

Oliver, C. (1992) The Antecedents of Deinstitutionalization. *Organization Studies* 13, 563–588.

O'Neil, T. (2007). *Background Note 1: Neopatrimonialism and Public Sector Performance and Reform.* London: Overseas Development Institute.

Ostiguy, P. (2009). Argentina's Double Political Spectrum: Party System, Political Identities, and Strategies, 1944–2007. *Kellogg Institute Working Paper #361.* Notre Dame: Kellogg Institute.

Ostrom, E. (1990). *Governing the Commons.* Cambridge: Cambridge University Press.

Ostrom, E. (2008). Design Principles of Robust Property-Rights Institutions: What Have We Learned? In K. G. Ingram and Y.-H. Hong (Eds.). *Property Rights and Land Policies.* Cambridge, MA: Lincoln Institute of Land Policy, 25–51.

Patton, M. Q. (1990). *Qualitative Evaluation and Research Methods.* New York: Sage.

PEFA. (2006). Public Expenditure and Financial Accountability Performance Measurement Framework. http://www.pefa.org/pfm_performance_file/the_framework_English_1193152901.pdf.

Pendel, G. (1968). The Past behind the Present. In J. Barager (Ed.). *Why Peron Came to Power.* New York: Knopf, 258–266.

Pettersen, I. J. (1995). Budgetary Control of Hospitals – Ritual Rhetorics and Rationalized Myths? *Financial Accountability and Management* 11(3), 207–221.

Piotti, B., Chilundo, B., and Sahay, S. (2006). An Institutional Perspective on Health Sector Reforms and the Process of Reframing Health Information Systems: Case Study from Mozambique. *Journal of Applied Behavioral Science* 42, 91–109.

Pollit, C. (2008). Moderation in All Things: Governance Quality and Performance Measurement. Paper for the Structure and Organization of Government Meeting, Gotenburg, November 2008.

Porter, D., Wescott, C., Andrews, M., and Turkewitz, J. (2011). Public Finance Management and Procurement in Fragile and Conflicted Settings. *International Public Management Journal,* 14(4), 369–394.

Pritchett, L., and Woolcock, M. (2004). Solutions When the Solution Is the Problem: Arraying the Disarray in Development. *World Development* 32(2), 191–212.

Pritchett, L., Woolcock, M., and Andrews, M. (2010). *Capability Traps? The Mechanisms of Persistent Implementation Failure – Working Paper 234.* Washington, DC: Center for Global Development.

Purdy, J. M., and Gray, B. (2009). Conflicting Logics, Mechanisms of Diffusion, and Multilevel Dynamics in Emerging Institutional Fields. *Academy of Management Journal* 52(2), 355–380.

Qureishi, H. (2011). *Saving Lives: Stories from the Fight. Fighting HIV/AIDS in Pakistan.* Geneva: Global Fund.

Ramo, J. C. (2004). *The Beijing Consensus.* London: The Foreign Policy Center.

Riddle, V. (2009). Policy Implementation in an African State: An Extension of Kingdon's Multiple-Streams Approach. *Public Administration* 87(4), 938–954.

Rimmer, M., MacNeil, J., Chenhall, R., Langfield-Smith, K., and Watts, L. (1996). *Reinventing Competitiveness: Achieving Best Practice in Australia.* South Melbourne: Pitman.

Roberts, A. (2010). *The Logic of Discipline: Global Capitalism and the Architecture of Government.* New York: Oxford.

Roberts, J., and Scapens, R. (1985). Accounting Systems and Systems of Accountability: Understanding Accounting Practices in Their Organisational Contexts. *Accounting, Organization and Society* 10(4), 443–456.

Rodrik, D. (2007). *One Economics, Many Recipes: Globalization, Institutions, and Economic Growth.* Princeton, Princeton University Press.

Rose, R. (2003). What's Wrong with Best Practice Policies – And Why Relevant Practices Are Better. *On Target? Government by Measurement.* London: House of Commons Public Administration Select Committee HC 62-II, 2003, 307–317.

Rosenbaum, E. F. (2001). Culture, Cognitive Models, and the Performance of Institutions in Transformation Countries. *Journal of Economic Issues* 35(4), 889–909.

Rothstein, B. (2005). Anti-Corruption Strategies in Africa: What Works and Why? Application for research grant from Sida/SAREC, April 18, 2005. http://www.qog.pol .gu.se/research/applications/Application-Sarec_Rothstein.pdf.

Sadler, E. (2002). A Profile and the Work Environment of Black Chartered Accountants in South Africa. *Meditari Accountancy Research* 10, 159–185.

Sahay, S., Sæbø, J., Molla, S., and Asalefew, A. (2009). Interplay of Institutional logics and Implications for Deinstitutionalization: Case Study of HMIS Implementation in Tajikistan. *Proceedings of the 10th International Conference on Social Implications of Computers in Developing Countries*, Dubai, May 26–28, 2009. Dubai School of Government.

Said, E. W. (1978). *Orientalism.* New York: Vintage Books Edition.

Salter, S. B., and Niswander, F. (1995). Cultural Influence on the Development of Accounting Systems Internationally: A Test of Gray's (1988) Theory. *Journal of International Business Studies* 26, 379–397.

Schein, E. H. (1996). Kurt Lewin's Change Theory in the Field and in the Classroom: Notes toward a Model of Managed Learning. *Systems Practice* 9, 27–47.

Scher, D. (2010). *The Promise of Imihigo: Decentralized Service Delivery in Rwanda, 2006–2010.* Princeton, NJ: Innovations for Successful Societies, Princeton University.

Schick, A. (1998). Why Most Developing Countries Should Not Try New Zealand Reforms. *The World Bank Research Observer* 13, 123–131.

Schneiberg, M. (2007). What's on the Path? Path Dependence, Organizational Diversity and the Problem of Organizational Change in the US Economy, 1900–1950. *Socio-Economic Review* 5, 47–80.

Schneper, W., and Guillén, M. (2004). Stakeholders Rights and Corporate Governance: A Cross-National Study of Hostile Takeovers. *Administrative Science Quarterly* 49, 263–295.

Scott, G. (2001). *Public Sector Management in New Zealand: Lessons and Challenges.* Wellington: Australian National University.

Scott, W. R. (1987). *Organizations.* 2nd edition. NJ: Prentice Hall.

Scott, W. R. (2001). *Institutions and Organizations.* Thousand Oaks, CA: Sage.

Scott, W. R. (2008). *Institutions and Organizations.* 3rd edition. Thousand Oaks, CA: Sage.

Scott, W. R., Ruef, M., Caronna, C.A., and Mendel, P. J. (2000). *Institutional Change and Healthcare Organizations: From Professional Dominance to Managed Care.* Chicago: University of Chicago Press.

Seo, M. G., and Creed, W. E. D. (2002). Institutional Contradictions, Praxis and Institutional Change: A Dialectical Perspective. *Academy of Management Review* 27(2), 222–247.

Sewell, W. H., Jr. (1992). A Theory of Structure: Duality, Agency, and Transformation. *American Journal of Sociology* 98, 1–29.

Serrat, O. (2009). *The Five Whys Technique. Asian Development Bank Knowledge Solutions,* 30. Manila: Asian Development Bank.

Shirley, M. (2005). Can AID Reform Institutions? Ronald Coase Institute Working Paper No. 6. http://www.coase.org/workingpapers/wp-6.pdf.

Sian, S. (2006). Inclusion, Exclusion and Control: The Case of the Kenyan Accounting Professionalisation Project. *Accounting, Organizations and Society* 31(3), 295–322.

Sian, S. (2007). Reversing Exclusion: The Africanisation of Accountancy in Kenya, 1963–1970. *Critical Perspectives on Accounting* 18(3), 831–872.

Skoog, G. E. (2000). *The Soft Budget Constraint. The Emergence, Persistence Logic of an Institution.* Dordrecht: Kluwer Academic Publisher.

Slack, T., and Hinings, C. (1994). Institutional Pressures and Isomorphic Change: An Empirical Test. *Organization Studies* 15, 803–827.

Snow, D. A., and Benford, R. D. (1992). Master Frames and Cycles of Protest. In A. D. Morris and C. McClurg Mueller (Eds.). *Frontiers in Social Movement Theory.* New Haven: Yale University Press, 133–155.

Spivak, G. C. (1990). The Making of Americans: The Teaching of English, the Future of Colonial Studies. *New Literary History* 21, 2–26.

Stewart, R. (2010). Afghanistan: What Could Work? *New York Review of Books,* January 14, 2010. http://www.nybooks.com/articles/archives/2010/jan/14/afghanistan-what-could-work/?pagination=false.

Stone, S. F. (2008). Asia's Infrastructure Challenges: Issues of Institutional Capacity. ADB Institute Working Paper No. 126. Manila: Asian Development Bank.

Streit, M., Mummert, U., and Kiwit, D. (1997). Views and Comments on Cognition, Rationality, and Institutions. *Journal of Institutional and Theoretical Economics* 153, 688–692.

Suchman, M. (1995). Localism and Globalism in Institutional Analysis: The Emergence of Contractual Norms in Venture Finance. In W. R. Scott and S. Christensen (Eds.). *The Institutional Construction of Organizations: International and Longitudinal Studies.* Thousand Oaks, CA: Sage, 39–63.

Sulemane, J. (2006). Mozambique: Better Budget Machinery – First Focus of Reform. In CABRI. *Budget Reform Seminar. Country Case Studies.* Proceedings from First Annual CABRI Seminar, Pretoria, South Africa, December 1–3, 2004. Pretoria: CABRI.

Sunaryadi, A. (2005). *Donor Support for Anti-Corruption.* Presentation at 5th Regional Anti-Corruption Conference. Beijing, PR China. September 28–30, 2005.

Sunaryadi, A. (2007). Indonesia and the UNCAC Review Mechanism. Keynote address at the conference. Making International Anti-corruption Standards Operational. Bali, Indonesia. September 5–7, 2007.

Swidler, A. (1986). Culture in Action: Symbols and Strategies. *American Sociological Review* 52(2), 273–286.

Thelen, K. (2003). How Institutions Evolve: Insights from Comparative Institutional Analysis. In J. Mahoney and D. Rueschemeyer (Eds.). *Comparative Historical Analysis in the Social Sciences.* Ithaca, NY: Cornell University Press.

Thornton, P. H., and Ocasio, W. (1999). Institutional Logics and the Historical Contingency of Power in Organizations: Executive Succession in the Higher Education Publishing Industry, 1958–1990. *American Journal of Sociology* 105(3), 801–843.

Thornton, P. H., and Ocasio, W. (2008). Institutional Logics. In R. Greenwood, C. Oliver, S. K. Andersen, and R. Suddaby (Eds.). *Handbook of Organizational Institutionalism.* Thousand Oaks, CA: Sage, 99–129.

Tolbert, P. S., and Zucker, L. G. (1983). Institutional Sources of Change in the Formal Structure of Organizations: The Diffusion of Civil Service Reform, 1880–1935. *Administrative Science Quarterly* 28, 22–39.

Tolbert, P. S., and Zucker, L. G. (1996). Institutionalization of Institutional Theory. In S. Clegg, C. Hardy, and W. Nord (Eds.). *The Handbook of Organization Studies.* Thousand Oaks, CA: Sage, 175–190.

Tomasic, R. (2001). *Some Challenges for Insolvency System Reform in Indonesia.* Paper presented at the Forum for Asian Insolvency Reform, Bali, Indonesia, February 7–8, 2001.

Townley, B. (1997). The Institutional Logic of Performance Appraisal. *Organization Studies* 18(2), 261–285.

Tushman, M. L., and Anderson, P. (1986). Technological Discontinuities and Organizational Environments. *Administrative Science Quarterly* 31, 439–465.

Uche, C. U. (2002). Professional Accounting Development in Nigeria: Threats from the Inside and Outside. *Accounting, Organizations and Society* 27(4–5), 471–496.

Ueno, S., and Sekaran, U. (1992). The Influence of Culture on Budget Control Practices in the USA and Japan: An Empirical Study. *Journal of International Business Studies* 23(4), 659–674.

United Nations Office on Drugs and Crime (UNODC). (2011). Group of Experts Evaluate the Coordination and Supervision Function of the Corruption Eradication Commission. *UNODC Indonesia Newsletter* 13 (March 2011), 1–2.

Van Dijk, R. (1999). Pentecostalism, Gerontocratic Rule and Democratization in Malawi: The Changing Position of the Young in Political Culture. In J. Hanyes (Ed.). *Religion, Globalization and Political Culture in the Third World*. London: Macmillan Press, 165–188.

van Kerkhoff, L. (2006). How Do Global-Scale Institutional Experiments Affect Knowledge? A Case Study of the Global Fund to fight AIDS, Tuberculosis, and Malaria. Paper presented at IDGEC Synthesis Conference, December 6–9, Bali, Indonesia.

Webb, S. B. (2002). Argentina: Hardening the Provincial Budget Constraint. In J. Rodden, G. Eskeland, and J. Litvack (Eds.). *Decentralization and Hard Budget Constraints*. Boston: MIT Press.

Werenfels, I. (2002). Obstacles to Privatization of State-Owned Industries in Algeria: The Political Economy of Distributive Conflict. *Journal of North African Studies* 7(1), 1–28.

Wescott, C. (2008). World Bank Support for Public Financial Management: Conceptual Roots and Evidence of Impact. World Bank Independent Evaluation Group Working Paper. http://ssrn.com/abstract=1169783.

Whitford, A., and Lee, S.-Y. (2009). Government Effectiveness in Comparative Perspective. *Journal of Comparative Policy Analysis* 11(2), 249–281.

Whittle, A., Suhomlinova, O., and Mueller, F. (2010). Dialogue and Distributed Agency in Institutional Transmission. *Journal of Management and Organization* 17(4), 548–569.

Wildavsky, A. (1992). Budgeting as a Cultural Phenomenon. In J. Rabin (Ed.). *Handbook of Public Budgeting*. New York: Marcel Dekker, 51–56.

Wilder, A. (2009). The Politics of Civil Service Reform in Pakistan. *Journal of International Affairs* 63(1), 19–37.

Wong, K. C. (2011). Using an Ishikawa Diagram as a Tool to Assist Memory and Retrieval of Relevant Medical Cases from the Medical Literature. *Journal of Medical Case Reports* 5, 120–123.

World Bank. (1985). *President's Report: Malawi Third Structural Adjustment Operation*. Washington, DC: World Bank.

World Bank. (1988). *Public Finance in Development: 1988 World Development Report*. New York: Oxford University Press.

World Bank. (1990a). *Malawi: Growth Through Poverty Reduction*. Washington, DC: World Bank.

World Bank. (1990b). *Malawi Public Expenditure Review*. Washington, DC: World Bank.

World Bank. (1992). *Governance and Development*. Washington, DC: World Bank.

World Bank. (1993a). *Argentina: From Insolvency to Growth*. Washington, DC: World Bank.

World Bank. (1993b). *Malawi: Public Sector Management Review.* Washington, DC: World Bank.

World Bank. (1995). *Implementation Completion and Results Report: Argentina Public Sector Reform Loan Project.* Washington, DC: World Bank.

World Bank. (1998a) *Support to the Government of Malawi's Anti-Corruption Program.* Washington, DC: World Bank.

World Bank. (1998b). *Uganda: Recommendations for Strengthening the Government of Uganda's Anti-Corruption Program.* Washington, DC: World Bank.

World Bank. (1998c). *Project Appraisal Document: Rwanda Community Reintegration and Development Project.* Washington, DC: World Bank.

World Bank. (2000a). *Reforming Public Institutions and Strengthening Governance.* A World Bank Strategy. Washington, DC: World Bank.

World Bank. (2000b). *Bolivia: From Patronage to Professional State. Bolivia Institutional and Governance Review.* Washington, DC: World Bank.

World Bank. (2000c). *Malawi: Country Assistance Evaluation.* Washington, DC: World Bank.

World Bank. (2003a). *Implementation Completion Report: Niger Public Expenditure Adjustment Credit (PEAC).* Washington, DC: World Bank.

World Bank. (2003b). *Implementation Completion Report: Benin Population and Health Project.* Washington, DC: World Bank.

World Bank. (2003c). *Pakistan: HIV/AIDS Prevention Project. Project Appraisal Document.* Washington, DC: World Bank.

World Bank. (2003d). *Implementation Completion and Results Report: Rwanda Community Reintegration and Development Project.* Washington, DC: World Bank.

World Bank. (2003e). *Combating Corruption in Indonesia.* Washington, DC: World Bank.

World Bank. (2004). *Project Appraisal Document: Rwanda Decentralization and Community Development Project.* Washington, DC: World Bank.

World Bank. (2005a). *Implementation Completion Report: Second Niger Public Expenditure Adjustment Credit (PEAC 2).* Washington, DC: World Bank.

World Bank. (2005b). *Implementation Completion Report: Bangladesh Health and Population Program Project.* Washington, DC: World Bank.

World Bank. (2005c). *Implementation Completion Report: Cote d'Ivoire Integrated Health Systems Development Project.* Washington, DC: World Bank.

World Bank. (2006). *Assessing World Bank Support for Trade, 1987–2004.* Washington, DC: World Bank.

World Bank. (2007). *IEG Review of World Bank Assistance for Financial Sector Reform.* Washington, DC: World Bank.

World Bank. (2008). *Public Sector Reform: What Works and Why?* Washington, DC: World Bank.

World Bank. (2009a). *Improving Effectiveness and Outcomes for the Poor in Health, Nutrition, and Population: An Evaluation of World Bank Group Support since 1997.* Washington, DC: World Bank.

World Bank. (2009b). *Implementation Completion Report: Burundi Multisectoral HIV/AIDS Control and Orphans Project.* Washington, DC: World Bank.

World Bank. (2010a). *Afghanistan Public Expenditure Review.* Washington, DC: World Bank.

World Bank. (2010b). *Implementation Completion Report: Pakistan HIV/AIDS Prevention Project.* Washington, DC: World Bank.

World Bank. (2010c). *Implementation Completion Report: Afghanistan Health Sector Emergency Reconstruction and Development Project.* Washington, DC: World Bank.

World Bank. (2011a). *Implementation Completion Report: Nepal Health Sector Program Project.* Washington, DC: World Bank.

World Bank. (2011b). *Implementation Status and Results Report. Angola HIV/AIDS, Malaria, and TB Control Project (HAMSETs).* Washington, DC: World Bank.

World Bank. (2011c). *Implementation Completion Report: Rwanda Decentralization and Community Development Project.* Washington, DC: World Bank.

World Bank. (2011d). *IEG Annual Report 2011.* Washington, DC: World Bank.

World Bank. (2012). *World Bank Approach to Public Sector Management 2011–2020: Better Results from Public Sector Institutions (Draft).* Washington, DC: World Bank.

Wright, J., and Winters, M. (2010). The Politics of Effective Foreign Aid. *American Review of Political Science* 13, 61–80.

Wuthnow, R., Davison Hunter, J., Bergesen, A., and Kurzweil, E. (1984). *Cultural Analysis: The Work of Peter L. Berger, Mary Douglas, Michel Foucault, and Jürgen Habermas.* London: Routledge and Kegan Paul.

Yao, Y. (2010). The End of the Beijing Consensus: Can China's Model of Authoritarian Growth Survive? *Foreign Affairs*, February 2.

Yeager, T. J. (1999). *Institutions, Transition Economies and Economic Development.* Boulder: Westview Press.

Zak, P. J., and Knack, S. (2001). Trust and Growth. *Economic Journal* 111, 295–321.

Zakocs, R. C. (2006). What Explains Community Coalition Effectiveness? *American Journal of Preventive Medicine* 30(4), 351–361.

Zeghal, D., and Mhedhbi, K. (2006). An Analysis of the Factors Affecting the Adoption of International Accounting Standards by Developing Countries. *International Journal of Accounting* 41(4), 373–386.

Zaccaro, S. J., Rittman, A. L., and Marks, M. A. (2001). Team Leadership. *The Leadership Quarterly* 12(4), 451–483.

Index

CPSIA information can be obtained at www.ICGtesting.com
Printed in the USA
LVOW07s2130090316

478480LV00001BA/135/P